Holiness through Work

Other Books of Interest from St. Augustine's Press

Giulio Maspero, *After Pandemic, After Modernity:*
The Relational Revolution

Giulio Maspero, *The Mystery of Communion: Encountering the Trinity*

Maurice Ashley Agbaw-Ebai, *Light of Reason, Light of Faith:*
Joseph Ratzinger and the German Enlightenment

Rocco Buttiglione, *The Metaphysics of Knowledge*
and Politics in Thomas Aquinas

Peter Kreeft, *Socrates' Children: The 100 Greatest Philosophers*

Peter Kreeft, *Socratic Logic (3rd Edition)*

Marvin R. O'Connell, *Telling Stories that Matter: Memoirs and Essays*

Richard Peddicord, O.P., *The Sacred Monster of Thomism*

Karol Wojtyła, *Man in the Field of Responsibility*

Catherine Godfrey-Howell, *Consensual Incapacity to Marry*

Josef Pieper, *Exercises in the Elements: Essays–Speeches–Notes*

Josef Pieper, *A Journey to Point Omega: Autobiography from 1964*

Joseph Bottum, *The Decline of the Novel*

Gene Fendt, *Camus' Plague: Myth for Our World*

Gabriele Kuby, *The Abandoned Generation*

Roger Scruton, *The Meaning of Conservatism: Revised 3rd Edition*

Roger Scruton, *The Politics of Culture and Other Essays*

Anne Drury Hall, *Where the Muses Still Haunt: The Second Reading*

Allen Mendenhall, *Shouting Softly: Lines on Law, Literature, and Culture*

Chilton Williamson, *The End of Liberalism*

Daniele Lorenzini, *Jacques Maritain and Human Rights: Totalitarianism,*
Anti-Semitism and Democracy (1936–1951)

Charles R. Embry and Glenn Hughes, editors, *The Timelessness of Proust:*
Reflections on In Search of Lost Time

Holiness through Work
Commemorating the
Encyclical *Laborem Exercens*
EDITED BY MARTIN SCHLAG, ED.

ST. AUGUSTINE'S PRESS
South Bend, Indiana

Manufactured in the United States of America.

1 2 3 4 5 6   26 25 24 23 22 21

Library of Congress Control Number: 2022930358

Paperback ISBN: 978-1-58731-320-2
Ebook ISBN: 978-1-58731-321-9

∞ The paper used in this publication meets the minimum requirements of the American National Standard for Information Sciences – Permanence of Paper for Printed Materials, ANSI Z39.48-1984.

St. Augustine's Press
www.staugustine.net

Table of Contents

Holiness through Work:
Commemorating the Encyclical *Laborem Exercens*. Introduction.
Martin Schlag 1

The Bible and the Fathers of the Church on Work
Giulio Maspero 6

Work Theology in the High Middle Ages
Patricia Ranft 34

John Paul II's Metaphysics of Labor
Angela Franks 60

Confronting a Technocratic Future:
Women's Work and the Church's Social Vision
Dr. Deborah Savage 78

Contemplation at Work:
A Theological Conversation Between John Paul II and Josemaría Escrivá
Martin Schlag 110

Laborem Exercens: A Protestant Appreciation
Richard Turnbull 134

Good Work: Insights from the Subjective Dimension of Work
Michael Naughton 163

Subjects and Objects in Meaningful Work
Christopher Michaelson 183

The Worker and the Transistor:
The Dignity of Work and Business Ethics in Global Corporate Practices
Javier Ignacio Pinto Garay and Alvaro Pezoa Bissieres 189

The Real Work: Making the Encyclical *Laborem Exercens* Operational
Gonzalo Flores-Castro Lingán 212

Laborem Exercens and the Subjective Dimension
of Work in Economics and Finance
Geoffrey C. Friesen 224

Index 257

Holiness through Work: Commemorating the Encyclical *Laborem Exercens*. Introduction.

Martin Schlag

The Inuit have a series of different words for ice. Our language must make do with one word. We notice a similar lack of nuance when it comes to addressing the varied reality of "work." The *Oxford English Dictionary* describes work as an action or activity involving physical or mental effort and undertaken to achieve a result, especially as a means of making one's living or earning money. It is also labor, one's regular occupation or employment. Work has to do with exerting oneself for a definite purpose, especially to produce something or to earn a living. In contrast to play or diversion, which regenerates us from our efforts, it is usually associated with toil.[1] But for some, it is so integral to life that it is a cause for great joy and can even seem effortless.

Work thus designates a wide span of human activities, from the harsh struggle for survival to artistic creativity, from uplifting intellectual work to backbreaking drudgery. Work is a polysemic word, i.e., a word that possesses multiple meanings, senses, and connotations. It appears in many contexts and is relevant for many aspects of our lives. Work makes up most of our days. For this reason alone, it is inseparable from our individual biographies and narratives. Like the roots and branches of a tree, work penetrates the soil and air in which we grow and thrive. It is constitutive of the human person. It is in work that our character is

---

1 See *Oxford English Dictionary*, accessed on October 8, 2021, https://
   www.oed.com/. I have summarized the meaning of "work" as noun and as
   verb and edited the wording.

formed and forged, where we develop our ideals and put them into practice, where we slowly discover our purpose in life. From a personalistic perspective, like that of Karol Wojtyla, later John Paul II, the word "work" implies yet another wide range of topics: meaning, values, purpose, narrative, virtues, ethics, society, business, and not least faith.

Utopian thinkers like Karl Marx and even non-utopian economists like John Maynard Keynes anticipate a future without work. Would such a future be desirable? A world without exploitation of workers, without slavery and degradation; a world with economic equity and inclusion, with safety for all laborers, and respect for their priceless contributions to society; a world in which the right to work and the rights of workers in work are recognized and protected. This would certainly be a world worth fighting for. But this need not be a world without work. Such a world would be a nightmare, and against God's explicit plan for his creation. God created the world and all it contains but left it unfinished. He created clay but not bricks, grain but not bread.[2] He wants us to continue the work of creation, and that is how he placed us in this world—as workers.[3]

As Giulio Maspero explains in his chapter, Christian faith inherited an attitude of respect and appreciation for work, also manual work, from Judaism. This attitude is expressed in the Bible and the Talmud. The early Christian teachers, especially Augustine, had to enculturate this mindset into the Hellenistic environment of their time, which generally considered manual labor as demeaning, unfit for free men. While Christian faith could not and cannot accept such a prejudice, it also calls on political and economic leaders, employers, employees, and all men and women to strive for institutions of work that foster virtues and thus true freedom. This was partially recognized by the early monastic tradition of the first Christian millennium, in which work was esteemed mainly as a cure against idleness. All kinds of temptation beset the monk, and the Christian in general, in moments of boredom and idleness. Work keeps the temptations away, or at least reduces them.

However, work is much more than just an ascetic cure: it shapes the

---

2   See Dan Bricklin, "Natural-Born Entrepreneur," *Harvard Business Review* (September 2001): 3–8.
3   See Gen 2:15.

world according to God's plan and will. Therefore, work is irreplaceable and integral to a Christian's witness to the world. We are judged in the eyes of our fellow citizens by how we as Christians join in the common effort of building a better, happier, and healthier world for all. This is part of our testimony as believers. However, there is a further dimension. Secular, inner-worldly work contributes to the coming of the Kingdom of God, and thus has an eschatological dimension. In her chapter, Patricia Ranft develops these ideas and shows how the medieval religious revival in Europe cherished work. This is in opposition to the prevailing scholarly conviction, which depicts the Middle Ages as a time in which there was hardly any theological reflection on work and ordinary life. Christianity supposedly had to wait for the Protestant reformers for that to happen.[4] Rather, Ranft's chapter shows how much work was esteemed in the Middle Ages. In fact, the Protestant Reformers were able to tap into older, preexisting Christian traditions when they pointed to ordinary work and professional activity as a path for the full realization of the Christian's calling to holiness. Richard Turnbull presents some of their teachings in his chapter in this volume.

Cutting a complicated and long history extremely short, Catholic theologians, thinkers, and pastors—as diverse as Francis de Sales, Thomas Merton, Jacques Maritain, and Josemaría Escrivá—refocused the Catholic tradition on ordinary work. By rediscovering the universal call to holiness of all Christians, this led up to the Second Vatican Council's program of Christian humanism and its renewed call for cultural transformation from inside the world. Pope John Paul II was firmly committed to this cause.

On September 14, 1981, the Feast of the Triumph of the Holy Cross, he published his encyclical *Laborem Exercens*. It is written by a Pope who had already experienced two forms of totalitarianism, one of which was a regnant communist regime that extolled theoretical materialism. He arrived in the West only to experience the dehumanizing effects of

---

4 See Charles Taylor, *Sources of the Self: The Making of the Modern Identity* (Cambridge, MA.: Harvard University Press, 1989), 211–33; classically expressed in Max Weber, *The Protestant Ethic and the Spirit of Capitalism*, first published in 1905 in German, multiple editions.

practical materialism. In opposition to both forms of inhuman material-ism, he proposed Christian humanism, the counterprogram of redeemed humanity. As a philosopher, John Paul II takes up the strands of intel-lectual discourse that lead us from the Bible, the Church fathers, the me-dieval reception and renewal of patristic theology, into the Reformation, and on to modern thought on work, especially Hegel and Marx. This monumental encyclical deserves a reflection 40 years after its publica-tion.

In her chapter, Angela Franks shows how the notion "work" in John Paul II's teaching fits within a larger metaphysical and aesthetic person-alistic commitment, summarized in the key phrase: "Action expresses the person." Deborah Savage puts *Laborem Exercens* in context with other writings of John Paul II, *Centesimus Annus* and *Mulieris Digni-tatem* in particular. Her chapter will be of interest also to those who, with Pope Francis, are concerned about the technocratic paradigm that is so deeply entrenched in modernity. She reflects on the specific calling of women in work, society, and culture. Martin Schlag concentrates on the encyclical's final section on spirituality. He brings John Paul II into con-versation with Josemaría Escrivá, showing how their teachings have dif-ferent emphases and thus complement each other. And for a panoramic vision of *Laborem Exercens* and its impact on a personal scholarly bi-ography, one should open Michael Naughton's chapter. It gyrates around the notion of "good work" and its institutional implications in business. Naughton's chapter ends with a case study and concludes the first part of the book, forming a bridge to its second, more practical part.

The aim of our book is to illustrate the lasting relevance and fertility of *Laborem Exercens* for intellectual life. In different ways, the authors in part two of the book show how the encyclical inspired them in their own field of business expertise. For Christopher Michaelson, a business ethicist, the concepts of the "objective" and "subjective" dimensions of work are important. The way *Laborem Exercens* distinguishes between the two dimensions of work aligns with his own scholarship and that of many other ethicists who study meaningful work. Javier Ignacio Pinto Garay and Alvaro Pezoa Bissieres reflect on the dignity of work and business ethics in global corporate practices. They start out asking what place Catholic social teaching can have in business ethics. As they argue in a framework of virtue ethics, they employ the principles of Catholic social teaching as bedrock for ethical reflection. Their chapter focuses on technology. They argue that *Laborem Exercens'* principles on good technology can be guidelines in a world of increasing surveillance and new forms of Taylorism. In his chapter, Gonzalo Flores-Castro undertakes the "real work" of making *Laborem Exercens* operational. John Paul II leaves the concrete realization of his vision in the hands of the subject of work: the worker. Flores proposes the theory of action developed by Pérez López (1934–1996) as a way to bring the principles closer to real, everyday work. Finally, as a professor of finance, Geoffrey C. Friesen highlights the changes to our financial logic when the subjective dimension of work is given its proper place in economic and financial models.

All authors in this book seem to agree on the importance of the distinction between the subjective and objective dimensions of work. Here we can probably find the most important, and perhaps most lasting, contribution of *Laborem Exercens* to intellectual history. We sincerely hope that our work as authors has made a little contribution of its own to further research and reflections by others. As editor of this volume, my gratitude goes to all authors who were willing to write their chapters, frequently in competition with other pressing chores and tasks. I thank St. Augustine Press and its Director, Catherine Godfrey, for accepting the book in its collection and for quick and unbureaucratic procedures. I gratefully acknowledge Frank Scarchilli's patient work of editing. I wish all readers insight and joy.

The Bible and the Fathers
of the Church on Work

Giulio Maspero

1. Introduction: An Anniversary

The encyclical *Laborem Exercens*, published forty years ago, begins by referring to work as an essential element of Christian humanism: "Only man is capable of work, and only man works, at the same time by work occupying his existence on earth. Thus work bears a particular mark of man and of humanity, the mark of a person operating within a community of persons. And this mark decides its interior characteristics; in a sense it constitutes its very nature."[1]

In fact, according to the Bible, God created the world through His work and He created the human being to work. This implies that the very covenant between the Creator and the only creature created in His image and likeness has at its core work itself. In the New Testament this revelation is reaffirmed with unimaginable force as Jesus links His own activity to the truth that His Father always works.[2] So our Lord had a specific profession, characterized by tools that are precisely those with which the Incarnate Word was crucified.

The Fathers of the Church had to rethink the classical conception of work in the light of this revelation and introduced a new relational vision of work with profound social consequences, such as he condemnation of slavery and the care of the weak. This chapter seeks to illustrate the essential steps along this path, highlighting the ontological novelty of

---

1   John Paul II, Encyclical *Laborem Exercens* (Vatican City: Libreria Editrice Vaticana, 1981), preamble. Henceforth the encyclical is quoted as LE.
2   Cf. John 5:17.

the Christian conception of work, which overcomes every possible ambiguity about it, founding human activity and its dignity in that relational dimension infused by the triune God in reality through the act of creation. In LE, John Paul II speaks in a way that takes relation not only into consideration but realizes its central importance for human work.[3] Work is embedded in society, thus in relationships between persons, who are much more than mere factors of production. First and foremost, however, work relates the human person to God, the Creator.

2. Work not Fight: The Biblical Novelty

To grasp the novelty and relevance of the Biblical and Patristic teachings on work, it is necessary to take a metaphysical perspective. It is not a question of entering into technical and excessively speculative details, but of taking as a starting point the difficulty of reconciling the one and the many that characterizes human thought in the search for the first cause of everything and the meaning of life. The very core of the issue is that this cause should be one, while reality is marked by multiplicity and by conflicts. The material world is shaped by clashes and struggles, illustrated in narrative form by myths. It is sufficient to think of the Babylonian and Greek examples, where a first couple of gods engenders and gets in conflict with its own offspring. For example, Uranus and Gaia, personifications of heaven and earth, are the first divinities, and one of their sons, Cronus, castrates the father and starts eating his own sons to avoid ending up like him, but Zeus, born by Cronus and Rhea, escapes his destiny and defeats his father. In Babylonia the narrative is analogous, as everything also begins with a couple whose children give rise to a conflict. Again the origin of the cosmos is from a dysfunctional "family" through a sort of mafia war. On a philosophical level this translates into the confrontation between Parmenides and Plato, where the former claims that being is one, while the latter affirms its multiplicity though analogy and dialectics, defining his stance as a sort of parricide against Parmenides himself.[4]

---

3   See, e.g., LE, n. 16.
4   Plato, *Sophista* 241d.

The Biblical picture is completely different. In the Genesis account,[5] in fact, the one God is the origin of everything, as He in the beginning creates (*bārā'*) out of nothing a relational pair consisting of heaven and earth.[6] The very Jewish verb points to the action of cutting not simply at a material level, but as distinction within the very created reality. The difference with respect to the previous cases is apparent: it seems that the biblical narrative could go back a step further beyond the dyad towards the unitary origin that was in the beginning and is the source of everything. Matter thus has a spiritual origin, as it flows from the spirit of God (*rûḥa 'ĕlōhîm*) and cannot be opposed to it.[7] The biblical text does not offer a chronological description or an explanation in the line of modern science, but presents the ultimate causes of why we are as we are. So the narrative has a liturgical dimension expressed by the "rhythm" and "pattern" in the succession of days. God vertically brings into being something that was not there before and this something is always structured as a relational couple characterized by numerical or vital fecundity: this happens with light and darkness,[8] with day and night,[9] with the waters below and the waters above,[10] with the sea and the mainland,[11] with the sun and the moon[12] up to the male and female human being.[13] The very terminology expresses a sort of reciprocity between the two elements brought into being, as if one were at the heart of the other, but precisely through their distinction.

Why is this important for the biblical understanding of work? The central point is that this relational texture that constitutes created reality does not originate from a conflict, but from the work of the One, who freely brought it into being. This multiplicity is the result of the work of

---

5   For a commentary, see Claus Westermann, *Genesis 1–11* (Minneapolis: Fortress Press, 1994).

6   Gn 1:1.

7   Gn 1:2.

8   Gn 1:4.

9   Gn 1:5.

10   Gn 1:6–7.

11   Gn 1:10.

12   Gn 1:14–18.

13   Gn 1:27.

the One and expresses His inner life. God creates by working, in fact, as it is said in Gn 2:2: on the seventh day He completed His work and this completion consisted in resting, where both actions have a liturgical significance. The first in Greek indicates a relational dimension that recalls both the plural that cmcrgcd from the heart of the Creator when He called man into being according to Gn 1:26, and the human being that so became a partner of God through His blessing that has the form of a mission, as we will see below. The second action is in Hebrew *wayyišəbōṯ*, where the conjunction (*w* = and) is essential to grasp that the two verbs constitute an endiad, according to a tendency typical of biblical language. The Hebrew verb is linked to the Sabbath revealing in this way that rest is not a mere cessation of doing, but the relational fulfillment of work in contemplation. Labor is not only about producing, but more deeply about enjoying the relationship with the fruit of one's work, taking care of it.

This is profoundly different from classical philosophical interpretations, as both in the Platonic perspective of the idea and in the Aristotelian doctrine of the form identity and otherness are opposed in an irreducible and dialectical way. On the contrary, in Gn 1:26 the one God shifts to the plural before creating the human being in His image and likeness, expressing in the latter's relationality His inner triune Life, as the New Testament will show. This is the point of arrival of a crescendo that reveals more and more the ontological depth of God's work in creating, accomplished through His own word, which places a relational ontological structure in being. In the sequence, clearly organized in a liturgical sense, each new act of God corresponds to the declaration of the goodness of the relational couple so created, up to the qualitative leap constituted by man and woman, in the light of which the Creator declares that all creation is now not just good, but very good.[14]

Thus the origin of the world is not in the conflict inherent in a initial dyad that produces dialectics, but in the One God, from whose interiority through the act of working flows a fabric of relationships that constitute reality in its depth. It could be said that the God of the Bible works precisely because He is One and He works from within Himself,

14 Gn 1:31.

9

communicating to creatures, through His work, the capacity to be in mutual relationship and to be in relationship with Him. This is shown by the speaking capacity of the human being, who is called to the dialogue with the Creator and sent to take care of creation through a blessing in the form of a mission,[15] as the the Hebrew text uses *məla'ḵət*, a term that recalls "angel" and, therefore, "mission," radically different from the Greek translation *ta erga* in the Septuagint. Here the Greek spirit fails to express in full what the sacred text is communicating: it is not a matter of working in order to then be able to devote oneself without disturbance to the theoretical sphere that recognizes the intelligible as the deepest ontological root of the real and, for this reason, seeks to go beyond the visible and the material, as the Platonic myth of the cave suggests.[16] The wonder that gave rise to philosophical activity in the face of the multiplicity of the cosmic world (*ta physika*) is betrayed by the theoretical outcome of Greek metaphysics itself, as María Zambrano has keenly observed,[17] for the dialectical opposition of the one and the many. The Aristotelian God is one but does not work, just as It has no word or relationship, because It is perfect and does not need anything. Its only activity is the theoretical contemplation. So, in this framework, the multiplicity of the world is in some sense the result of the dialectics with this First Principle. In contrast, the Jewish Sabbath is not opposed to the first six days of creation, but is its dynamic fulfillment.

What seems fundamental to highlight is that, according to Genesis, work is constitutive of the human being on two counts. We have seen how it refers back to the image and likeness of God. At the same time, it is precisely the mission and the dynamics that flow from creation that place the human being in a constitutive relationship with the earth. In Gn 2:5–6, at the beginning of the second account of creation, which is more ancient and anthropological than the more liturgical and refined first one in Gn 1, after work has made its appearance in relation to God, as seen in Gn 2:2, there is the extraordinary recurrence of work itself,

---

15 Gn 1:28–30.

16 Plato, *Respublica*, 514b–520a.

17 María Zambrano, *Filosofía y poesía* (Ciudad del Mexico: Fondo de Cultura Económica, 1996).

now in relation to the human being who however, in this second narrative, has not yet been created.[18] Beyond historical and philological considerations, it is evident that the text tries to show that without the "partnership" between God and the human being the world cannot be itself: the earth is described as a desert, without grass, because the Creator had not made it rain and the human being did not work the land (*'āḏām 'ayin la'ăḇōḏ 'eṯ-hā'ăḏāmâ*). This last sentence is extremely significant, because the one who, according to Gn 2:7, will be molded by God from the dust of the ground, is in some way presupposed to the perfection of the earth itself through the ability to work, which derives from having been created in the image and likeness of God. This relational correspondence between the human being and the earth is also present at the terminological level in Hebrew, because "man" is *'āḏām*, while "earth" is *'ăḏāmâ*, a term composed of exactly the same letters joined to the feminine sign, which does not exist in the case of "man." And the verb "to work" (*'ăḇōḏ*) is found right between the two terms placed in constitutive relation by the Creator. The construction is analogous to how in Gn 2:23, at the moment of the creation of the woman from the rib of the man, this says that she will be called "woman," i.e., *'iššâ*, because from the man, i.e., *'îš,* had been taken away. Without the reference to the Hebrew, this translation would remain unintelligible. Instead, like the relationship between Adam and the earth, here too the original reveals the relational identity in the feminine sign added to the first term. So, work is at the center of the relationship between the human being and the world.

In conclusion, God creates by working because He is one, and from within Himself He infuses created reality with a relational identity, so that the human being works precisely because he or she is the image of this God. Therefore, from the biblical perspective, human work too is born from within, from (wo)man's relational identity, and is at the service of the relational fabric that constitutes the world. Thus, paradoxically, the human being is de-*fined* by a relationship with the *infinite* that characterizes his or her immanence, for the creation in the image of God.

---

18 Filippo Serafini, "Vocazione al lavoro dell'uomo in Genesi 2," in *Verso una spiritualità del lavoro* (2018).

And the Genesis narrative explains why this vertical relationship is always translated also horizontally in the relationship with the other, both cosmic and personal. Human action, therefore, according to the biblical perspective, even if it is external, is never extrinsic, but is always at the same time for communion with God and for communion with others. Adoration and action are thus linked in the metaphysical depth of the human being's ultimate origin, preventing any dialectical opposition between inside and outside, between the One and the many.[19] The rain that irrigates the earth passes through the heart of man, of every man, through his capacity to let himself be generated and through the relational dimension that constitutes him. So work is understood, from the biblical point of view, as being married to the world, as making love with reality.

3. The Exile of Work

But dialectics are present in the world and the image of work presented in the first two chapters of Genesis clashes with the fatigue and burden that led Aristotle to assert that the citizen should not work, because work, especially material work, belongs to the dimension of means and not to that of ends. Thus, according to the Greek ideal, work is only for slaves, while the freedom of the *polis* is freedom also from work.[20] What does the Bible have to say about this? Is the picture it presents really idyllic and unrealistic? Here the narrative in Genesis seems to reach one of its peaks, because its etiological perspective also embraces the experience, or rather the evidence, of evil. Precisely because of the ontological-relational depth of the first principle according to the biblical description, for the human being, who is created in God's image, it is possible to address the Creator in order to say no to the gift that constitutes her. Gn 3:1–7 describes the temptation of the serpent, who makes a false statement as the premise of its reasoning, namely that God had forbidden the human being to eat of every tree in the garden. The metaphysical

---

19   Jean Daniélou, *Prayer as a Political Problem* (New York: Sheed and Ward, 1967).

20   See Aristotle, *Politics*, 1277b2–6 and 1329a21.

connection between good and truth emerges here in narrative form. The woman responds to the false premise by trying to correct it, through the assertion that God has forbidden eating only the fruit of the tree in the center of the garden, the mere contact of which would have caused her and Adam to die. Note that the grammar of the dialogue indicates that the temptation is directed at the couple, thus that it embraces their relationship, as this is revealed by the Creator as a constitutive element of being. At this point the lie reveals its violent face because the serpent, at the moment in which it denies God's affirmation, reinforces the verb to die, with a doubling typical of the Semitic language. Scott Hahn reads the text as a threat to the life of the original couple by the serpent: Adam was called to sacrifice his own human life to defend Eve, standing between her and the serpent, dying a simple death to protect against the "death-death" that concerns the relationship with God, who is Life.[21] According to the tempter, the Creator would have imposed this extrinsic law to prevent the human being from becoming like Him, when in fact Adam and Eve have already been created in God's image and likeness. The gulf between the ontological and gnoseological dimensions is immediately evident, because the knowledge of good and evil is presented by the serpent as gain, when, in the perspective of the first two chapters of Genesis, evil is only the absence of good, the negation of relationship. To take from the tree of life is to deny one's filiation, to renounce being children, that means to be generated. It is not a question of violating an extrinsic law, but of rejecting the founding and gratuitous relation through which the human being is constituted. Thus Adam and Eve, beginning to judge apart from the source, "think finite," i.e., in a finite horizon. This is why their infinite desire comes into tension with creaturely finitude, a tension which is the origin of all dialectics, because one cannot be himself or herself without reference to a dimension beyond, something or someone else that cannot be conquered but only received as a gift.

It is important to stress that the usurpation is only cognitive, because reality remains under the absolute power of the Creator: the world and the human being are still the work of God. But when the vertical

---

21 Scott Hahn, *First Comes Love* (New York: Doubleday, 2002), 62–70.

relationship with Him is wounded, because it is rejected by the human being, the horizontal relationship also becomes difficult, as revealed by the consciousness of being naked that problematically arises in the original couple.[22] It should be stressed here that the response to this disturbance is through the human being's work, of which he or she is capable being the image of God. In fact, Adam and Eve weave fig leaves and make belts out of them, acting in such a way as to protect and embrace physically and culturally those limits that without the relationship with the infinite source are now unbearable. Thus original sin has wounded, but not destroyed, that good which is contained within those limits. In fact, the Creator continues to uphold the efficacy of His work, as demonstrated by the call "Adam, where are you?"[23] The curse that follows is extremely relevant from the perspective of the theology of work, because it precedes the human being's expulsion from paradise in the form of a mission. In fact, despite the wound, the creature continues to belong to God and to represent Him in the world, so much so that man is sent to work that earth from which he was taken. It is essential to remind that human work was present in God's plan even before the creation of the human being, as a constitutive element of the image impressed by the Creator in the only creature capable of addressing Him and saying "we." Therefore, the curse itself cannot be read only as a punishment or an extrinsic imposition, but it acquires the value of a statement of fact: it is declarative and not constitutive. Fatigue in work, pain in childbirth, relational dependence, weariness and the sweat of the brow to the extreme of returning to that earth from which (wo)man was drawn by the creative word[24] are the consequences of (wo)man's choice, who has withdrawn from the relationship with the Source and therefore suffers because of his or her own limitations. But just as the ability to work remains, so too the divine judgement in showing that what the human being has committed with its consequences also indicates the path of return. In fact, speaking to the serpent, the Creator affirms that the enmity between its descendants and that of the woman would end with the victory of the

22 Gn 3:7.
23 Gn 3:9.
24 Gn 3:16–19.

latter, even if through a mortal blow to the heel of someone who would have originated from her.[25] Tradition has read in these words an announcement of the paschal mystery, when the idolatrous power of representation over reality would be overcome by the voluntary entry into the limit by the Son of God made flesh.

This shows how the dyad, uprooted from its unitary root, comes into conflict, thus accounting for the ambivalence of work in human perception. So Abel's blood is shed by Cain "in the field,"[26] therefore in the latter's sphere of work, as a consequence of the different value attributed to the fruits of their labor. In fact the two brothers, probably twins, because the text says that Abel himself was born after Cain without Adam reuniting with Eve, are different because the second-born is a shepherd of flocks, while the first-born toils the land.[27] But at the moment of sacrifice, that is, in the act of bringing the work to completion in worship, in imitation of what the Creator had done on the seventh day, only Abel's offering is appreciated.

Thus, after the original sin, work shows a certain ambivalence, which will induce idolatry, that according to the Bible is the transition of the human being from accepting to have been made by God to the idea of producing one's own divinities, i.e., idols. And this shift transforms the world into a battlefield, as in the myths, because the reference to the One who founds human relationships and differences is lost. Work can become clash.

But in spite of the violence, the Creator continues to preserve through the vertical relationship with His creatures the latter's horizontal relationality. In the fourth generation Lamech was born, whose children devoted themselves to different jobs, from shepherding, to playing the zither and the flute, to metalworking. But Lamech was a murderer like Cain.[28] Here it is significant that the narrative points out that it is at this very moment that Adam begets Set, who in turn has a son named Enos, who first began to call upon the name of God.[29] It seems that everything repeats itself and

25 Gn 3:15.
26 Gn 4:8.
27 Gn 4:1–2.
28 Gn 4:19–22.
29 Gn 4:26.

only adoration can put a limit to the tension that manifests itself in the relational and working life of man. The horizontal dimension cannot be sustained without a return to the vertical dimension with the Creator, that is, to the gift that from the infinite is poured into the finite.

Thus, in Adam's descendants we come to Noah, who has three sons: Shem, Ham and Japheth.[30] Here begins the narration of the universal deluge,[31] caused by the proliferation of evil committed by men.[32] As in the curse at the end of chapter three, here too the statement must be read from an etiological perspective, which makes possible a relational reading that can illuminate the biblical ontological and moral meaning of work. In fact, the flood consists precisely in the closing of the space between the waters above and the waters below, opened by the creative Word on the second day of God's work. The human beings are violently closing this space that makes life and relationships possible.[33] But the Creator points precisely to work as the path to salvation, giving instructions on the construction of the ark from cypress wood.[34]

Salvation is accomplished through a family and the work of a family put at the service of relationships on three levels: with God, among the members of Noah's family, and with respect to the animals, which are introduced in pairs into the ark.[35]

From a metaphysical point of view, one can see here the Creator's desire to preserve the relational variety of the different couples of animals that violence always tends to reduce by eliminating otherness. After forty days and forty nights, the fruit of the work of Noah and his family allows life to begin again and God promises not to curse the ground any more as long as the earth lasts.[36] The text is particularly significant if read from the ontological-relational perspective of work, because the Creator affirms that "seed and harvest, cold and heat, summer and winter, day and night" will not cease, indicating four pairs that refer back to

30   Gn 5:32.
31   Cf. Gn 6–9.
32   Gn 6:5.
33   Gn 6:11–12.
34   Gn 6:14–16.
35   Gn 6:18–20.
36   Gn 8:20–22.

that horizontal relationship that God's Word had put in place through the act of creation. It is about a new beginning, a new creation, signaled by the repetition of the blessing-mission to be fruitful and multiply,[37] of which the rainbow is a symbol.[38]

But the work immediately appears in connection to a further sin, which disturbs this new beginning. Noah, in fact, after the Flood begins to cultivate vines and produces wine with which, he becomes drunk.[39] Ham found his father asleep naked in the tent and told his brothers the shameful fact. Shem and Japheth went in where their father lay walking backwards, so as not to see him, and covered him with their cloaks.[40] The question is fundamental from a moral point of view, because it shows the crossroads that opens up in front of every human being before the limit of the other: if one execrates it, one ends up falling into that same limit and being enslaved to it, as will happen to the descendants of Ham, while if one embraces and covers the limit of the father, one is free to be oneself, generating in freedom. The question is always onto-logical-relational, because the other, and the parent *in primis*, belong to one's own identity. The condemnation of the other's limit becomes a condemnation of oneself, which prevents generativity and fertility. Thus the curse hurled by Noah on Ham, who will be the "slave of slaves" of his brothers, is once again a simple statement of what relational ontology requires starting from the creative act itself.

The Genesis narrative also continues to present the ambivalence of human work, which can be lived in a relational or idolatrous sense. Babylon dramatically exemplifies the latter possibility: through the technique of bricking, men try to build a city that is a tower as high as the sky.[41] This attempt to conquer the vertical relational dimension on their own, starting from the ground up with their own strength, ends in confusion, to which the very name of the city alludes, as the Hebrew word *bābel* refers through the repetition of the *b* to stammering. The human beings thus lose a

37 Gn 9:1–7.
38 Gn 9:12–16.
39 Gn 9:20–21.
40 Gn 9:22–23.
41 Gn 11:3–4.

common language, a *logos* that makes it possible for them to enter into relationships. And this is a consequence of the wrong use of labor.

The biblical narrative can therefore be reread from a contemporary perspective as an example of the impossibility of not taking a position in the face of the tension towards the infinite that every man carries in his heart. Even if only implicitly, each person with his or her own choices decides what the meaning of his or her existence is and works at the service of a first principle, a foundation of that meaning, which can be a valid path towards the very source of being, or a usurper that has symbolically taken its place. The result is simple: freedom in the first case, slavery in the second. The criterion here is the *a posteriori* relational dimension and not merely the *a priori* conceptual one.

The rest of Genesis shows how God rebuilds human unity through the covenant with Abraham, that is, with a family. The land to be worked is at the center of this relationship, which will be as fruitful as numerous are the stars in the sky and the sand in the sea. But Isaac's father must undergo the terrible test in which the Creator is reaffirmed as the origin of life and its true guardian. And with Jacob and his twelve sons, the foundation is laid for the vital unity of mankind to be reconstituted by God. The story of Joseph again reveals the relational exchange between the slave and his free brothers, who have sold him but find themselves receiving salvation just from him.

So, Egypt is the place par excellence where Israel knew God's providence but also experienced the slavery of labor. The Exodus recounts precisely this journey of liberation, in which the people must learn to live again by means of their relationship with the Creator, rather than placing the divine under their own power of production, as the episode of the golden calf reveals. The amazement before the manna reconstructs the working capacity of Abraham's descendants who conquer and build their home in the promised land on the covenant with the Creator. Then they will be constantly exposed to the danger of relapse, as the story of David or the new exile in Babylon show.

4. Work Redeemed

In the New Testament, in a certain sense, the path is repeated but now with Christ, true God and true man, as the protagonist. As it has been shown, according to the Old Testament God creates through His word and this is a real work that infuses a relational structure into the world, as both work and word implies processions and multiplicity. This is a key element to approach the fourth Gospel which starts with the Word that is in the beginning and is the origin of creation. This means that work itself can now be rooted in the Trinitarian immanence, in the relational intimacy of God. God's Word in creation in reality speaks of the second divine Person, the Son, who in His relationships with the Father and the Holy Spirit is the origin of reality, as everything was made through the Word Himself. So the narrative in the Gospel begins with Jesus being hastily taken to Egypt, to the very land that symbolizes slavery and the ambivalence of work, from where He returns to His homeland, retracing the path of His people. Work touches every moment of His life, because it defines His identity and, therefore, His double filiation, as son of man and Son of God. Everything revolves around the term *'abbā*, which means "father," according to the alternative root of *pater*. The former in Indo-European languages indicates the familial term with which the son addresses only his own parent, and not the ancestors, the rulers, or the gods.[42] But Jesus of Nazareth calls with this word both the Creator and Joseph, for whom He is called the "carpenter's son"[43] and, therefore, is a "carpenter" Himself.[44] This was blasphemous to a Jew, because it meant that Jesus, evidently a man, made Himself God. But if His words are recognized as true, for example in the light of the events after Easter, then this means that Jesus' profession is not only linked to that of Joseph, but in a certain sense also to that of His *'abbā*. We could say that our Lord works on the earth precisely because He is God, revealing the immense dignity of work, which is not bound only to necessity but, from the perspective of His Divinity, is connected to the freedom of love and gift, that is the origin of everything according to biblical faith.

Thus, the hidden life of Jesus is marked by the "work" of both

42 Emile Benveniste, *Le vocabulaire des institutions indo-européennes*, I (Paris: Munit, 1969), 210–11.

43 Mt 13:55.

44 Mk 6:3.

Joseph, who communicates to Him his position in the society of the time, and the Father, the Creator. In public life, with the beginning of the preaching, all the words and signs performed by Christ demonstrate that He is capable of doing the works that only God can accomplish. The question put to Him is "what work do you do?":[45] for this reason He forgives sins, cures lepers, heals the blind, raises the dead.[46] The controversy over the Sabbath revolves around this very point, because the religious authorities identify such actions as servile work, therefore forbidden on the Sabbath.[47] The Gospel of John is particularly valuable for the Christian understanding of work, since the reason that Jesus gives to explain His action is, according to the fourth evangelist: "my Father always works and I also work."[48] All the actions of the Son are related to those of the Father, because He does the latter's works. As a commentator has written: "In John's Gospel we find a surprising statement by Jesus about God who never rests, not even on the Sabbath, because one can be born and can die even on this day, therefore the Father gives life and exercises judgment even on the Sabbath; He continues His creative action even on this day, as the ancient Jewish theology recognizes."[49]

It is not by chance that the parables of the two sons narrated by Jesus have work as their background. Even more, the Pascal Mystery, the culmination of Christ's mission on earth, is presented as God's work, an expression found at the end of Psalm 21(22) which the Crucified begins to pray during His passion, punctually described in the text.[50] And the crucifixion takes place with the very tools of a carpenter.

At the same time Jesus says not to worry about tomorrow, showing how His Father cares for the flowers in the field and the birds in the sky:

---

45 John 6:30.
46 John 3:17 and 12:47.
47 Lk 13:14.
48 John 5:17.
49 Salvatore A. Panimolle, "Il Padre lavora sempre!" in *Lavoro-progresso-ricerca nei Padri della Chiesa*, Dizionario di Spiritualità Biblico-Patristica 35 (Roma: Borla, 2003), 7.
50 Psalm 21(22):32.

"Therefore I tell you, do not worry about your life, what you will eat (or drink), or about your body, what you will wear. Is not life more than food and the body more than clothing? Look at the birds in the sky; they do not sow or reap, they gather nothing into barns, yet your heavenly Father feeds them. Are not you more important than they? Can any of you by worrying add a single moment to your life-span? Why are you anxious about clothes? Learn from the way the wild flowers grow. They do not work or spin. But I tell you that not even Solomon in all his splendor was clothed like one of them. If God so clothes the grass of the field, which grows today and is thrown into the oven tomorrow, will he not much more provide for you, O you of little faith? So do not worry and say, 'What are we to eat?' or 'What are we to drink?' or 'What are we to wear?' All these things the pagans seek. Your heavenly Father knows that you need them all. But seek first the kingdom (of God) and his righteousness, and all these things will be given you besides. Do not worry about tomorrow; tomorrow will take care of itself. Sufficient for a day is its own evil."[51]

These words proved to be extremely important for the early church. They had to be interpreted as an affirmation of the priority of the Father's work over that of the human being who, as a creature, works as a partner of God, but is not omnipotent. Instead, it was necessary to avoid any interpretation along the lines of denying the value of human activity. It should be noted that here, too, the work is illuminated by the teachings of the Gospels and stripped of any ambivalence which, in the final analysis, still comes back to the relationship between the one and the many: does the Creator—the One—do everything, or must the human beings do their part—the many—in such a way that history have a real value?

The teachings and the example of Paul were very important in this respect,[52] in particular his "if anyone was unwilling to work, neither

51   Matt 6:25–34.
52   Cf. Acts 18:3 and 20:34; 1 Thess 2:9 and 1 Cor 9:15–18. On Paul's work,

should that one eat."[53] In the light of these words, one can also explain the admonition in the *Didache* not to trust Christians who remain idle and do not want to work.[54] The lives of the early Christians was the most effective exegesis of the references to work in the New Testament. This showed that all work is possible for the believer if he or she does it in relationship with God:

> If you are a farmer, then tend the land, but acknowledge God as you tend the land; sail, you who love navigation, but call upon the heavenly pilot. While you were a soldier the knowledge of God seized you: listen to the general who shows you what is right.[55]

Once again, the relational dimension is the key to overcoming all ambivalence, presenting work in all its transcendence as the place where the human beings live and express themselves as partners of their Creator.

Later, in the fourth century, after the Constantinian turn, it will be highlighted that Peter worked after Christ's resurrection, thus showing the value of history and the secular dimension, which is taken care of by the work done in communion with God. This will be the teaching of Chrysostom,[56] who gathered the fruits of a precious theological reflection that was particularly fruitful in the Cappadocian and Antiochian Fathers.

5. The Fathers' Humanism: East

Indeed, in the fourth century it was necessary to oppose not only Arianism, an heterodox doctrine which reduced the Son of God to a mere creature, but also Apollinarism, which denied the full humanity of Christ.

see Ronald F. Hock. *The Social Context of Paul's Ministry: Tentmaking and Apostleship* (Philadelphia: Fortress, 1980).
53   2 Thess 3:10.
54   Cf. *Didache,* 12, 3–5.
55   Clement of Alexandria, *Protrepticus*, X 100, 4.
56   Cf. John Chrysostom, *In epistulam ad Corinthios* 20, 6:PG 61, 168D.

Gregory of Nyssa became acquainted with the latter only on his journey to Jerusalem in 382, a turning point in his thought, when, like Jerome, direct contact with the places where Christ had lived was reflected in his thought with greater attention to the corporal and historical dimension.[57] Thus, the Cappadocian wrote a "Reply (*Antirrhetikos*) to Apollinaris" in response to the "Demonstration (*Apodeixis*) of the divine Incarnation, which took place in accordance with the human being" by the bishop of Laodicea.

From the very first lines of Gregory's refutation one can see that his main concern is the fact that Apollinaris' theology would make the bodily and historical life of Christ, including His conception, merely apparent. The dogmatic knot of the relationship between time and eternity is, therefore, at the heart of the matter. In this way, the history of salvation would be reduced to mere appearance, compared to immanence. The theological discussion thus becomes a diatribe on the reality and value of all history, since the humanity of Jesus can only derive from Adam and the series of all successive generations. This is immediately linked to freedom and, therefore, to the reality of the choices made by the human being.[58]

In this context, the Pauline anthropological tripartition, to which Apollinaris refers, plays a fundamental role. The distinction between carnal, psychic, and spiritual men in which the bishop of Laodicea exegetically frames 1 Cor 3:3, does not imply a distinction of nature, but rather a moral reading. Here lies the dogmatic core of the bishop of Nyssa's answer, according to which the reference to carnal men simply indicates an excessive inclination to the carnal dimension.[59]

The distinction of the human being into three elements, spirit, soul, and body (*pneuma, phychê, sôma*),[60] preached by the bishop of Laodicea

---

57 Jean Daniélou, "Le Symbole de la caverne chez Grégoire de Nysse," in *Mullus. Festschrift Theodor Klauser*, eds. A. Stuiber, A. Hermann (Münster: Aschendorff, 1964); Jean Daniélou, La chronologie des oeuvres de Grégoire de Nysse, *Studia Patristica* 7 (1966): 159–69.

58 Cf. Gregory of Nyssa, *Antirrheticus adversus Apollinarem*, GNO III/1, 140, 5–11.

59 Cf. *ibidem*, 141, 32–142, 2.

60 *Id.*, 209, 2.

with reference to the Pauline doctrine in 1 Thess 5:23, is applied to Christ who, to be truly man, must in turn be composed of these three elements. But Gregory counters:

> According to us, when Paul writes this to the Thessalonians, praying to the Lord that they may be sanctified wholly in body, soul and spirit, he does not divide the human being into three parts, but discusses which is the considerably higher philosophy concerning the use of freedom in this life, as he also does in his writings to the Corinthians. For there he refers to a carnal man and a spiritual man and to the psychic man who is between the two, calling carnal the one who is subject to the passions and matter, calling spiritual the one who is not weighed down by the ballast of the body, but has his mind turned to higher realities, and meaning by psychic the one who is exactly between the two and participates in the one and the other.[61]

The reference to freedom is fundamental here, because it places the interpretation of the Pauline passage in a moral and not a *physical* and necessary context. In fact, the name follows the element that the human person chooses as a guide in his or her existence. Thus the carnal man is not devoid of the operation proper to the intellect, nor is the spiritual man alien to the body, but the designation refers to the activities (ἐνέργεια) that man himself decides to carry out through his will.[62] The spiritual man is also bodily and psychic, so the psychic man has the possibilities offered to his nature by both the spirit and the body. But it is the exercise of freedom that determines the disposition to the more or less elevated concrete element.

The Pauline designations correspond, therefore, to what is seen in life,[63] including every aspect of reality which, as such, is an opportunity for personal sanctification:

61 *Id.*, 209,19–210,1.
62 Cf. *id.,* 210,3.
63 Cf. *id.*, 210,14–15.

Therefore [Paul], since he desires that those who are perfect in virtue should not only witness it in the higher life, but that they should turn their gaze to God even if they accomplish something that concerns the bodily dimension, and that they should not turn away from Him even if they accomplish some activity in between—for he says whether therefore you eat or drink or do anything else, do everything for the glory of God (1 Cor 10:31), so as not to be distracted from the goal of divine glory even in bodily occupations —therefore he invokes with his blessing on the Thessalonians, who are already fully turned to the best, a complete sanctification, saying God will sanctify you to perfection, and all that is yours, spirit, soul and body (cf. 1 Thess 5:23), i.e., wishing that every bodily, psychic and spiritual activity be directed to sanctification (πρὸς ἁγιασμὸν).[64]

The affirmation of the possibility of accessing union with God through every activity, even the most material, could not be clearer, as its Christological foundation. The second divine Person, in becoming flesh, has in fact sanctified his entire life in its bodily aspects. But this life of Christ is inserted into the fabric of human lives, and is relationally inseparable from them. The human being and God cannot be conceived dialectically, just as time and eternity cannot be opposed to each other.[65]

Gregory of Nyssa's conception is very daring because, through an *ante litteram* phenomenological analysis, he traces the erect structure of the human body back to creation in the image and likeness. Man would be able to look at the sky precisely because of his relationship with God. Not being forced to move on all fours, with the head always turned towards the earth, would be linked to a sort of evolution, which would have freed the front limbs for those functions that in animals are carried out by the mouth, allowing the development of language. Thus the human body would be impregnated with *logos*, in the sense of being configured for speech and work, i.e., for relationships.[66]

64 *Id.,* 210,21–211.2.
65 Cfr. *id.*, 194,28–195–14.
66 *Id.*, *De hominis opificio*, 8, PG 44, 144ª–149A.

This doctrine reflects the spirit of Cappadocian theology and will have a great influence through the monastic rule of Basil,[67] later resonating also in the West in the Benedictine *ora et labora*.

From the theological point of view, we see that the affirmation of the value of work passes through the simultaneous recognition of the absolute difference between the creature and the Creator, but also of the relationship that unites them precisely in the ability to work:

> God gave man the faculty of participating in creativity, in the manner proper to the creator of the universe, and which he reproduces in himself, although to an absolutely lesser degree than God [...] Man does create objects that were not there before, and in this respect he has in himself a certain analogy with divine creativity: he creates houses, ships, cities, walls, harbors, seats and beds, in short, small and large things that did not exist before; but he is not able to produce substances.[68]

The quoted text is profoundly modern, because it highlights the value of human creativity as a reflection of the Creator's perfection and, therefore, as the content of the divine image and likeness instilled by God in man.

These teachings did not remain theoretical, but had a profound effect on ancient society, leading to the first clear condemnation of slavery.[69] The absence of freedom made forced labor inhuman and therefore unworthy of the divine image impressed on the human being. The same can be said for work in the service of the poor and defenseless. Lepers themselves began to be treated as human persons and, therefore, as citizens, even though the disease attacked the very human aspect of the

---

67 Basil, *Regulae,* 37,2.
68 Theodor of Mopsuestia, in Philoponus, *De opificio mundi*, 6, 14: W. Reichardt, 256, 16–19; 21–27 (Teubner: Leipzig, 1897).
69 Ilaria Ramelli, *Social Justice and the Legitimacy of Slavery: The Role of Philosophical Asceticism from Ancient Judaism to Late Antiquity* (Oxford: Oxford University Press, 2016).

sick.[70] Basil had a hospital city built—Basiliad—in which the sufferers were taught a trade so that the social distancing imposed by medical necessity would not be at the expense of their dignity.[71] This work is probably linked to the severe famine that had struck Cappadocia between 368 and 369, but was built on a scale that transcended the simple hospice for the poor and sick.[72] In fact, Basiliad was first and foremost a real city, indeed a "new *polis*" (τὴν καινὴν πόλιν).[73] As Martin Schlag has written: "They [the Fathers] inverted the pyramid of honor in pagan society: dignity was no longer conquered by prowess in battle and through merits recognized by the Senate, but was rather granted to all by God, independently of the social standing of the person involved."[74]

6. The Fathers' Humanism: West

It is extremely important to note that these practical consequences do not move at a purely moral level but are the result of theological progress that has reshaped the philosophical and metaphysical image of God in the light of Trinitarian revelation to develop a new anthropological conception. This is confirmed by the Latin tradition, which is more pragmatic and concrete because of its Roman heritage. In this sphere too, the Fathers based their interpretation of the value of work in creation, as Ambrose shows:

> It does not seem out of place to explain why Jesus had a carpenter for a father. In fact, through this typology, he shows

70 Cfr. Sozomen, *Historia Ecclesistica*, 34, 9.
71 Marcello La Matina, "Il posto del malato tra Ethos e Logos. Luoghi di cura e saperi nel mondo antico e tardoantico," *MEDIC* 15/2 (2007): 17–30.
72 Benoit Gain, *L'Église de Cappadoce au IVe siècle d'après la correspondance de Basile de Césarée (330–379)* (Roma: Pontificium Institutum Orientale, 1985).
73 Gregory of Nazianzus, *Oratio* 43 (*Funebris oratio in laudem Basilii*), 63, 1, 3 (Paris, 1908).
74 Martin Schlag, "The Historical Development of Christian-Catholic Humanism," in *Humanism in Economics and Business*, eds. D. Melé and M. Schlag (Dordrecht: Springer, 2015).

that his Father is the One who, as the author of all things, created the world, as it is written: "In the beginning God created the heavens and the earth" (Gn 1:1). It is true that one should not compare the human with the divine, but the typology is clear, since the Father of Christ works in fire and in the Spirit (Mt 3:11), and like a good carpenter of the soul He planes our faults all around, promptly putting the axe at the root of the shriveled trees (cf. Mt 3:10 and Lk 3:9), skillful in cutting down the stunted branches, leaving the lofty ones on the summit, flexing the hardness of the soul with the fire of the Spirit, and shaping the whole human race for different tasks with the different quality of ministries.[75]

The divine nature is transcendent and infinite, thus radically different from creation, but the Creator has left His own personal imprint on His work, so that the history of salvation, the life of Christ and the life of every human being are linked by a profound ontological relationship.

The value of work even in its most material aspects is strongly affirmed. Augustine, who had been attracted to Christianity by Ambrose's preaching, had to show the radical nature of this doctrine in his confrontation with some monks, who interpreted 2 Thess 3:10 as referring only to spiritual work, but not to physical labor.[76] The answer is based on the exegesis of the Fourth Gospel and the Ambrosian heritage.

In his commentary on John, Augustine, with a dizzying progression of theological thought, dissolves the possible conflict caused by an overly literal exegesis of John 5:17 and Gn 2:2: Jesus said that his Father always works, but in the creation narrative it is said that God rested on the seventh day. How is this possible? As always, theological reasoning must start by showing the difference between the Creator and the creature. This is why the Bishop of Hippo immediately explains that God does not need to rest like a human being after working.[77] This difference also indicates the reason that makes it possible for Him to rest while continuing to work:

75 Ambrose, *Expositio evangelii secundum Lucam*, 8,10ss.
76 Cf. Augustine, *De Opere Monachorum*, 1, 2.
77 Cf. *id.*, *In Evangelium Ioannis*, 17, 14.

I think it can be said, rather, that God's rest on the seventh day was a great mysterious sign of our Lord and Savior Jesus Christ himself, who declared: "My Father continues to act, and I also act." (John 5:17) The Lord Jesus is also God. He is the Word of God, and you have heard that in the beginning was the Word; and not just any word, but the Word was God, and all things were made through Him (John 1:1.3). Here perhaps is the meaning of God's rest from all His works on the seventh day. For read the Gospel and see how many wonderful things Jesus accomplished. He was crowned with thorns, He was hung on the cross, He said, "I thirst" (John 19:28), and He took the vinegar with which the sponge was dipped, so that the prophecy might be fulfilled: "In my thirst they have watered me with vinegar" (Ps 68:22). But when all His works were done, on the sixth day, He bowed His head and yielded his spirit, and on the Sabbath He rested in the tomb from all His labors. So it is as if He said to the Jews: Why do you expect me not to work on the Sabbath? The Sabbath law was given to you in reference to me. Turn your attention to the works of God: I was there when they were done, and they were all done through me. I know that my Father continues to act. The Father created the light; He said: Let there be light (cf. Gn 1:3); but if He said, it means that He worked through the Word. And I was, I am his Word; by me through those works the world was created, and by me through those works the world is governed. My Father worked then, when he created the world, and He still works now, governing the world. In creating He created through me, in governing He governs through me. This the Lord has said, but to whom? To the deaf, to the blind, to the lame, to the sick who did not want to know about the doctor, and in their madness wanted to kill Him.[78]

Augustine's reading takes up Ambrose's *Exameron* where the purpose of creation is identified with the incarnation, in the sense that God's

78 *Id.*, 17, 15.

rest would be a prophecy of Good Friday, because the Creator could rest after the creation of the human being having someone to forgive.[79] In the interpretation of the Bishop of Hippo, the act of creation is seen in its Trinitarian depth, showing that salvation is not a different act from creation. God is not a filler who intervenes only when something goes wrong, but is a loving and infinitely omnipotent Father who has imprinted His image on man and cares for him to the extreme of offering His Son for him. The passion of Christ is thus presented as the culmination of God's work, which corresponds precisely with His rest.

In the light of this interpretation of John's gospel, in the line of the prologue where creation is presented from within God, Augustine dispels the doubts of the monks who considered that some works were not worthy, returning to Paul's teaching, in particular to 1 Cor 10:31–32 already seen in Gregory of Nyssa as a key element of his teaching on work:

> The Apostle, therefore, would not have shunned some work in the field or some craft. For I do not know of whom he should have been in awe in this matter who had said, "Do not be an admirer either of the Jews or of the Gentiles, or of anyone in the Church of God" (1 Cor 10:32). If one should say: "For the Jews"; but the patriarchs also were shepherds of flocks. If: "For the Greeks," that is, those whom we call heathen; but certain philosophers whom they held in high esteem were also shoemakers. If: "For the Church of God"; it was a carpenter (cf. Mt 13, 55) that righteous man whom God chose to be the witness of the virginity of her who was to remain undefiled as a bride and then forever, he—I say—to whom the Virgin Mary, mother of Christ, was betrothed. Any of the above professions is therefore good, as long as it is performed faithfully and without fraud.[80]

The affirmation of the goodness of all work, provided it is done with a righteous intention, cannot be clearer. This also removes any possible tension in interpretation with respect to Matt 6:25–34:

79 Ambrose, *Exameron* IX, 10, 76: CSEL 32.1.2, 418.
80 Augustine, *De Opere Monachorum*, 13, 14.

If one were to make an objection to them on the basis of the birds of the air that do not sow or reap or fill the granaries, or the lilies of the field that do not work or spin, they would have no difficulty in answering in this way: If we for a just reason, for example, sickness or urgent duties, could not work, surely He would give us food and shelter, as He does with the birds and the lilies who do not do any such work. But as long as we are able to work, we should not tempt our God. For to have this ability is a gift from God, and when we live by our work, we live by the gift that He bestows upon us, for it is God who grants us the ability to work.[81]

The possibility of working is, therefore, defined in terms of a divine gift, i.e., the personal relation with God, because it belongs to the very image impressed by the Creator in that one creature that He created for dialogue with Himself and as His own representative in the world. The difference with respect to Greek philosophical thought is clear, so much so that work itself is presented as a path to unity with God. But the theological foundation of this novelty is the possibility of rereading the world in the light of the Trinity, in such a way as to overcome any possible opposition between the one and the many, thus dissolving the ambivalence of the work itself.

7. Conclusion: Hope for Postmodernism

Work can make us more human or less human. Some people suffer from dependence on work, other from a lack of it. The biblical-patristic perspective explains why. We have been created by the One God who is in Himself relational and who created the world out of nothing, constituting it as a fabric of relationships. The human being is the only one in the cosmos to be in the image and likeness of the Trinity, since (wo)man was conceived in order to call the Creator "you." This makes us capable of free and caring relationships, making it possible for us to be God's representative in the world. But because of this very freedom we can also say no, falling into the necessary dimension.

81   *Id.*, 27, 35.

Thus, human work lies metaphysically between the one and the many, between freedom and slavery, where relationship is precisely what discriminates between these two possibilities. In myths, everything originates in conflict, and work can lead to conflict, as the examples of Cain and Abel, Babel and Egypt show. But reality originated from the one and only Creator, who gave us the Son who became flesh for us. Thus, through His work, at once Creator and creature, the path for work to return to human care is reopened. The Fathers analyzed these tensions and recognized the relationship as the fundamental element of this path. Thus work is conceived as a filial gift, which constitutes (wo)man as radically dependent on the One who created him and her and preserves them in being, but also as a partner of this God who loves relationships because He is relations. The condemnation of slavery and the affirmation of the need to care for the weakest with one's own work have their premise here, in the relational dimension that makes work good as expression of the divine image in the human being. This is what we desperately need in this post-modern age, suspended between the acute perception of the need for caring for the human in all its forms, even the most fragile or rejected, and the temptation to overcome the human through a techno-gnosis, which promises nothing but more manipulation and slavery. The biblical-patristic perspective may, therefore, prove valuable so that post-modernity can continue to be human.

Thus, the proposed biblical-patristic pathway also highlights the prophetic force of *Laborem Exercens*, which highlights the fundamental role of Genesis in understanding human work,[82] to affirm the primacy of the subjective dimension of work over the objective one. The Church Fathers' reading of scriptural data shows that "the primary basis of the value of work is man himself, who is its subject," because "work is *for man* and not man *for work*."[83] This magisterial text can therefore be considered a real guide for dealing with postmodernism, without reducing

---

82 "The Church finds in the very first pages of the Book of Genesis the source of her conviction that work is a fundamental dimension of human existence on earth" (*Laborem exercens*, n. 4).

83 *Ibidem*, n. 6.

it simply to a radicalization of modern assumptions, but discovering in it, through the light of Christ, that "it is always man who is the purpose of the work."[84]

84   *Ibidem.*

Work Theology in the High Middle Ages

Patricia Ranft

1. Introduction

Just as John Paul II's *Laborem Exercens* has had impact well beyond Catholicism, so too did the work theology of medieval religious.[1] Recognition of the relationship between creation, end times, change, stewardship, labor, individualism, social equality, and communal responsibility owes much to the theology developed by these religious. Unfortunately, they have been almost exorcised from Western history—along with the tenth through the thirteenth centuries in general. Despite a century and a half of superb research into the High Middle Ages, and despite the documentation of the innumerable critical advances made during those centuries, the connotation in popular culture of the word medieval is still overwhelmingly negative; when a teenager calls his or her parents medieval it is not a compliment! As the following article will show, none of these connotations are deserved. The theological, theoretical, social, and practical advances that medieval religious made in connection with work are examples *par excellence* of their genius.

---

1   I use the words "work" and "labor" interchangeably, although I realize some make distinctions between the two. For one of the few recent discussions of medieval work theology, see John van Engen, "Medieval Monks on Labor and Leisure," in *Faithful Narratives: Historians, Religion and the Challenge of Objectivity*, ed. Andrea Sterk and Nina Caputo (Cornell, NY: Cornell University Press, 2014), 47–62. For a much more detailed history of medieval work theology, see my *Theology of Work: Peter Damian and the Medieval Religious Renewal Movement* (New York: Palgrave Macmillan, 2006). Unfortunately, due to a change in editors as the book was going to press, the uncorrected draft was published instead of the final one. I take this opportunity to apologize to readers for any errors therein.

2. Cluny

While patristic writers did much to define Christian attitudes toward work, their theology did not much influence early medieval society's attitude towards labor or laborers. Society continued antiquity's view of labor as inherently demeaning, limited to manual labor, and assigned to the lower classes. Although regrettable, it is somewhat understandable: given society's struggle to establish a secure, flourishing environment, it needed a large, compliant workforce to achieve that end. By the tenth century, however, increased stability created an environment that permitted society to attend to needs other than basic survival. Warmer temperatures gave birth to an agriculture revolution, technology increased output, and the population grew, creating more free time to reflect upon the abstract. Medieval society could now commence to create a distinct culture of its own, and it did. One result was a monastic renewal. From the tenth to the thirteenth centuries, multiple religious orders were founded or reformed. This began within Benedictine monasticism and culminated in the mendicant orders, all of which introduced lasting social innovations. It is within these orders that we find the formulation of a sophisticated theology of work and the application of that theology to real-world situations. This time secular society gradually adopted it.

The pre-formulation of medieval work theology is found in Cluny, a French Benedictine monastery founded in 909. Its daughter houses spread rapidly throughout the West during the next two centuries, and with it spread a distinctly Cluniac eschatological spirituality. Eschatology is a powerful tenet in any spirituality, potent beyond its benign appearance, because it contains a call to action in the face of death. Contrary to a view of death as threatening societal collapse, belief in the *Parousia* demands society to ready this world for the next. Thus, Christian eschatology "creates a perennial source of strength for strenuous activity."[2] To "make

2   Colin Morris, *The Discovery of the Individual, 1050–1200* (London: SPCK, 1972), 145; and Ernest Troeltsch, *The Social Teaching of the Christian Church*, 2 vols. (New York: Macmillan, 1931), 2:1005–06. Troeltsch continues: "Eschatology does not, as short-sighted opponents imagine, render this world and life in this world meaningless and empty; on the contrary, it stimulates human energies." 2:1006.

straight the way of the Lord" (Jn 1:23) requires "an expenditure of physical and/or mental effort": this is Webster's definition of labor.

What was new in Cluniac eschatological spirituality is its emphasis on the prophetic nature of eschatology: The future gives meaning to the past and present.[3] Thus, Cluny reshaped its old rituals and invented new ones to reflect the belief that people can transcend the limitations of death. By so doing, it gave society hope for a future beyond the grave, and along with that, power. Power is only power in relation to the future; without a future, power is inconsequential and futile. Thus, eschatology and power are joined at the hip. To believe in Cluniac eschatology is to believe one has the power to change the present to ensure the intended future. Cluniacs' self-definition provided them with motivation to change their world in anticipation of life after death:[4] "Some men, seeing death approaching them and knowing they have led evil lives, are smitten with terror and bitterly ask themselves," writes Bernard of Cluny, "what shall I do?"[5] Cluny's charter answers: "No one can come to [heaven] unless he prepares the way here by giving generously of his sustenance to those who are laboring in the Lord's vineyard."[6] Clearly, Cluniac eschatology insists on labor, and labor produces change.[7] True, Cluniac spirituality places greater emphasis on prayer as an instrument of change, but it recognizes work as necessary in the construction of a

3   There are broadly two types of Christian eschatology, prophetic and apocalyptic. The former sees continuity between present and future through change; the latter believes in their discontinuity, the future attained through sudden divine intervention. See John Wilson, *Pulpit in Parliament* (Princeton: Princeton University Press, 1969), 198–208.
4   See Kassius Hallinger, "The Spiritual Life of Cluny in the Early Days," in *Cluniac Monasticism in the Central Middle Ages*, ed. Eileen Hunt, 1–10 (London: Macmillan, 1971).
5   Bernard of Cluny, "Sermon on the Unjust Steward," in *The Source of Jerusalem the Golden*, tr. H. Preble, ed. S. Jackson (Chicago: 1910) 8:194–95.
6   H. E. J. Cowdrey, "Unions and Confraternity with Cluny," *Journal of Ecclesiastical History* 16:2 (1965), 152–62.
7   Patricia Ranft, "The Maintenance and Transformation of Society through Eschatology: Cluniac Monasticism," *Journal of Religious History* 14:3 (1987), 246–55.

society fit for the Last Judgment. Thus, with Cluniac eschatology's recognition of this need to work, it was left to Peter Damian to construct a theology expanding on the implications of this mandate.

3. Peter Damian

Damian (1007–1072) was born in Ravenna of humble origins, but, fortunately, this did not hinder him from receiving a sound education in Faenza, Parma, and, perhaps, Ravenna. He acquired immediate fame as a teacher upon completion of his education, but sometime around 1034 he abandoned teaching and entered Romuald of Ravenna's (952–1027) new monastery at Fonte Avellana, where Cluniac influence was extensive; Romuald had spent years at Cluny before founding his monasteries. Teacher, rhetorician, monk, prior, bishop, cardinal, theologian, papal legate: By the time of his death Damian was known throughout the West as one of its premier leaders. While modern scholarship has been remiss in failing to acknowledge his importance, medieval society was not. In Dante's *Divine Comedy*, it is Damian who stands at the highest level of Paradise.[8]

That Cluniac spirituality influenced Damian is well documented. He wrote exemplary stories about Cluny's Abbot Maiolus and had a close relationship with Abbot Hugh, perhaps Cluny's greatest abbot.[9] When Cluny owed Peter payment for a service rendered, he asked for the payment to be the "support [of] one poor man with food and clothing," stating "this is the fruit of my labor."[10] That Damian saw Cluniac eschatology and work to be intimately connected is clearly seen in his discussion of the etymology of the name Cluny: "This word derives from haunch

---

8 Dante Alighieri, *Paradise*, tr. Dorothy Sayers and Barbara Reynolds (Harmondsworth, BG: Penguin, 1962; repr.1986), canto 21, 43–44; 105–10; 114–19; 121. See also, Bernard Hamilton, "S. Pierre Damien et les Mouvements Monastique de son temps:" *Studi Gregoriani*, 10 (1975), 175–202.

9 See Letter 106:26–30, in *Peter Damian Letters*, tr. Owen Blum, vols 1–3, 5; Blum and Irven Resnick, vols. 6–7 (Washington, DC: Catholic University of America Press, 1989–2005), 5:188–91. All future references will follow this form: L106:26–30, *Letters* 5:188–91.

10 L 103.3 in *id.*, 5:143.

(*clunis*) and goad (*acus*), indicating the practice employed with oxen used for plowing." Thus, Cluny is etymologically and historically a place of work: "And as a man's spirit is made to dread the terror of the Last Judgment, it is like the point of the goad piercing his posterior. It pierces the rear, that we might direct our effort toward that which lies ahead."[11]

After entering Fonte Avellana, Damian did not abandon the academic world entirely. He was determined to resolve the main tension between the world he left and the world he entered. How can Christians, especially religious, justify pursuing truth in secular subjects when they had vowed themselves to the pursuit of spiritual matters? His answer is simple and profound: Resolution is in the word truth. All knowledge, secular or sacred, is found in God, because God is *Truth Itself*, a phrase Damian employed frequently when referring to God.[12] The search for Truth, regardless of where, is the search for God. Moreover, Damian's emphasis on the universal obligation to pursue Truth had the further consequence of equalizing people. Truth is found in everyone: "We have as teachers not orators but fishermen...men who are meek and simple."[13]

Damian's next step was the construction of a social theology. At its center was eschatology, from which his work theology flowed naturally. As Cluny intimated, only through work would the present world change into a world faithful to its eschatological end. "As to our beginning and to our end, these we cannot alter," but work can change what happens "between these two limits."[14] Work changes life after birth, but after death "nothing more can be changed" because work ceases.[15] Failure to work is "dissolute negligence" of the eschatological mandate to make

---

11 L 113.4, 5 in *id.*, 5:287–88.
12 L 8.4, *id.*, 1:102; L 23.20, *id.*, 1:225; L 115.6, *id.*, 5:308; L 108.19, *id.*, 5:205; L 28.14, *id.*, 1:263; L 39.9, *id.*, 2:105; L 50.37, *id.*, 2:307; L 81.31, *id.*, 3:221. See Patricia Ranft, "The Role of the Eremitic Monk in the Development of the Medieval Intellectual Tradition," in *From Cloister to Classroom*, ed. E. Rozanne Elder (Kalamazoo, MI: Cistercian Publications, 1986), 80–95.
13 *Patrologicae cursus completus, series Latina*, ed. Jean-Paul Migne, vols. 221 (Paris, 1844–64) 144:824, 828. Here after PL–
14 L 104.31, in *Letters*, 5:161.
15 L 111.6, *id.*, 5:251.

ready for the eschaton.[16] Spread throughout his writings, his work theology is neither systematic, self-conscious, nor methodical. Its underlying tenets must be teased out of his other, more explicit theologies, a difficulty that partially explains why it has been ignored in modern times. However, its excavation is more than worthwhile; for without knowledge of Damian's contribution, the history of work theology is incomplete: Damian leads us directly to John Paul II. That said, I will now offer a brief sketch of Damian's theology.

He begins with Creation. "The perfect man…is rightly made in the image of his Creator," and must "strive, insofar as is possible, to imitate the example of God himself" by rendering creation perfect.[17] Damian resurrects a Platonic metaphor to illustrate the relationship between humanity and creation: "Just as in Greek man is called a microcosm, that is to say, a little world,…so also each of the faithful seems to be, as it were, a little Church, with all due respect to the mystery of hidden unity" of all creation.[18] The metaphor has many presumptions: a unified universe, a unified humanity, humanity's participation in nature, and a shared destiny. As such, humanity's interest in the wellbeing of creation is of the highest priority. People are God's stewards on earth.

Work in all its innumerable forms is how humanity fulfills its role as stewards; it perfects the imperfections caused by sin. All activity—be it intellectual, physical, or spiritual—that readies creation for end times is work. It is not the sole domain of one class, but the obligation of all persons. The specific task of each individual varies, but not its intrinsic value. It is only when the work of each person is united with the work of every other person that creation is ready for the eschaton. Damian utilizes a body metaphor to explain this relationship between the individual and the community: "All are from one, and all are one… and, therefore, even though she seems to be divided into parts with respect to her physical circumstances, the mystic integrity of her inmost unity can in no way be broken up."[19] Thus, for Damian there is no

16 L 54.10, *id.*, 2:350.
17 L 49.11, *id.*, 2:278.
18 L 28.25, *id.*, 1:270.
19 L 28.13–14, *id.*, 1:263.

ascending ladder of importance in labor. Every individual's work is of equal importance. He continues:

> In the human body, moreover, the eyes, the tongue, the feet, the hands, each have a function naturally proper to them. But the hands do not touch for their own benefit, or the feet walk, or the tongue speak, or the eyes behold just for themselves,... [thus] the part functions for the whole and the whole for its parts. This is why Paul's tongue can truly say: "On account of the Good News of Christ I labor."[20]

Damian's recognition of the unbreakable bond between the work of the individual and the welfare of the community is one of his most significant contributions to Western culture, no less Christian theology. Damian then explains how this bond applies to religious communities, specifically with respect to the lay brotherhood. The origin of lay brothers (religious who are "under vows, dedicated to a life of toil") is hazy.[21] Even though the Benedictine Rule mandates labor, when monasteries like Cluny expanded liturgical duties, the manner of doing manual labor had to be newly addressed and communities increasingly turned to lay religious to perform manual tasks.[22] We know lay brothers were members of Romulad's monastery at Camaldoli by 1012. Eventually the Carthusians, Grandmontensians, Fonte Avellanans, Gilbertines, Premonstratensians, Vallombrosians, and Cistercians all had lay brothers; at a minimum Fontevrault and the Gilbertines had lay sisters.[23] Damian's comments concerning lay

20 L 28.22, *id.*, 1:267–68.
21 Conrad Greenier, "The Laybrother Vocation in the Eleventh and Twelfth Centuries," *Cistercian Studies* 15 (1980), 39.
22 See Kassius Hallinger, "Woher Kommer Die Laienbrüder?" *Analecta S. Cisterciana* (1956), 26–42. Unfortunately, little research has been done on laysisterhoods. For Romuald, see Colin Phipps, "Romuald—Model Hermit," in *Monks, Hermits and the Ascetic Tradition*, ed. W. J. Shields (Oxford: Blackwell, 1985), 65–77.
23 Katherine Smith, "Laybrothers and Laysisters, Christian," in *Encyclopedia of Monasticism* ed. William Johnson (Chicago: Fitzroy Dearborn, 2000), 1:748.

brothers are the earliest, his recording of their vows the first, and his inter-action with them among the most significant. Moreover, he argues that lay brothers are not auxiliary but rather full members of the community whose work is equally as virtuous as all other members. They are not hired labor-ers or servants but religious, the same as choir monks are. Damian's support of lay brothers is but a natural extension of his work theology. He saw all work as an apostolate, a way to become an *imago Dei*. He writes of his own various labors as an apostolate to the community. No task was beneath him; no task was more or less worthy than another. What mattered was not the particular work a person does, but that one fulfills one's apostolate.

Damian also applied his work theology to another burgeoning phe-nomenon: the Canons Regular movement. Its origin is also obscure. We do know that it arose in mid-eleventh century Italy and that Romuald's monasteries were involved in it.[24] It is also documented that Damian was its chief champion, earning him the moniker "veritable founder."[25] He devoted two treatises to Canons Regular, urging them to make sure their words reflected their works.[26] The treatise of one anonymous Canon Regular is clearly influenced by Damian's theology. He begins by ac-knowledging that "there are very many pursuits necessary for the monas-tic life," and then lists thirty-six different kinds of labor: reading, singing, preaching, writing, illuminating, ruling lines, scoring music, binding books, sewing new clothes, repairing old clothes, carving spoons, mak-ing candlesticks, building beehives, gardening, farming, grafting and pruning trees—and on and on. He treats all labor as equally valuable and useful. Anonymous concludes by reminding the canons that "although certain people believe it is disgraceful and indecent" that canons should do manual labor, it is not; all labor is sanctifying.[27]

---

24 The first legislation concerning the canonical life was in 755. The Caro-lingians also issued legislation to regulate those attached to churches. Ca-nons "Regular" refer to canons who lived by a set rule (*regula*). See L 50.20, in *Letters*, 2:299–300.

25 Augustin Fliche, *La réforme grégorienne*, vols. 3 (Paris: E. Champion, 1924–27), 1:337.

26 L 39, in *Letters* 2:98–110 and L 98, *ibid.*, 5:87–102.

27 Translated in J. C. Dickenson, *The Origins of the Austin Canons* (London: SPCK, 1950), 193.

Perhaps more significant is the fact that, unlike the canons, most of society did not consider it self-evident that Anonymous' thirty-six activities were indeed labor. The canons helped society accept them as so not only by their theology, but by the permanent mark on Western culture their work left: Geoffrey of Hanlawe pioneered in medicine, Humphrey of Llanthony in secular literature; William of Newburgh and Richard of Hexham reinvigorated historiography; Godrey, Richard, Walter, and Hugh of St. Victor were intellectual giants of the period; the canons' house of St. Ruf was the center for architects and sculptors.[28] In short, the Canons Regular lived Damian's theology.

Canons in fact expanded Damian's theology to include a greater emphasis on the utilitarian nature of work. "A man does not do all the good which he is capable so long as he refuses to be useful to others," wrote Hildebert of Lavadin.[29] Adam of Dryburgh reminded his fellow canons that they have an obligation to be sure that their work is "efficacious and useful" and that their counseling offers "useful advice."[30] Hugh of St. Victor comments thus: "Indeed the works of saints which are very much in the estimation of men pertain not to dignity but to utility." Even the study of Scripture is good only "if I work to know and to perform good and useful acts."[31]

Damian did not limit his message to religious. He chided the laity to change their attitude towards work and to fulfill their own obligation to labor. He reminded Duchess Beatrice of Tuscany of her obligation "to bring forth a harvest of good works." Beatrice must follow Empress Galla's example and "display to the world the miracle of the productive fir tree" which, although it bears no fruit, "is useful in erecting buildings and...serves the needs of construction."[32] When writing to the Countess Guilla, Damian expands on the nobility's responsibility to address social injustices through their labor. If all have an obligation to work, then it is

---

28 See C. Stephen Jaeger, *The Envy of Angels* (Philadelphia: University of Pennsylvania Press, 1994), 244–68.

29 PL 171:141–43.

30 PL 198:554, 557, 492.

31 PL 176:932–33, 640.

32 L 51.2, in *Letters*, 2:335.

unjust to live off the labors of others. Therefore, "you should not delight in savoring the small holdings of orphans or the fattening birds of widows" but work as good stewards to ensure their comfort. He implores: "O noble daughter, do not by plundering the poor but recoil from food acquired through violence," and "break the pattern of customary evil that you have found, abolish the practice of confiscating the property of the poor, prevent unjust taxes and impositions on the serfs, and, following the example of King Josiah, establish a new order."[33] It is the assigned task of rulers to labor for justice. He instructs her on the precise type of work needed to accomplish this. "And since the Apostle commands everyone to work with his own hands 'so that he may have something to share with the needy' you should intensify your farming, and thus your barns will be filled with abundant crops to be used in assisting the poor."[34] Consistent with these admonitions, Damian did not hesitate to reprimand Duke Godfrey of Tuscany for his failure to work assiduously towards establishing peace in his territory. Because the Duke "refrains from exercising the control of government" there is unchecked violence in his territory.[35]

Damian also praises lay persons who conscientiously do their assigned labor. Damian's letter to Beatrice of Tuscany focuses on the duties of secular rulers to "bring forth a harvest of good works."[36] He tells Duchess Adelaine to "never abandon the practice of generosity and justice." Her exemplary legal work in clerical reform assures her that "when you have finished your stewardship...the kingdom of heavenly glory" awaits.[37] Damian also commends Margrave Bernard because his farm "produced bumper crops of various kinds."[38]

Akin to his teaching on the relationship between work and social justice is Damian's promotion of the division of labor. Damian finds this principle

33 L 143.5, 4, 8, *id.*, 6:144–45.
34 L 143.8, *id.*, 6:145–46.
35 L 67.12, *id.*, L 3:75.
36 L 51.2, *id.*, 2:335.
37 L 114.18, *id.*, 5:304. During the eleventh century simony was a vehicle for social mobility. The laity reacted to the resulting scandals by asserting their right to judge clergy.
38 L 110.28, *id.*, 5:242.

in Scripture: "Each one has an undivided gift from God, one after this manner, another after that" (1 Cor 7:7). Consequently his model for the division
of labor is found in the *vita apostolica*: "The apostles themselves, the leaders of the Christian teaching and those foremost in our discipline, had different tasks among themselves."[39] In practice, division of labor was present
from the beginning of Western civilization, but it was used to divide society.
Damian sees division of labor as a source of unity and equality, both so inseparable from Damian's eschatological vision. He cites 1 Cor 12.4–6:
"'There are all sorts of service...[and] varieties of workings,'" and it is God
who "determines in each the merit and variety of functions."[40] Because all
tasks are necessary for the perfection of the *Parousia*, division of labor is
essential. It is the laity's duty to supervise secular matters, and the clergy's
to "supervise ecclesiastical matters." Thus, the priest "must be the soul of
compassion" while the secular judge must "punish the guilty."[41] As the
Body of Christ requires diverse functions, so too a cleric's work must differ
from a layperson's: "In truth, what business has a monk involving himself
with the trifling affairs of laymen? To what purpose should I carry within
the confines of the monastery the noisy courts of justice?"[42] When all complete their tasks, the community thrives. In monks' cells, for example, "various duties are performed in harmony, where here one is chanting, there
one is praying, in another one is writing, and in still others various kinds of
manual labor are performed"; paradoxically, the result of this diversity is
communal unity.[43] "Even though she [the Church] seems to be divided into
parts with respect to her physical circumstances, the mystic integrity of her
inmost unity" remains intact.[44] Whether cleric or lay person, noble or serf,
man or woman, it is God, not humans, who "examines the deeds of every
person and office, of every rank and order."[45]

In our modern culture work is usually promoted as a way out of
poverty, but "work" here refers to paid labor enabling the purchase of

39 L 153.19, *id.*, 7:25.
40 L 40.4, in *id.*, 2:115–16.
41 L 67.6, *id.*, 3:72.
42 L 132.25, *id.*, 6:69.
43 L 28.54, *id.*, 1:287.
44 L 28.14, *id.*, 1:263.
45 L 153.5, *id.*, 7:17.

things. Damian instead promotes the non-material benefits of work. Work gives one freedom. It frees one from demeaning reliance and control, as was the plight of many serfs. Conversely, lack of work limits one's independence. This has the potential to be detrimental. When monastics "fail to practice useful trades...they employ laymen, even evil ones" because the work must be done.[46] Importantly, work also provides access to the rest found only in God, for "this rest is only acquired if first the person is engaged in the various labors."[47] Jacob had "to toil in service" for two seven-year periods because "the labor of a good work comes before the rest of contemplation" of God.[48]

As time passed, society agreed more and more with Damian's insights concerning work. Menial, manual tasks were gradually viewed as vehicles for reward, not humiliation, and secular vocations were slowly recognized as equal to religious callings. The tripartite division of society into fighters, prayers, and workers became popular, and it was generally accepted that all these laborers were equal, necessary, and admirable. Common people heard from the pulpit that their labor, no matter how servile, was not demeaning. Laborers were encouraged to perform those monumental tasks medieval society completed in its quest for control of their world. The great accomplishments of Western Christendom would not have been possible if that society had not taken a new look at the nature of work. Damian demanded that it do just that. His preaching and writings stimulated reflection and prodded society into reassessing its appraisal of labor. His immediate influence is seen in the theology of work that emanated from the religious reformers that followed in his wake.

4. Cistercians

At the beginning of the medieval reform movement, the order that rivaled the canons in popularity was the Cistercian. It evolved from the Benedictines, gradually incorporating existing reform monasteries into its own family. Early Cistercians simply thought of themselves as strict

46 L 54.10–11, *id.*, 2:350–51.
47 L 153.31, *id.*, 7:32.
48 L 153.34, *id.*, 7:34.

interpreters of the Rule of St. Benedict, but by the mid-twelfth century they were generally acknowledged to be their own order. While in many aspects they were innovators, their understanding of work followed the basic theology of Damian. They too rooted work theology in eschatology: "It is only human, I know," writes Guerric of Igny, "to be distressed about the moment of passage from the earth," but one should be "confident about the day of judgment" as long as one's "life does not cease to produce fruit."[49] His commentary on Is 40:3 and Mk 1:3, "Prepare the way of the Lord," acknowledges that the preparation is difficult, but "the labors of the penitents" will bring about the necessary changes and "the prizes that await us."[50] He places labor in an eschatological setting: "'Look,' [the Lord] says, 'I am coming quickly and bringing with me reward to bestow on everyone in proportion to his labors.'"[51] Guerric urges his contemporaries to imitate John if they desire heaven, for there is neither "justification without good works" nor "holiness without toil." If there were, then "John's life should be laughed at rather than preached."[52] Guerric acknowledges the hardships of work. Manual labor wearies the body and is in fact burdensome. The body yearns for rest. He places this desire for rest in eschatological terms. When you labor you "will find rest in your soul…joy in your work" and be "consoled in your toil by the hope of the reward."[53] That reward is, of course, the rest found in God. Thus, the apparent conflict between labor and rest disappears when placed in an eschatological context. In the anticipation of the Parousia, which is present *already but not yet*, a person "is at rest even when he is working."[54]

We hear echoes of Damian in other Cistercian theologians, if not all. Baldwin of Ford lists numerous occupations that are rightfully called labor.

---

49 Guerric of Igny, *Liturgical Sermons*, vols. 2, tr. Monk of Mt Bernard (Spencer, MA: Cistercian Publications, 1970), 3.1, 2; and 23.6. For origins of Cistercians, see Constance Berman, *The Cistercian Evolution* (Philadelphia: University of Pennsylvania Press, 1996).
50 Guerric, *ibid.*, 5.2 and 5.5.
51 *Id.*, 1.4.
52 *Id.*, 43.3
53 *Id.*, 25.4.
54 *Id.*, 49.2.

He includes no derogatory remarks, no modifying descriptions, no hierarchical placement of work or workers. He assigns no social status to any, thus opening the door even further to the social mobility that medieval society pursued. Like Damian, Baldwin turns to the Mystical Body to support his work theology. "We who are many are yet one body," and each has a specific job to "work for a common end." With "different sorts of service, and different sorts of working" each type of labor "becomes of benefit to another because its usefulness is shared."[55] In his discussion of rest, he also sheds light on the relationship between work and rest: "God is a certain peace and supreme rest, for he is always the same, always immutable and unchanging." Humans work to change the temporal world so they can attain union with the unchangeable God in heaven. "Perfect rest cannot be found in the place of affliction," Baldwin admits, but "here our rest is begun" through work.[56] Isaac of Stella encourages all to work "while you can do good," for our model is Christ who "came not to have service done for him, but to serve others."[57] And throughout Bernard of Clairvaux's writings, eschatology looms large in his consideration of labor. "Temporal works are as seeds of an eternal reward," and they must "do good purposefully."[58] Aelred of Rievaux harkens back to Damian's reminder of the individual's relationship with the community via the Mystical Body: "Whatever one does, this belongs to all; and whatever all do, this belongs to each...let not our lay brothers bewail that they do not sing or watch as much as the monks. Nor the monks, that they do not work as much as the lay brothers." It is from the labor of both that "one tabernacle is made."[59] Guibert of Hoyland's sermons echo Damian's concern for the poor and labor's ability to alleviate the plight of the poor. Workers "eat

---

55 Baldwin of Ford, *Spiritual Tractates*, vols.2, tr. David Bell (Kalamazoo, MI: Cistercian Publications, 1986), 15.

56 *Id.*, 5.

57 Isaac of Stella, *Sermons on the Christian Year*, vols.2, tr. Hugh McCaffery (Kalamazoo, MI: Cistercian Publications, 1979), 23.13 and 12.5.

58 Bernard of Clairvaux, *Sermons of Conversion*, tr. Marie-Bernard Said (Kalamazoo, MI: Cistercian Publications, 1981), 8.16 and 13.20. See also, *The Letters of Bernard of Clairvaux,* tr. Bruno Scott James (Chicago: Henry Regnery, 1953), 105.

59 PL 195: 249.

from their manual labor, but from their slender reserves they share with the needy."[60]

One should note the practical, visual results of Cistercian work theology, for their labor had a major impact on Western civilization. As Constance Bouchard concludes, "the Cistercians were involved from the beginning with the rapidly developing economic practices of the twelfth century and were in some instances prime movers of their evolution."[61] They constructed the first medieval irrigation system in northern Italy, introduced fulling mills into southern France, mined coal and quarried stone for the architectural masterpieces of the Middle Ages, were the mainstay of numerous markets and fairs at the heart of economic growth, and aggressively pursued overseas trade.[62] The list goes on and on. Without belief in the spiritual goodness of labor, motivation for their labor would be hard to explain.

5. Women's Contributions

Unsurprisingly, women's work theology is hard to document, given the lack of extant sources and various prohibitions of women's engagement in theology. Fortunately, these attempts did not erase their theology of work completely, and it certainly did not inhibit nuns from engaging in work similar to the monks. Herman of Tournai records his personal knowledge of Cistercian women's work: they "labor constantly with their hands, not only spinning and weaving, which are well known to be women's work, but also in digging in the fields, in clearing the filled woods with axes and hoes, and in tearing out thorns and brambles."[63] Hildegard of Bingen (1098–1179) is the first woman to write extensively

---

60 Gilbert of Hoyland, *Sermon on the Song of Songs*, vols.3, tr. Lawrence Braceland (Kalamazoo, MI: Cistercian Publications, 1979), 23.3.

61 Constance Bouchard, *Holy Entrepreneurs* (Ithaca, NY: Cornell University Press, 1991), 187.

62 See Constance Berman, "Medieval Agriculture, the Southern Countryside and the Early Cistercians," *Transactions of the American Philosophical Society*, 75:5 (1986); and David Williams, *The Cistercians in the Early Middle Ages* (Leominster: Fowler Wright, 1998).

63 PL 156: 1001–02.

on work theology. At age eight, she was enclosed in an anchorhold with the recluse Jutta, who "labored with such unrelenting effort."[64] Jutta's emphasis was not unique; the *Ancrene Wisse*, a popular rule for women recluses, insists that "holy people often used to live by their hands."[65] Jutta passed on this wisdom to Hildegard who, in turn, was both a theologian of work and a model worker. Honored as a Doctor of the Church, Hildegard was a musician, scientist, preacher, monastic founder, spiritual director, prophet, abbess, medical scholar, philosopher, and, thankfully for posterity, an author. In every labor she undertook, she did so because she believed work would change the world for the better.

Hildegard's mature thought on work is found in *Book of the Rewards of Life*, although almost her entire corpus references labor's significance.[66] She supplies an additional element to Christian work theology by focusing on the Incarnation. During the Early Middle Ages, resurrectional theology dominated Western religious culture; the Risen Christ, for example, is pervasive in the period's art. Even Christ's crucified corpus was often clothed in royal garments.[67] In the waning days of the eleventh century, theology began to speak more about an immanent, incarnational God, and such emphasis prompted theologians like Hildegard to place work theology in a more dynamic context. In both resurrectional and incarnational theology creation is embraced, but because resurrectional theology envisions a regal, distant God, divine presence in the world is not as evident as it is with the indwelling, immanent God of incarnational theology. The Incarnation immerses the human Jesus in the world and changes it forever. Hildegard considers

64 *The Life of Jutta*, 4,6, in *Jutta and Hildegard: The Biographical Sources*, tr. Ann Silvas (University Park, PA: Pennsylvania State University Press, 1999), 71,74.

65 *Ancrene Wisse*, part 8, in *Anchorite Spirituality: Ancrene Wisse and Associated Works*, tr. Anne Savage and Nicolas Watson (New York: Paulist Press, 1991), 201.

66 *The Book of the Rewards of Life*, tr. Bruce Hozeski (Oxford: Oxford University Press, 1994).

67 See Celia Chazelle, *Crucified God in the Carolingian Era* (Cambridge: Cambridge University Press, 2001). In the High Middle Ages a bleeding, suffering corpus is more common.

it her special task to persuade others that people, *imago Dei*, must change the world too. When incarnational theology dominates and rational endeavors are conducted in theological language, the relationship between people and creation is seen in a particular light. God "is known through creation," Hildegard reminds us, and therefore the desire to know God is the same as the desire to know creation. In her *Physica* and *The Book of Divine Works*, this thesis dominates. In both, she insists that creation must be embraced in order to better understand it and thus God.[68]

Hildegard explains how this is accomplished: "When God created man, he told him to work with the other creatures. Just as man will not end unless he is changed into ashes and as he will rise again, as also his works will be seen."[69] The responsibility to work is "part of His divine plan," therefore, "a worker who does not do the work he is capable of doing...will became a rustic."[70] Hildegard's mild name-calling reflects more disappointment than condemnation. Work is the means by which we share in God's creative power, so the person who fails to work is refusing a gift, the gift of power: "Therefore, as long as I live on this earth, I will acquire the things I want by thinking, speaking, and working."[71] When work's power is used incorrectly, the whole of creation, not just creatures, will "bring their complaints to their Creator" and become hostile to humanity, as in the case of floods, thorny plants, etc.. "If we do not care for earthly things, the earth will sprout thorns and thorny plants. We would then be sinning," Hildegard warns.[72] Because they "are more changeable in their actions than any other creature," people must think carefully about the changes their work brings about, including personal changes: "You have the power to master yourself." Given the power of

---

68 *Liber divinorum operum*, eds. A. Derolez and Peter Dronke (Turnhout: Brepols, 1996); and *Physica*, tr. Pricilla Throop (Rochester, NY: Inner Tradition,1995).   She relies heavily on 2 Cor 5:17: "There, if any man is in Christ, he is a new creature; the old passed away, behold new things have come."

69 Hildegard, *Rewards*, 6:17.18.

70 *Id.*, 1:40.52; 4:7.11.

71 *Id.*, 4:9.14.

72 *Id.*, 4:59.76.

work to "overturn the whole world," people must ensure the usefulness of their work.[73]

Here Hildegard harkens back to the eleventh-century theologians. "God gave man the ability to work...[and] as a result man should look forward to what is useful."[74] She places this utilitarian aspect of work in its eschatological context. "Those who put their effort and care into their present life and who do not put any effort into their future life" do not understand the *raison d être* of work.[75] Their work must mirror divine work: "The Maker of the world undertook creation first, and thus set the example for His servants to labor after His fashion."[76] And again: "For God created man and subjected the rest of creation to him, in so far as man may work with the rest of creation so that God's work may not be blotted out."[77] Thus, work is useful to humans both "carnally and spiritually, because one thing proceeds from another. Man highly prizes his useful works, because he conceives them in his mind and brings them into effect by his actions. So too it is God's will that His power be manifested in all his creatures, because they are His work."[78]

Hildegard reinforces her predecessors' insistence on work's social leveling power, particularly between women and men. "The human form is seen in the inmost nature of the Deity," although these humans "are widely divergent in bodily form."[79] Rather than being divisive, these multiple forms are the basis for mutual dependence and unity. "Male and female were joined together in such a way that each one works through the other. The male would not be called 'male' without the female, or the female named 'female' without the male. For a woman is man's work, and man is the solace of woman's eyes, and neither of them

73 Letter 84r, in *Letters of Hildegard of Bingen*, vols.3, tr. Joseph Baird and Radd Ehrman (New York: Oxford University Press, 1994–2004), 1:188; and Hildegard of Bingen, *Scivias*, tr. M. Columba Hart and Jane Bishop (New York: Paulist Press, 1990), 3.10.2.
74 *Rewards*, 4:8.12.
75 *Id.*, 4:59.76.
76 Letter 156r, in *Letters of Hildegard*, 2:103.
77 *Rewards*, 5:75.94.
78 Letter 31r, in *Letters of Hildegard*, 1:96.
79 Hildegard, *Scivias*, 3:1.7, 8.

could exist without the other."[80] She continues in a memorable passage on the equality of women and men: "Woman was created for the sake of man, and man for the sake of woman. And…they should work as one in one work, as the air and the wind intermingle in their labor."[81] Hildegard's life is testimony to her work theology; her pioneering work in theology, music, literature, medicine, and art opened up new vistas in the West, just as her work theology urged her to do.

While Hildegard is the most significant woman theologian to treat work, she is not alone. Unfortunately, others did not author the abundant sources that Hildegard did, so they are harder to document. Their lives, on the other hand, are evidence of the dedication of these women to living up to the theses of medieval work theologians. The women formed many of the fringe apostolic groups of the era: Poor Lombards, Cathars, Poor Catholics, Waldensians, Humiliati, and the Beguines, to name a few of the more successful ones. Some flirted with heresy, a few were officially sanctioned, but all had a definite impact on work, workers, and society's perception of both. Most importantly, they had an actual impact on society's economic landscape as it transitioned from a barter economy to a profit economy. They embraced and promoted the attitudes necessary to make the transition successful. And this was likely possible because, unlike the monastic orders, these fringe groups had intimate contact with the urban population. In fact, the Cathars were so associated with cloth workers that they were commonly called *texterants*, weavers. Moreover, Humbert of Romans identified Humiliati as those who "live by the work of their own hands."[82] Their order was divided into three orders, the second and third for lay people, who were indispensable to the Commercial Revolution; chronicler Jacques de Vitry claims that in 1216 there were one hundred fifty Humiliati in Milan alone, excluding members living at home.[83] A few decades later, there were 227

---

80 PL 197: 885.

81 Hildegard, *Scivias*, 1:2.12.

82 Humbert of Romans, quoted in *Gli Umiliati nei loro XIIeXIII* (repr: Roma: Multigrafica, 1970), 261–63.

83 *Lettres de Jacques de Vitry*, ed. R. B. C. Huygens (Leiden: E. J. Brill,

communities in Milan, and Humiliati were present everywhere in the booming Italian cloth industry.[84] Clearly, the Humiliati considered labor to be an irreplaceable opportunity to be materially and spiritually useful to society.

Robert of Grosseteste tells us that Beguines, a group exclusively for women, flourished in the Low Countries and "are the most perfect and holiest religious because they live by their own labor and are not burdensome of their fellow humans with pecuniary demands."[85] Unfortunately, they too suffer from lack of documentation, but Jacques de Vitry provides us with some key observations. He recognized the significance of these women and of how their attitude toward work stirred many to follow suit. When writing a *vita* for a Beguine named Marie D'Oignies, he places her labor in the center of his narrative. She persuaded her husband "to imitate his companion" and serve with her at a leprosarium called Williambrouck. Here she became a Beguine, and continued to labor for "the necessities of life for the poor." De Vitry reports that "even strong men could barely endure a third part of her labor." At one point Marie "made plans to flee so that…she might beg from door to door," but eventually decided against begging.[86] As we shall see, the choice between working and begging plays a major role in the schism within the Franciscan Order in the Late Middle Ages. Fortunately, Marie and fellow Beguines chose correctly: work.

Another woman, Juliana of Mont Cornillon, best known for her role in establishing the Feast of Corpus Christi, provided another model of the new worker.[87] She began her religious life by asking to milk the cows

1960), 73. For further background on the impact religious had on urban centers see Ray Benton, *Economic Theology of the High Middle Ages* (New York: Routledge, 2020).

84 See Sally Brasher, *Women of the Humiliati* (New York: Routledge, 2003), 113.

85 Cited in Brenda Bolton, "Some Thirteenth Century Women in the Low Countries," *Nederlands archief voor kergeschiedenis* 61:1 (1981), 7–8.

86 Jacques de Vitry, *Life of Marie D'Oignies*, tr. Margot King (Toronto: Peregrina Publishing, 1993), prologue; bk 1.38; and bk 1.40.

87 The feast was the first universally observed feast in the Roman calendar and the first promoted by a woman.

daily: "Unwilling to eat her bread in idleness…she chose a humble and abject task which would serve the common good." Her reasons reflect a sound grasp of medieval work theology: "She considered that by her manual labor she would have a share in the penance of the sick and all the good works accomplished by the congregation that enjoyed the milk."[88] Intent upon giving "posterity an example," she "kept up both kinds of exertion, physical and spiritual, as long as she was able."[89] Proof of the power of her example is evident in the role that the Corpus Christi Feast played in this history of Western labor. Within generations of her successful promotion of the feast, it became the major vehicle workers employed to ensure recognition of their guilds—the predecessors of today's labor unions.[90] The only other female religious groups we have abundant sources for are Flemish women. Christina of St. Troud, Lutgard of Aywieres, Margaret of Ypres, Beatrijs of Nazareth, Ida of Nivelles, Ida of Louvain, Ida of Léau, Yvette of Huy, Elizabeth of Spalbeck, and Catherine of Louvain are all women few are familiar with today. However, medieval society recognized their significance and documented their contributions to the new work ethic in hagiographic form. They spoke about work's value; they worked. The tide was turning. Manual labor and laborers began losing their social stigma. As historian Jacques LeGoff aptly concludes, "With the beginning of the thirteenth century, the working saint was losing ground, giving way to the saintly worker."[91]

The mendicant orders were born during this transition, the Franciscans being of particular importance in the history of work. While they originally

---

88 *The Life of Juliana of Mont Cornillon (1192–1258)*, tr. Barbara Newman (Toronto: Peregrina Publishing, 1989), bk 1:5.

89 *Id.*, bk 1:7–8.

90 Miri Rubin, *Charity and Community in Medieval Cambridge* (Cambridge: Cambridge University Press, 1987), passim.

91 *Time, Work and Culture in the Middle Ages*, tr. Arthur Goldhammer (Chicago: Chicago University Press, 1980), p.115. Of course, the advances medieval society made in eliminating social stigma from certain kinds of work was hardly complete. As late as the eighteenth century French noblemen endorsed a longstanding tradition that barred them from commercial professions. To do so was to suffer "dérogeance," the loss of prestige and privilege attached to nobility.

embraced the work theology first articulated by Damian, within a few generations segments of the male branch were rejecting it.[92] The female branch stayed true to Damian's theology and even made their own contribution. *The Rule of Clare of Assisi* states that "the Lord has given the grace of working," and so all "are to work faithfully and devotedly in gratitude." It should be utilitarian and communal, that is, "work which pertains to a virtuous life and to the common good."[93] Francis of Assisi's original rule did enunciate a work theology, but it also included the following instruction: "And when it should be necessary, let them seek alms like other poor people."[94] Unfortunately, this permission became the crux of a conflict that tore the friars asunder and turned much of society against them in the Late Middle Ages. Most often viewed as a conflict over voluntary poverty, at the heart of the schism was actually the issue of work. Certain factions of Franciscans, insistent upon observing voluntary poverty, ultimately rejected manual labor. But by the early fourteenth century, society had been largely converted to medieval work theology and saw voluntary poverty and its subsequent begging as a denial of that theology.[95] If friars could work to support themselves, why should other people's work support them? Had not Damian already made it clear that one should "not live by plundering the poor but recoil from food acquired through violence…since the Apostle commands everyone to work with his own hands"?[96] Critics of these Franciscans argued that mendicancy was *ipso facto* sinful, because it rejected personal responsibility to work for survival. This in turn was a refusal to contribute to the well-being of self and society. The friars' "willful begging" rankled society. It violated scripture, papal rulings, patristic

---

92 See Patricia Ranft, "Franciscan Work Theology in Historical Perspective," *Franciscan Studies* 67 (2009), 41–70.
93 *Rule of St. Clare*, 7, 1–3, in *Francis and Clare: The Complete Works*, tr. Regis Armstrong and Ignatius Brady (New York: Paulist Press, 1982), 219. Clare's personal labor was cited in her "Bull of Canonization," as a reason for her sainthood. See Nesta de Robeck, *St. Clare of Assisi* (Milwaukee: Bruce Publishing, 1951), 234.
94 *Early Rule of Francis*, 7.3–9, in *Francis*, 115.
95 See *The Middle Ages at Work*, ed. Kelli Robertson and Michael Uebel (New York: Palgrave, 2004), esp. 88–125.
96 L 143.8, in *Letters* 6:145–46.

writings, and, most importantly, the *imitatio Christi*: Christ was a carpenter.[97] True imitation of Christ is achieved by working as Christ worked. Evidently, in a society that had imbibed medieval work theology and now saw labor as an individual and communal duty with the power to save and change society, voluntary poverty lost its religious appeal. Refusal to work was now seen as a vice, not a virtue.

Of course, Franciscan work history is not all negative. The criticism cited thus far pertains to the refusal to support themselves through manual labor. Society acknowledged and appreciated the labor of the Franciscans and the contribution that their fellow mendicants, the Dominicans and the Carmelites, made to Western intellectual culture, particularly the work they engaged in while establishing the great university centers that are still the mainstay of modern academia. Moreover, mendicant ministry to laborers in the new urban centers is to no small decree responsible for the cities' survival, and their preaching therein was crucial to the success of the Commercial Revolution. Nevertheless, it cannot be denied that many friars failed to appreciate how work theology had altered society's view of physical labor. In many ways, criticism of the friars allows us to see how thoroughly work theology permeated society. By the end of the fourteenth century, work theology and the work ethic it produced had almost universal acceptance. Able friars who voluntarily begged were the same as those who "lazed in idleness," condemned by society. In 1359, and again in 1376, England codified the Christian work ethic into law, and other countries soon followed.[98] Clearly, voluntary poverty and manual labor communicated different messages in the fourteenth century than they did in the tenth. Both were now judged though the lens of work theology.

97 See Richard FitzRalph, *Defensio curatorum*, 1405–08, in *Trevisa's Dialogue*, ed. John Perry (Cambridge: Cambridge University Press, 1925), 80–89.

98 B. Putnam, *The Enforcement of the Statute of Laborers during the First Decade of the Black Death* (New York: AMS Press, 1970), 11 and appendix. Spain, Portugal, France, Poland, Venice, Genoa, Bavaria and Hanault passed similar legislation. For comments on current view of labor laws, see Eve Tushnet, "Labor Laws: Lessons from Recovery Culture on the Meaning of Work," *America* 2222 (April 27, 2020), 26–28.

6. Reflections

The High Middle Ages was a period of extreme positive change. Unfortunately, this is rarely celebrated. The history of work theology provides an opportunity to do so. At the beginning of the period, society was struggling to survive; at its end it was thriving. At the heart of this progress is a new work ethic and the religious who perpetuated it, both in word and in deed. By identifying the sanctifying aspects of labor, the religious provided a new motive for labor. Work is not merely for survival, self-sufficiency, or repentance; it is for repairing and preparing creation for the *Parousia*. By firmly placing work in an eschatological setting, theologians opened up a different way of viewing labor. The punitive connotations of manual labor and the denigrating status of the manual laborer were challenged. Rather than hearing that work is burdensome, society learned that it is a gift of the highest order because it gave people the power to change the world. Again and again, theologians insisted that all people—man or woman, noble or commoner, saint or sinner—must respond gratefully. They argued that, whether physical, spiritual, or intellectual, all labor is valuable, and all laborers deserve equal respect. Their stress on work's utility led to a deeper appreciation of work's role in the pursuit of social justice. Recognizing the connection between work and the rest that is found only in God, they urged society to engage in the former in order to attain the latter.

What needs to be remembered here is how innovative these ideas were. Nowhere in the ancient world do we see the ruling class joyfully engaging in manual labor. Nowhere do we see a society questioning class divisions or recognizing the relationship between labor, laborers, and social justice. Nor did the ancients judge labor by its communal utility or view work as a source of both individual growth and societal unity. It is medieval work theology, unique in its time, which gave society the ability and motive to transform self, society, and nature. Yes, everything in medieval work theology flowed directly from Scripture and Tradition, but it was only when the theologians considered here explored, explained, and extrapolated from the preexisting theology that the West absorbed it into its culture. It was the adoption of this theology that empowered society to become the powerhouse known as Western Christendom. As a result, the Agricultural Revolution increased population, the economy burst forth, the Commercial Revolution established cities still thriving today, technology changed the relationship between person and nature, an intellectual awakening gave birth to universities, architecture defied gravity with its soaring cathedrals, and modern science sowed its first seeds. Each and every one of these medieval achievements was made possible by the labor of its people.

The debt *Laborem Exercens* owes to medieval theology is seldom mentioned for the simple reason that medieval work theology is rather unknown.[99] Once familiar with it, the continuity between it and John Paul II is obvious. In the encyclical's Blessing, John Paul II tells us that "work means any activity by man, whether manual or intellectual, whatever its nature or circumstances, it means any human activity that can and must be recognized as work...within a community of persons"; this could have been written by Damian.[100] "That human work is a key, probably the essential key to the whole human question" was argued a near millennium before John Paul II included it in his encyclical.[101] Before John Paul II claimed that once the dignity of the worker was recognized, "the basis of ancient differentiation of people into classes according to the kind of work done" would cease; medieval theologians preached the same.[102] Moreover, we have seen how many medieval theologians

99   Van Engen, "Medieval Monks," 61, agrees with its essential inclusion: "No history of labor and leisure in premodern Europe or even modern secular Europe will make sense of persisting attitudes and practice apart from their reshaping by medieval religious teaching and practice."

100 Blessing, at www.Vatican.va/content/john-paul-ii/en/encyclical/document/ hf_jp_ii_enc_14091981_laborem-exercens.html. For recent discussions about the relationship between work and social justice, see Emmanuel Pic, "La relation comme fondement de la dignité de la personne," *Bulletin de Littérature Ecclésiastique* 111:1 (2020), 13–22; Wayne Stumme, "The missing dimension of work and witness: a passion for workplace justice," *Word and World* 25.4 ( ) 413_23; Wilfred Sumani, "Work and the Promotion of Justice, Peace and Reconciliation in Africa," AFER; and Zachery Settle, "Work and Its Discontents: On Contemporary Theology's Response to the Question of Work," *Modern Theology* 37:1 (2021), 165–90. Issue 25:4 of *Word and World* is devoted completely to work.

101 *Id.*, 3.

102 *Id.*, 6.

reminded their contemporaries how, now in John Paul II's words, "man's work is a participation in God's activity."[103] From the Cluniacs to the mendicants, work theology was anchored in eschatology, and John Paul II follows suit: "The expectation of a new earth must not weaken but rather stimulate our concern for cultivating this one…foreshadowing of the new age."[104] Most importantly, medieval theologians gave living witness to the veracity of their theology. One may reasonably argue, that the religious of the High Middle Ages did far more than any other group to establish the foundation of Western civilization. In no small part is this due to their development of and adherence to Christian work theology.

---

103 *Id.*, 25. See Patricia Ranft, "Getting to Work: Entitlement Societies and the Devaluation of Labor," *America* 2000:5 (February 18, 2013), 16–18.
104 *Id.*, 27.

John Paul II's Metaphysics of Labor

Angela Franks

Anglophone debates over John Paul II's theory of labor are often concerned with his agreement with a neo-conservative economic program. While this is a worthwhile question, its terms do not do justice to the pope's capacious worldview. John Paul II's theory of labor fits within a larger metaphysical and aesthetic commitment, summarized in the key phrase from *Person and Act*: "Action expresses the person."[1] This personalistic commitment is central to the metaphysics of labor in *Laborem Exercens*.[2]

This chapter will begin by developing the context for John Paul II's understanding of labor. Using the work of Brad S. Gregory and Charles Taylor, the first two sections will engage in a brief historical survey. I will examine the late-medieval/early-modern shift in the valorization of work as part of ordinary life, a shift that was part of a larger divide created between being and action. The early-modern rejection of formal and final causality elevated instrumental reason, a move that also reconfigured human labor as purely instrumental. Combined with the ascendency of voluntaristic pictures of God, the result was, as Joseph Ratzinger puts it, "man's complete devotion to his own work as the only

---

1   The same idea is found in the theology of the body audience talks: "The body expresses the person." John Paul II, *Man and Woman He Created Them: A Theology of the Body*, trans. Michael Waldstein (Boston, MA: Pauline, 2006), 7:2, p. 154; 9:4, p. 164; and *passim*. See Angela Franks, "Deleuze, Balthasar, and John Paul II on the Aesthetics of the Body," *Theological Studies* 81, no. 3 (Dec. 2020): 649–70, https://doi.org/10.1177/0040563920960056.

2   John Paul II, Encyclical Letter *Laborem Exercens* On the Ninetieth Anniversary of *Rerum Novarum* (Vatican City: Libreria Editrice Vaticana, 1981), Prologue. Future references to this work will be abbreviated *LE*.

certainty."[3] In the third section, I turn to John Paul II and *LE* to see how he affirms the ordinary life of work in a way distinct from that of the early moderns. I will argue that John Paul II's aesthetic philosophy of the person provides a distinctive way of reconnecting being and action through expression. He returns to a sacramental, or semiological, account of action as revelatory of being, prior to any utilitarian purpose. I will conclude by showing how his approach bears fruit in the spirituality of work that he presents in *LE*. Such a spirituality prizes the "subjective" or personalistic meaning of labor before its "objective" use.

1. The Industrious Revolution

Recently, Charles Taylor and Brad S. Gregory have repristinated the labor theory of Max Weber's *Protestant Ethic and the Spirit of Capitalism* (1904–1905). For mostly different reasons than those found in Weber, Taylor and Gregory argue for the social significance of the attitudes and social conditions that began in the late medieval age and flourished in the Reformation.

Gregory emphasizes the universal condemnation of avarice in the patristic and medieval worlds. Money was understood to be conducive to idolatry, in that it can easily become an end in itself rather than a means to an end.[4] Gregory cites Aristotle, whom Thomas Aquinas followed on this point: "Consequently those who place their end in riches have an infinite concupiscence of riches; whereas those who desire riches, on account of the necessities of life, desire a finite measure of riches, sufficient for the necessities of life, as the Philosopher says."[5]

---

3 Joseph Ratzinger, *Introduction to Christianity*, second ed., trans. J. R. Foster and Michael J. Miller (San Francisco: Ignatius Press, 2004), 61–62. Similarly, Balthasar labels this the modern "Prometheus principle"; see Hans Urs von Balthasar, *Theo-Drama*, vol. II: *The Dramatis Personae: Man in God,* trans. Graham Harrison (San Francisco: Ignatius Press, 1990), 417–24.

4 Brad S. Gregory, *The Unintended Reformation: How a Religious Revolution Secularized Society* (Cambridge, Mass.: 2015), 246–47.

5 *Summa Theologiae*, Ia-IIae, q. 30, a. 4, English Dominican translation, available at www.newadvent.org. For commentary, see Angela Franks,

The virtue of almsgiving imprints medieval life with ideas and practices that relativized monetary gain.[6] Even though increasing urbanization, beginning in the eleventh and twelfth centuries, began to depersonalize economic exchange, the larger Christian context meant that "even in cities such behaviors remained market *activities* in what had not yet become a market *society*."[7] This was true throughout the late Middle Ages.

On the face of it, little of this changed with the Reformation. Like Catholic moralists, Reformers were just as opposed to the love of luxury, especially when found among the Catholic hierarchy.[8] Nevertheless, Reformed soteriology refused to allow a salvific importance to one's economic actions. Because it tended to deny that avarice or almsgiving could hurt or help one's chances for salvation, economic activity was disaggregated from the divine and given its own relative independence.[9] As seen especially in the "Industrious Revolution" of the Dutch Republic in the mid-seventeenth century, this disaggregation also seemed to lead to economic and political supremacy, brought about "by bracketing questions of Christian truth rather than letting doctrine dictate political decision-making."[10] This intentional separation of

"End-less and Self-Referential Desire: Toward an Understanding of Contemporary Sexuality," *National Catholic Bioethics Quarterly* 18, no. 4 (Winter 2018): 629–46 at 637.

6   I do not mean to imply that avarice was uncommon. (See Gregory's summary in *The Unintended Reformation*, 253, 258.) It was not, however, justified theoretically. For the importance of almsgiving, see *ST*, II-IIae, q. 187, a. 3, which makes the ability to give alms one of four reasons to work, and the commentary in Marc Vincent Rugani, "St. Thomas Aquinas on the Goodness and Right to Work Today," *The Downside Review* 136, no. 4 (2018): 193–210 at 198–200.

7   Gregory, *The Unintended Reformation*, 260, emphasis mine; see also 249–51, 258–60.

8   Summarized in *ibid.*, 262–64, 266–69.

9   *Id.*, 265, 269–72.

10   *Id.*, 274. Gregory points out that from the mid-seventeenth century on, European states foreswore wars of religion and fought instead for economic and political supremacy (282–83). For the importance of the Dutch Republic and the shape of early capitalism, Gregory relies heavily on Jan de Vries in *The Industrious Revolution: Consumer Behavior and the House-*

economic and political action from doctrine and salvation is new with the modern validation of work.

The economic rejection of the traditional Christian view of avarice is expressed clearly (and controversially) in 1705, by Bernard Mandeville in his poem "The Grumbling Hive, or Knaves Turn'd Honest," republished in 1714 as *The Fable of the Bees*. Avarice is now seen to be the necessary driver of the economy, producing good ends through bad means.

> The Root of Evil, Avarice,
> That damn'd ill-natur'd baneful Vice,
> Was Slave to Prodigality,
> That noble Sin; whilst Luxury
> Employ'd a Million of the Poor,
> And odious Pride a Million more …

Here vice becomes almost providential, turned to good economic benefit: "Thus every part was full of vice, / Yet the whole mass a paradise …"

2. The Affirmation of Ordinary Life

Gregory helps us to understand the ascendency of the economic in our social imaginary. Charles Taylor provides further insight into how "production and reproduction," which were previously seen as secondary compared to the primary end of virtue and contemplation, become more central.[11] He treats these themes under the heading of "the affirmation of ordinary life."[12]

hold *Economy, 1650 to the Present* (Cambridge: Cambridge University Press, 2008), and Albert O. Hirschman, *The Passions and the Interests: Political Arguments for Capitalism before Its Triumph* (Princeton: Princeton University Press, 1977), among many other sources.

11 Charles Taylor, *Sources of the Self: The Making of the Modern Identity* (Cambridge, Mass.: Harvard University Press, 1989), 211. I will not treat the changing status of marriage here; Taylor addresses it at 226–27.

12 *Id.*, 209–302; cf. Charles Taylor, *A Secular Age* (Cambridge, Mass.: The Belknap Press of Harvard University Press, 2007), 176–85. See Patricia

According to Taylor, this affirmation begins in the Reformation but does not become widespread until the end of the seventeenth and beginning of the eighteenth centuries. He locates its inspiration in the Reformation rejection (shared by many Catholic reformers) of a spiritual elitism that viewed the religious life as more fully "Christian" than the life of the ordinary layman.[13] "The institution of the monastic life was seen as a slur on the spiritual standing of productive labor and family life, their stigmatization as zones of spiritual underdevelopment." Luther himself lives out the theological shift by abandoning the monastery and marrying a former nun.[14]

Puritan clerics placed a particular emphasis on a dual Christian calling, both to faith in Christ and to a specific kind of labor. The important thing was not how elevated this labor was but how well one did it. Hence, preacher Joseph Hall argued, "God loveth adverbs; and cares not how good, but how well."[15]

In many ways, of course, this was simply a basic Christian conviction, a point Taylor does not completely grasp. In Christianity, the important thing was not how much the widow gave, but the degree of love and abandonment to God that marked her gift (Mk 12:38–44). For Thomas Aquinas, non-burdensome work was found in the garden before the fall and hence is an intrinsic part of human life created in the image of God, who is pure act.[16] Modern Catholic spiritual writers, such as St. Francis de Sales, emphasized the salvific potential of doing little things well, a trend that reached its apex in St. Therese of Lisieux's "little way."

Nevertheless, for metaphysical reasons that I will unpack shortly, the Protestant emphasis on adverbs, while not novel, had a distinct flavor.

Ranft's chapter in this volume for the principles guiding the medieval Catholic affirmation of ordinary life.

13 Taylor, *Sources of the Self*, 217; cf. *A Secular Age*, 61–76, on "reform."
14 Taylor, *Sources of the Self*, 218.
15 *Id.*, 223–24.
16 On the garden, see Thomas Aquinas, *Summa Theologiae*, Ia, q. 102, a. 3. On Thomas concerning human labor, see Rugani, "St. Thomas Aquinas on the Goodness and Right to Work Today"; and Sylvester Michael Killeen, O.P., "The Philosophy of Labor According to Thomas Aquinas: A Study in Social Philosophy" PhD diss, Catholic University of America, Washington, DC, 1939.

That flavor was due to the rejection of hierarchy, both ecclesiastical and ontological. For the Protestant, it was suspect to elevate one way of life—such as vowed continence—over another—such as marriage. As a result, hierarchies of all kinds became subject to a leveling process.

If it is no longer tenable that the life of the evangelical counsels is objectively superior to other forms of life, then the superiority of a life must be found not in its objective status within a hierarchy but only in the subjective way one lives it out. While the Catholic theology of work emphasized both objective and subjective excellence, the Protestant anti-hierarchical move allowed only for the subjective.[17] Hence all the weight was placed on the adverbial, on "how well" one did one's work.

In this scenario, idleness becomes a grave spiritual matter, as the preachers of the day repeatedly stressed. The opposition to idleness began to lend an increasingly moral valence to wealth, and poverty likewise became more morally suspect.[18] The elevation of industriousness was also an important theoretical element supporting the "Industrious Revolution" of early modernity. Further, along with diligence comes enjoyment, as long as it is rightly ordered: "there is no question of renunciation."[19] Renunciation of pleasure was itself renounced as popish elitism and works-righteousness.

This validation of ordinary life within Puritanism was mixed up with a surprising streak of Pelagianism. How could this happen? First, Taylor argues that the sacred/profane distinction, which smacks of popish spiritual elitism, was replaced by the order/disorder tension.[20] Calvinists believed that the elect must act responsibly to prevent vice from taking hold in a society. This responsible action entailed striving to order the community to virtue (as seen in Geneva or New England). An elite religious

---

17 See Thomas's relativization of work dependent upon one's state of life, with the life of the counsels as an objectively greater state, at *ST*, II-IIae, q. 182 and q. 183, a. 3.

18 See Gregory, *The Unintended Reformation*, 269–70. Cf. Victor V. Claar and Robin J. Klay, *Economics in Christian Perspective: Theory, Policy and Life Choices* (Downer's Grove, Ill.: Inter Varsity Press Academic, 2007) for a contemporary Protestant version of the moral elevation of wealth.

19 Taylor, *Sources of the Self*, 225.

20 Taylor, *A Secular Age*, 82.

life may have been out of bounds, theologically, but an ordered society was enjoined by the Gospel itself. Secondly, the wider culture began to shift toward what Taylor calls a "disciplinary society," which was marked by a great optimism about the possibilities of human malleability under social control.[21] As part of this, all denominations were influenced by an early-modern repristination of Stoicism. Thirdly, Puritans allied themselves with Francis Bacon's program of technological service to mankind, which again seemed to put Gospel requirements into a practical program of societal organization through science.[22]

This last point illuminates our question concerning the status of labor, so let us explore it more closely. Taylor finds the logic of this alliance with scientific technology in the emphasis of both Puritans and early-modern scientists on *using* (rather than renouncing) the goods of the world for the glory of God and the service of man. This is clear in Bacon. But also, as Taylor states, for the Puritans' Augustinian theology, "*instrumentalizing* things is the spiritually essential step."[23] This was the Protestant form of Ignatian indifference, and it was mixed with an innately Calvinist distrust of the goodness of the postlapsarian natural world. Instrumental reason seemed to subsume appropriately all the fallen things of the world under the aegis of the Kingdom of God, as managed by the God-fearing man with technological know-how. According to this mindset, the proper enjoyment of the world was enabled by the instrumentalizing of all things for God and humanity by means of a uniquely modern knowledge.

This embrace of instrumental reason is the key for understanding how the early Protestant valorization of labor differs from the Catholic one. I will explore this divergence in the next section; for now, let us attend more

---

21   *Id.*, 90–145; cf. Michel Foucault, *Discipline and Punish: The Birth of the Prison*, trans. Alan Sheridan (New York: Vintage Books, 1995).

22   Taylor, *Sources of the Self*, 212–14 and 230–32. Both Bacon and the Puritans felt themselves to be rejecting dead tradition (Aristotelian science and Catholicism respectively, but of course the two overlapped) for the sake of living experience.

23   Taylor, *Sources of the Self*, 232, emphasis in the original. This shift relies upon a certain reading of Augustine, as in, e.g., *De Doctrina Christiana* and its distinction between *uti* and *frui*.

closely to the philosophical commitments behind the Puritan welcome of the Baconian project.

The ability to instrumentalize things, in order to turn them toward the benefit of humanity, requires emptying those things of any final purpose they might have had. In this way, final causality was jettisoned. Further, in order to be plastic matter available for manipulation, things cannot already be marked by form. Yet formal and final causality make the cosmos meaningful, marked by an intrinsic order. In rejecting these forms of causality, the late-medieval *via moderna* of nominalism and its related voluntarism created conditions for a new vision of the cosmos. Now the universe is not the expression of the eternal divine ideas but rather held together by the power of God.[24]

In such a metaphysical context, the role of human labor is exaggerated. If the world is not supported by an intrinsic order but rather only by the free will of God, the divine *potesta absoluta* could have ordained a completely different reality, even one in which the moral law was exactly opposite to the one we now have.[25] In such a world, labor's ordering activity is all the more urgent to *make* the fallen cosmos into part of God's kingdom.

> It is no longer a matter of admiring a normative order, in which God has revealed himself through signs and symbols. We rather have to inhabit it as agents of instrumental reason, working the system effectively in order to bring about God's

---

24 Charles Taylor, *A Secular Age*, 97; cf. Thomas Pfau, *Minding the Modern: Human Agency, Intellectual Traditions, and Responsible Knowledge* (South Bend, Ind.: University of Notre Dame Press, 2015), 168. The loss of formal and final causality is traced in many other works, including Gregory, *The Unintended Reformation*; Louis Dupré, *Passage to Modernity: An Essay in the Hermeneutics of Nature and Culture* (New Haven: Yale University Press, 1993); Simon Oliver, "Physics without *Physis*: On Form and Teleology in Modern Science," *Communio* 46 (Fall-Winter 2019): 442–69; and many more.

25 Dupré, *Passage to Modernity*, 176–77. Dupré qualifies this by noting that, for most nominalists, *once* God ordains a web of secondary causes, the order of that causality is completely reliable. Nevertheless, created order comes about *after* and *as a result of* divine decision, rather than being a limited but true reflection of God's eternal *ratio*.

purposes, because it is through these purposes, and not through signs, that God reveals himself to the world.[26]

Joseph Ratzinger sees these trends culminating in Giambattista Vico,[27] who rejects the Scholastic conviction that *verum est ens* (being is truth) in favor of *verum quia factum*: truth is found in what we make ourselves.[28] "The dominance of the fact began, that is, in man's complete devotion to his own work as the only certainty."[29]

Lastly, along with the other things inhabiting the world, man himself loses form and telos, and he also becomes plastic matter that must be fashioned. This self-fashioning is merely one more piece of human labor, which more and more defines man. This trajectory reaches its apex in Marx (more on him shortly) and in the post-structuralists inspired by him.[30] Yet some nineteenth-century observers, like poet Matthew Arnold, decried the change: "Our preference of doing to thinking" is but "another version of the old story that energy is our strong point and favourable characteristic, rather than intelligence."[31]

26 Taylor, *A Secular Age*, 98. Taylor's analysis would be enriched by considering the theological status of post-lapsarian creation in mainstream Protestant thinkers.

27 For the Renaissance precedents to Vico, see Stephen Greenblatt, *Renaissance Self-Fashioning: From More to Shakespeare*, second ed. (Chicago: University of Chicago Press, 2005).

28 Ratzinger, *Introduction*, 59.

29 Ratzinger, *Introduction*, 61–62. Similarly, Balthasar labels this the modern "Prometheus principle"; see Hans Urs von Balthasar, *Theo-Drama*, vol. II: *The Dramatis Personae: Man in God,* trans. Graham Harrison (San Francisco: Ignatius Press, 1990), 417–24.

30 On Marx, see Angela Franks, "A Body of Work: Labor and Culture in Karol Wojtyła," in *Leisure and Labor*, ed. Anthony Coleman (Lanham, Md.: Lexington Books/Rowman and Littlefield, 2019), 127–40, excerpted at https://churchlifejournal.nd.edu/articles/jp2s-labor-on-marx/. On the labor of self-construction in post-modernity, see Angela Franks, "A Wojtyłian Reading of Performativity and the Self in Judith Butler," *Christian Bioethics* 26, no. 3 (December 2020): 221–42, https://doi.org/10.1093/cb/cbaa011.

31 *Culture and Anarchy*, cited in Pfau, *Minding the Modern*, 180.

3. Rooting the Ordinary in Being

What are we to make of this history? Many themes sounded by the Puritans are appealing to contemporary Catholics. Vatican II documents such as the fourth chapter of *Lumen Gentium* and the entirety of *Apostolicam Actuositatem* from the Second Vatican Council, as well as John Paul II's Apostolic Exhortation *Christifideles Laici*, have emphasized that the laity are not second-class citizens, but rather full Christians called to sanctity. As a result, the ordinary life of work and marriage— Taylor's "production and reproduction"—have received increased magisterial attention.

The Catholic revival of ordinary life shares some convictions with Protestantism, and, indeed, modernity itself is a complex reality that need not be utterly rejected.[32] But the voluntarist and then Baconian abandonment of formal and final causality remains the key problematic feature within the modern affirmation of ordinary life. As a result, modernity exaggerated the role of human labor, investing it with an excessive eschatological import, a trend seen in Marxist-influenced thought today.

A retrieval of the value of human labor must begin with the conviction that the world reflects the divine *Logos* and not merely divine power. If this is the case, then the retrieval of both ontological and ecclesial hierarchies becomes tenable. Those hierarchies reflect the interrelations of formal realities with each other and vis-à-vis the final end, God; hence, form and finality are intrinsic to the objective (and not merely subjective) aspect of the goodness of human work. Further, a metaphysics that accepts form and finality requires less of human labor. We do not need to work to make the world to be in accord with God's design, because all things are already ordered according to that design, even if the Fall destabilizes that order to

32 See Dupré, *Passage to Modernity*, 223–30 (on modern spirituality, especially Ignatian) and 237–48 (on the Baroque) for attempts to integrate the positive aspects of modernity with Catholicism, utilizing Hans Urs von Balthasar in *The Glory of the Lord*, vol. 5: *The Realm of Metaphysics in the Modern Age*, trans. Oliver Davies, et. al., ed. Brian McNeil, C.R.V., and John Riches (San Francisco: Ignatius Press, 1991), 78–140 and 169–88. In general, this volume of *Glory of the Lord* provides a critical yet sympathetic reading of modernity.

some degree.[33] But if this is the case—if Catholicism does not call us to labor because our instrumental reason is the primary way to order the world—then what grounds the value of human work for the Catholic?

John Paul II provides an answer to this question in *Laborem Exercens*. The Polish pope was quite conversant in modern philosophy and especially in Marxist thought, which surrounded him, in varying degrees of decadence, in Soviet-controlled Poland. *LE* begins with the conviction that human labor is one piece of the revelatory function of the human person who is and who acts as *imago Dei*. "Man is made to be in the visible universe an image and likeness of God Himself, and he is placed in it in order to subdue the earth."[34] In so *being and acting*, the human person is *fulfilled*: "Work thus belongs to the vocation of every person; indeed, man expresses and fulfils himself by working."[35] In this way, the formal and final causality that was lost in modern concepts of labor is reintegrated into the anthropology of work.

First, let us note the pope's formulation: Even before man "fulfills himself" through labor, he "expresses" himself. By making human labor a matter of revelation before it is a matter of achievement, John Paul II's theology is formally aesthetic, if we use the terms provided by Hans Urs von Balthasar's theological aesthetics.[36] Balthasar argues that, in the form of a beautiful thing, "the truth and goodness of the depths of reality itself are manifested and bestowed...."[37] Beauty entails the revelation of the

---

33 The degree to which the Fall destabilizes God's created order is a point of disagreement among different Catholic theological systems, but Catholic orthodoxy demands retaining some sense of the enduring goodness of post-lapsarian nature.

34 *LE*, Prologue.

35 John Paul II, Encyclical Letter *Centesimus Annus* On the Hundredth Anniversary of *Rerum Novarum* (Vatican City: Libreria Editrice Vaticana, 1991), §6.

36 I will here focus on the "production" side of Taylor's production-reproduction equation, but the aesthetic rationale that John Paul II uses to validate labor is formally identical to what is found in his theology of the body and of marriage. See Franks, "Deleuze, Balthasar, and John Paul II on the Aesthetics of the Body."

37 Hans Urs von Balthasar, *Glory of the Lord: A Theological Aesthetics*, vol. 1, *Seeing the Form*, trans. Erasmo Leiva-Merikakis (San Francisco: Ignatius Press, 1982), 118. See also Hans Urs von Balthasar, *Theo-Logic*, vol.

depths of being. This aesthetic approach anchors the ordinary not primarily in doing—and action's corresponding utility—but in being. This approach is sacramental, in that it assumes the semiotic powers of the material world. In the being of creation, the goodness, truth, and unity of its divine source are imaged and made visible, and this making-visible is beauty.

Let us see how this dynamic occurs in John Paul II's aesthetic personalism, summarized in the frequently repeated phrase from *Person and Act*: Action reveals the person. In the book's introduction, Wojtyła explains that an analysis of personal act is his method for approaching the mystery of the human person. *"The act is a particular moment of the vision*—that is, the experience—*of the person."*[38] The person is especially revealed through moral acts and moreover becomes either good or evil through his acts.[39]

Further, the revealed person is an interior reality.[40] The richness of personal interiority is an important modern theme; for John Paul II, however, this interiority depends first upon metaphysics. Each person is a *suppositum*, an individual and unrepeatable substance.[41] Further, each person is a substance of a rational nature, which is the "birth" or origin of our freedom (*natura* derives from *natus*). Human nature ensures that man labors, as *LE* emphasizes: "From the beginning...he is *called to work. Work is one of the characteristics that distinguish* man from the rest of creatures...Thus, work bears a particular mark of man and of humanity...."[42] Further, human nature gives a person the ability to "create

1, *Truth of the World*, trans. Adrian J. Walker (San Francisco: Ignatius Press, 2000), 88, 141, and 216–25; and Franks, "Deleuze, Balthasar, and John Paul II on the Aesthetics of the Body." Balthasar's *Gestalt* (translated as "form") is not simply synonymous with either Platonic or Aristotelian *eidos*, yet it is still "formal" in the broad metaphysical sense in which I am using the term here.

38 Karol Wojtyła, in *Person and Act*, trans. Grzegorz Ignatik, ed. Antonio López, FSCB, vol. 1: *Person and Act and Related Essays*, in The English Critical Editions of the Works of Karol Wojtyła / John Paul II, series ed. Antonio López, FSCB (Washington, DC: The Catholic University of America Press, 2021), 102. Future references will be abbreviated P&A.

39 *Id.*, 105.

40 *Id.*, 113.

41 *Id.*, 174–76.

42 *LE*, Prologue, emphasis in the original.

oneself" through free actions, while also limiting the possible field of actions.[43] Metaphysics is not the last word on the person, but it is the first and necessary word.

Already here we see the recovery of elements abandoned in early modernity, namely, the sign-value of human action and its relation to human nature. An affirmation of the existence of human nature reintroduces formal causality to the equation, which is a reality that both enables and puts limits upon self-fashioning. Personal action builds upon, rather than replaces, the formal causality of nature, and human action is expressive before it is instrumental. But Wojtyła also affirms some aspects of modern anthropology, namely, the (qualified) self-formation that happens in action. The person who acts is a dynamic reality, who can form himself for better or worse, for virtue or vice.

Wojtyła's metaphysical realism enables his aesthetic vision. Being and act reveal the depths of reality, depths that ultimately point to the Creator as origin and goal of all things. Because the world is already marked by form and oriented to telos, human persons do not have to conjure up order. It is already present, revealed effortlessly in the visible world, and developed freely by human persons. As poet James Matthew Wilson puts it, "All things declare their being and their goodness / By going out beyond themselves like seeds …"[44] Man does this consciously and freely through his action.

4. A Spirituality of Labor

We are now able to understand John Paul II's aesthetics of labor.[45] *Laborem Exercens* undertakes a theological treatment of man as revealed

---

43 On human nature, see *AP*, 178–81. On limited self-creation, see *id.*, 171–73.

44 James Matthew Wilson, "Seeds," *Evangelization and Culture*, vol. 1, no. 1 (fall 2019), 15.

45 For more detailed treatments of John Paul II's theology of labor, see Franks, "A Body of Work," and Angela Franks, "The Body, Alienation, and Gift in Marx and Wojtyła," Proceedings of "The Heart of Work" Conference, Oct. 19-20, 2017, in *Pensando il Lavoro*, edited by Giorgio Faro, vol. II/5. Rome: Edizioni Università Santa Croce, 2017, pp. 223–37.

through labor, much like *Person and Act* undertook a philosophical treatment of man as revealed through action.[46]

As noted, Wojtyła's philosophizing happened against the backdrop of official Marxist dialectical materialism. Marxist analyses of labor emphasize the motivation of human needs. We labor, according to Marx's early writings, to satisfy the needs that arise from our embodied reality.[47] Yet this formulation bakes a negative motivation into labor. As Marx writes in *Capital*, "[T]he realm of freedom actually begins only where labor which is determined by necessity and mundane considerations ceases...."[48] The goal is not more meaningful labor but simply less of it.[49] Work should be something that one chooses to do out of one's free inclinations (one's will), as *The German Ideology* famously emphasized.

> [I]n communist society, where nobody has one exclusive sphere of activity but each can become accomplished in any branch he wishes, society regulates the general production and thus makes it possible for me to do one thing today and another tomorrow, to hunt in the morning, fish in the afternoon, rear cattle in the evening, criticize after dinner, *just as I have a mind, without ever becoming* hunter, fisherman, herdsman or critic.[50]

The voluntarist freedom of indifference exhibited here is breathtaking.[51] The will is not constrained by reality—including the reality that cows might

---

46 *LE*, §1
47 See Karl Marx, *Comments on James Mill*, trans. Clemens Dutt, in vol. 3 of Karl Marx and Friedrich Engels, *Collected Works* (London: Lawrence and Wishart, 1975), 220 [XXIX]; and Karl Marx and Friedrich Engels, *The German Ideology*, trans. W. Lough, in vol. 5 of Marx and Engels, *Collected Works* (New York: International Publishers/Lawrence and Wishart, 1976), 41–42.
48 Karl Marx, *Capital*, vol. 3, trans. David Fernbach (New York: Penguin, 1981), 959.
49 See my analysis in "A Body of Work" and "The Body, Alienation, and Gift."
50 Marx and Engels, *The German Ideology*, 47 [17], emphasis mine.
51 For "freedom of indifference," see the work by Servais Pinckaers, O.P.,

require more from their owners than the occasional dabbling in husbandry. Even more: beyond the activity of the work, Marx and Engels also refuse to grant any formal causality to the *worker*. They emphasize that one need not "become"—that is, be formed as—a worker of a certain type (a hunter, fisherman, herdsman, or critic). Such a limitation would be unfreedom, even alienation, because it would entail the division of labor seeping into the worker's objectivity. The division of labor (along with its close relative, private property) is the source of alienation, and in Communism it must not be allowed to contaminate the worker through any formal causality.

This fear of the intrinsically alienating power of form is absent in *LE* and John Paul II's other writings on work. The pope takes seriously the question of alienation.[52] Yet he does not find the truth that work forms the worker to be inherently troubling, because he is not troubled by formal causality. Because of the metaphysical grounding of the person as a *suppositum* of a human nature, alienating labor cannot literally de-humanize him; indeed, nothing can. Rocco Buttiglione notes:

> As philosopher, Wojtyła has elaborated a particular philosophy of human action that is also defined as a *philosophy of praxis*. It develops with particular profundity the theme of the *self-creation of man through work*. This theme, typical of Marxism, is here developed in strict connection with the philosophy of being and of the good.[53]

especially *Sources of Christian Ethics*, trans. Sr. Mary Thomas Noble (Washington, D.C.: The Catholic University of America Press, 1995), 242–43.

52 See *Centesimus Annus*, §41–42, and Wojtyła's earlier treatment in his essay "Participation or Alienation?": "Despite its weaknesses,…the concept of alienation seems needed in the philosophy of the human being" (in *Person and Community*, trans. Theresa Sandok, OSM, Catholic Thought from Lublin, vol. 4 [New York: Peter Lang 1993], 197–207 at 205).

53 *L'Uomo e il Lavoro: Riflessioni sull'Enciclica* Laborem Exercens (Bologna: CSEO, 1982), 13, translation mine, emphasis in the original. Buttiglione considers this philosophy of praxis to be one of John Paul II's most important innovations; see also his *Karol Wojtyła: The Thought of the Man Who Became John Paul II*, trans. Paolo Guietti and Francesca Murphy (Grand Rapids, Mich.: William B. Eerdmans Publishing Co., 1987), 121.

But if this kind of metaphysical grounding is lost—as is the case with early modernism and with Marx's theory—human activity has the power of actual self-destruction, because the formal activity of human nature and the substantial reality of the human being as *suppositum* are absent: "Labor is *man's coming-to-be* for *himself* within *alienation*, or as *alienated* man."[54] Thus, there are no ontological safeguards that could protect the person against alienating labor. And for Marx, within capitalism, labor can only be alienating and therefore destructive.

Instead of this denigration of labor, John Paul II rewrites the "intransitive" element of work in *LE*: no longer inherently alienating, labor can now be in the service of the virtue of the subject. Of course, work is "transitive," in that it begins in a subject and is directed outwardly.[55] "Work [is] a 'transitive' activity, that is to say an activity beginning in the human subject...."[56] The person expresses herself and creates through action. But labor is also "intransitive": work must "serve to realize [the person's] humanity, to fulfill the calling to be a person that is his by reason of his very humanity."[57] Work expresses and forms the person, on the basis of his substantial reality. Through our labor, we form the products of our labor, and we also form ourselves. Contrary to the self-fashioning proposed by modernity, this formative power is based upon the prior reality of a formed cosmos. Labor works with and builds upon this formation, but our work is absolved of the urgent need to create form *ex nihilo*. This relativization of work is simultaneously its freedom.

Recall the Protestant preacher exclaiming that "God loveth adverbs; and cares not how good [the kind of work is], but how well [one does

---

54 Karl Marx, *Critique of Hegelian Philosophy*, in Marx and Engels, *Collected Works*, vol. 3, 333 (XXIII), emphasis in the original.

55 *LE*, §6. This distinction is not original to John Paul II; it is found in Aristotle, in *Metaphysics* ix, 16, as commented upon by Aquinas, *ST* Ia, q. 18, a. 3, ad 1.

56 *LE*, §4.

57 *Ibid*, §6. More on the "intransitive" is in Karol Wojtyła, "The Constitution of Culture through Human Praxis," in *Person and Community*, 265–67. See also Deborah M. Savage, *The Subjective Dimension of Human Work: The Conversion of the Acting Person According to Karol Wojtyla / John Paul II and Bernard Lonergan* (New York: Peter Lang, 2008).

it]." *LE* agrees with the Puritan conviction that the value of work is not rooted in a certain kind of work, but the encyclical puts less value on "how well" one performs work. Rather, the value of work is found in its personal dimension: "The basis for determining the value of human work is not primarily the kind of work being done *but the fact that the one who is doing it is a person.*"[58]

In other words, rather than an ethic of diligence and utility defining the value of work—an ethic closely tied to instrumental reason—work's value is defined by its personalistic content, an approach closely tied instead to formal causality. By relativizing effectiveness and elevating personhood, John Paul II presents a metaphysical theory of human work that escapes the utilitarian trap. "[I]t is always man who is *the purpose of the work....*"[59] For this reason, all work is a human good.[60]

The result is a true spirituality of work, as *LE* develops.[61] As Rocco Buttiglione puts it, the dynamism of human action and labor serves "as the place of the manifestation of being...."[62] Even the futility that marks all post-lapsarian labor is caught up in this spirituality. The toil of work reminds us of death, which entered into the world at the same moment as toil. Further, work's futility is a sign of the Cross. Both toil and death have meaning in light of the Resurrection, which gathers up all created futility and brings to fruition the seeds of a new life within it.[63]

58 *LE*, §6, emphasis mine.
59 *Id.*, emphasis in the original.
60 *Id.*, §9.
61 *Id.*, §§24–27; cf. Joe Holland, *Creative Communion: Toward a Spirituality of Work* (New York: Paulist Press, 1989); Przemysław Piątkowski, "The Spiritual Status of Work in Opus Dei," *Journal of Management, Spirituality & Religion* 4, no. 4 (2007): 418–31, https://doi.org/10.1080/14766080709518676; Vivian Ligo, "Configuring a Christian Spirituality of Work," *Theology Today* 67 (2011): 441–66; and James B. Murphey, "Opus Dei: Prayer or Labor? The Spirituality of Work in Saints Benedict and Escrivá," *The Charismatic Principle in Social Life*, Routledge Frontiers of Political Economy, ed. Luigino Bruni and Barbara Sena (New York: Routledge, 2012), 94–111.
62 Buttiglione, *L'Uomo e il Lavoro*, 13.
63 *LE*, §27.

The Resurrection transforms what, in human work, is already a natural image of the Creator God.[64] The Father creates men ultimately for Sabbath-rest on his bosom (Jn 1:18). Thus, "man ought to imitate God both in working and also in resting, since God Himself wished to present his own creative activity under the form of *work and rest*."[65] Work is a matter both of acting and of being: not only the "exercise of human strength in external action," but also the "becoming more and more what in the will of God he ought to be...."[66] In both the being and the acting, man images the God who is and who creates and saves.

In this way, John Paul II in *LE* seeks to validate human labor on metaphysical-aesthetic and personalist grounds. Human work is indeed useful, but it is not good simply for that reason. It is good primarily because it reflects and participates in the creativity of the God who creates and saves. Because of this imago-nature, Wojtyła can say, "Man is a being, so to speak, doomed to creativity."[67] In human labor, our doing is rooted in our being. Work expresses the goodness, truth, and beauty of created being, which is itself an echo of the Good, the True, and the Beautiful who is the triune God.

---

64 *Id.,* §25.
65 *Id.*, emphasis in the original.
66 *Id.*
67 Karol Wojtyła, *Love and Responsibility*, trans. Grzegorz Ignatik (Boston: Pauline Books and Media, 2013), 121.

Confronting a Technocratic Future:
Women's Work and the Church's Social Vision

Dr. Deborah Savage

Humanity has entered a new era in which our technical prowess has brought us to a crossroads.
Pope Francis
Laudato Si'

I saw death overtaking a life of infinite beauty, and I felt that this was not just an external loss that we could accept and remain who we were.
Romano Guardini
Letters from Lake Como: Explorations on Technology and the Human Race

Buried as it is in the panoply of ideas that have shaped the history of the West, few people realize that the roots of the contemporary fascination with the use of technology can be traced to a key moment in our long intellectual tradition. In 1537, Sir Francis Bacon famously declared that knowledge is power. And in the wake of this declaration, he persuaded those who followed that its purpose is to gain mastery over nature in order to make it conform to the demands of men.[1] That we now find ourselves at the crossroads Pope Francis points to in his 2015 encyclical, *Laudato Si'*, is no real surprise to anyone familiar with Bacon's influence.[2] For Bacon's key insight was that, when knowledge is embodied in the form of new technical

---

1 Francis Bacon, "The Advancement of Learning," in *Instaurian*. Quoted in Stanford Encyclopedia of Philosophy, https://www.iep.utm.edu/bacon/#SH2i.
2 Pope Francis, *Laudato Si'*, 2015, #102: *Humanity has entered a new era in which our technical prowess has brought us to a crossroads."* Quoted above.

inventions and mechanical discoveries, it is the force that drives history.[3] And so it did then, as modernity rose up to consume all that had gone before—and so it does now, amidst the confusion of our postmodern period, because humankind has been following Bacon's lead ever since.

It has become tragically clear that we have been pursuing a trajectory that has finally brought us to the point in our history at which we are presented with a dangerous choice: Shall we submit to the advent of technical advances that now appear poised to displace the human person as the prime actor in his own work, to replace him as the *subject* of work, developments often described as an inevitable and therefore unstoppable force? Or shall we continue to resist these forces with all our might, knowing full well that, unless we do, we will be complicit in a devil's bargain? We know the answer, for the life of man himself lies in the balance. The question that looms over these proceedings is: *How* shall we proceed? If every unstoppable force requires an equally unmovable force to combat it, where will we find the leverage we need?

The aim of this paper is to offer one possible response to that question. Along with John Paul II and others in this volume, I will argue that the first point of leverage will be found through a proper understanding of the subjective dimension of human work. I will demonstrate the profound truth at the core of John Paul's argument that work is the "key to the social question," articulated in *Laborem Exercens,* by offering an analysis of his later encyclical, *Centesimus Annus,* through the lens it provides. This will illuminate the fact that human work is the engine of human creativity and well-being; technology must never replace the person if we have any hope of preserving a truly human life.

That analysis will provide the point of departure for what I will argue is the second element in our search for maximum leverage. We will consider the convergence of John Paul's account of human work with another theme that is central to his project: his contribution to the Church's understanding of woman. I believe there is a critical link to forge between these two aspects of his thinking.[4] I will argue that any confrontation with the encroachment of technology on human life must leverage

---

3   David Simpson, "Francis Bacon," Stanford Encyclopedia of Philosophy, https://www.iep.utm.edu/bacon/#SH2i.

4   John Paul II, *Evangelium Vitae* (Vatican City: Libreria Editrice Vaticana,

in particular the specific contribution of women and the role they are called to play in the moral dimension of community life. It is the conjunction of these two themes in John Paul's thought—the meaning of work and the particular gifts that woman brings to the tasks of human living—that will constitute our focus in this paper.

My analysis begins by referencing the Church's own grasp of the connection between her social teaching and the teachings on women—expressed quite explicitly in the *Compendium on the Social Teaching of the Church*[5]—in order to consider more fully several points of convergence between these two distinct but organically intertwined threads. This will set the stage for a subsequent, fuller exploration of the significance of woman's vocation. A necessary preliminary step will be to establish the normative meaning of the term "feminine genius," which the authors of the *Compendium* repeatedly reference and which they argue is "needed in all aspects of the life of society."[6] This will lead to an exploration of the proper socio-economic context in which woman's vocation must manifest and develop, focusing primarily on woman's influence on the economic sphere from the perspective of her critical role in the moral-cultural dimension of human society, a prominent aspect of John Paul's argument in *Centesimus Annus*. We will conclude with some reflections on the nature of technology, not as reducible to machinery or *techne*, but as a particular way of looking at the world and the importance of the feminine principle in shaping our vision of the meaning of human life.

1. Women and Catholic Social Thought: A Deep Connection

The documentary heritage of Catholic Social Thought traditionally includes papal encyclicals and other writings concerned primarily with issues of justice in the economic sphere. As a result, scholars of the

1995), sec. 99, https://www.vatican.va/content/john-paul-ii/en/encyclicals/documents/hf_jp-ii_enc_25031995_evangelium-vitae.html.

5   Pontifical Council for Justice and Peace, *Compendium of the Social Doctrine of the Church* (Vatican City: Libreria Editrice Vaticana, 2005).

6   *Id.*, sec. 147.

tradition, especially for the last 125 years, have tended to focus their re-flections on the economic arena, resulting in a vast, if somewhat brack-eted, treasury of thought on how the human community might come to "live in peace secured by justice."[7]

But the publication in 2005 of the *Compendium of the Social Doc-trine of the Church* by the Pontifical Council of Justice and Peace re-vealed in a rather quiet but certainly dramatic way a much more comprehensive vision. Intended as *"a complete overview of the funda-mental framework of the doctrinal corpus of Catholic social teaching,"* the *Compendium* encompasses not only concerns for human dignity and community in the sphere of economics, but also the role of the family and the unique contributions of women in bringing about a just society. Though it went mostly unnoticed, documents such as John Paul II's Apostolic Exhortation on the family, *Familiaris Consortio*, and his let-ters to women, the Apostolic Letter of 1988, *Mulieris Dignitatem,* and the letter of 1995, are included and referred to at some length.[8] In a clear and systematic way, the *Compendium* appropriates for the Church's so-cial tradition not only the topic of women and their fuller participation in the workplace,[9] but also the equality and complementarity of men and women,[10] the teachings on human sexuality,[11] and the particular role of women in promoting the culture of life.[12]

7   William Byron, "The Social Question: Who Asks? Who Answers?" in *On the Condition of Labor and the Social Question One Hundred Years Later: Commemorating the 100th Anniversary of Rerum Novarum, and the Fiftieth Anniversary of the Association for Social Economics,* ed. Thomas O. Nitsch, Joseph M. Phillips, Jr., and Edward L. Fitzsimmons, Toronto Stu-dies in Theology, vol. 69 (New York: Edwin Mellen Press, 1994), 17. Fat-her Byron's way of putting the "social question" is considered its classic formulation.

8   Deborah Savage, "Women and the Catholic Social Tradition," in *Catholic Social Thought: American Reflections on the Compendium,* ed. D. Paul Sullins and Anthony J. Blasi (New York: Lexington Books, 1992), 155–68.

9   *Compendium*, sec. 248–51; sec. 295.

10   *Id.,* sec. 147.

11   *Id.,* sec. 231–33.

12   *Id.,* sec. 231. Quoting *Evangelium Vitae,* sec. 93.

The fact that the *Compendium* invokes the teachings contained in the documents on women and family should not be minimized; its significance needs to be fully understood. It would be difficult to find a more definitive indication of the connection between the Church's social teaching and her teachings on women. To women of faith, it seems self-evident that women occupy a critical place in the effort to spread the moral and social virtues necessary to a humane social existence.[13] But for the fathers of the Church to include all of these documents in such a historically important, systematic, and comprehensive overview unquestionably gives women and their contributions—both actual and potential—a prominent place in such considerations. In other words, it is not just an interesting fact. As Pope Francis says in *Evangelii Gaudium* section 25 (in a somewhat different context), it has "programmatic significance and important consequences," opening the door to a deeper reflection on the ways in which women might participate in advancing the aims of the Catholic Social Tradition.

The *Compendium* is punctuated throughout with references to the tradition's teachings on women and the family, too many to fully explore here. I will limit these preliminary reflections to a brief summary of what I consider to be the essential point of convergence between the teachings on women and the aims of Catholic Social Teaching: the complementarity that characterizes the nature of woman in relation to man and the particular "genius" women bring to these questions.

a) Complementarity as Mission

Catholic social thought is grounded in a particular understanding of what it means to be human; not surprisingly, prior to any analysis of the principles that govern it, the authors of the *Compendium* first establish the meaning of the human person. The chapter entitled "The Human Person and Human Rights" provides an extensive analysis of the anthropological framework at the heart of the Church's social teaching. The received tradition, including the personalism of Pope St. John Paul II, is fully

13 Paul VI, *Gaudium et Spes* (Vatican City: Libreria Editrice Vaticana, 1965), sec. 30.

explored. The unrepeatability of the person, the potencies and faculties he possesses, the origin and meaning of his dignity and his freedom, his social nature, and the rights that issue from these realities are all invoked. But the text also reflects a new intellectual commitment to several themes that emerged most explicitly during St. John Paul II's papacy: the nature of woman in relation to man, the complementarity that characterizes their relationship, and the significance of that complementarity for community life.[14]

In their chapter on the human person, the *Compendium's* authors include a particularly significant text from John Paul's Apostolic Exhortation on the mission of the laity (*Christifideles laici*), which specifies the work needed to illuminate a woman's place in the Church's mission and the life of society:

> The condition that will assure the rightful presence of woman in the Church and in society is a more penetrating and accurate consideration of the *anthropological foundation for masculinity and femininity* with the intent of clarifying woman's personal identity in relation to man, that is, a diversity yet mutual complementarity, not only as it concerns roles to be held and functions to be performed, but also, and more deeply, as it concerns her make-up and meaning as a person.[15]

The document commits the Church to a continuing reflection on the basis of femininity and asks us to pursue a critical understanding of the "values and specific gifts of [both] femininity and masculinity."[16] John Paul insists on this because without a grasp of these realities, the mission of the laity—to transform the temporal order—cannot be fulfilled.[17] Thus, as the authors of the *Compendium* affirm, the Church's social vision can only be realized by women and men who understand themselves to be

14 *Compendium,* sec. 145?
15 *Id.,* sec. 146. Quoting John Paul II, *Christifideles laici* (Vatican City: Libreria Editrice Vaticana, 1989), sec. 50.
16 *Christifideles laici,* sec. 50. Italics in original.
17 *Id.,* sec 50.

complements of each other, "not only from a physical and psychological point of view, but also ontologically";[18] and who, as a result, work intelligently together in light of this reality. The text reiterates the Holy Father's declaration, found in the *Letter to Women,* that "'to this unity of the two,' God has entrusted not only the work of procreation and family life, but the *creation of history itself.*"[19]

The *Compendium* reveals that this deeper understanding of the relationship of man and woman is not just an interesting anthropological development in the Church's understanding of the human person. It cannot be reduced to a response to the "woman question," nor is it simply a conceptual way to include women in an otherwise primarily masculine endeavor. The teaching on complementarity represents a *profound shift* in meaning: the Church is declaring that it is precisely this complementarity that gives us our mission—namely, to create not only human families, but human history itself. And by implication, if we are to complete that mission, if we are to return all things to Christ, we must understand and affirm the genius of women—and of men—in order to permit their full expression in the life of society. It will have enormous implications for the work they are each called to do in creating the socio-economic structures that sustain families—and civilizations.

b) The Feminine and Masculine "Genius"

If the doctrine of complementarity represents the essential convergence between the Church's social doctrine and her teachings on women, a brief synopsis of its meaning will serve as a next step in our investigation. As I have demonstrated elsewhere, a full account of the complementary nature of woman and man can be derived by returning, with St. John Paul II, to the two creation accounts in Genesis.[20] A comprehensive

18 *Compendium,* sec. 147.
19 *Id.*, sec. 147. Quoting John Paul II, *Mulieris Dignitatem* (Vatican City: Libreria Editrice Vaticana, 1988) sec. 11; and John Paul II, *Letter to Women* (Vatican City: Libreria Editrice Vaticana, 1995), sec. 8. Italics added.
20 See Deborah Savage, "Woman and Man: Identity, Genius, and Mission," in *The Complementarity of Women and Men,* ed. Paul Vitz (Washington,

explanation of the theory is beyond the scope of this present paper and so I will illuminate only its foundational aspects, introducing but a sketch of both the masculine genius and feminine genius. Though the Church has focused primarily on what might constitute the so-called "feminine genius," I contend that, if we are to articulate the particular gifts women bring to the tasks of human living, the feminine genius cannot be understood apart from the genius men bring to the world.[21] Since our main interest here is in exploring the contributions of woman, I will offer just a brief summary of my theory concerning the genius of man.

If we consider the order of creation described in Genesis 1–2, we know that man is created first. It is notable that he is (apparently) in the Garden alone with God and all the other creatures for some period of time before the appearance of woman. But aside from this special relationship with the Creator, man's first contact with reality is of a horizon that otherwise contains only lower creatures, what we might call "things" (*res*); God concludes that man is alone, without a "helper" fit for him, which leads ultimately to the creation of woman.[22]

D.C.: CUA Press, 2021), 89–131. In the *Theology of the Body,* St. John Paul II asserts that Genesis 1 is concerned with man *per se,* that is, man in the abstract, and associates that with the metaphysical anthropology of Aquinas. He argues that Genesis 2 describes man in the subjective sense and associates that account with the more modern sensibilities of the philosophy of consciousness school. I have demonstrated that this is a legitimate claim and taken it as a starting point in my effort to develop John Paul's account of complementarity somewhat further. The analysis illuminates both their essential equality and their physical and ontological complementarity.

21 Savage, *op. cit.* For more on the masculine genius, see "Adam's Gift: Man in the Order of Creation," *Humanum Review,* vol 3 (2016), https://humanumreview.com/articles/adams-gift-man-in-the-order-of-creation. A previous version of the theory was published as "The Genius of Man," *Promise and Challenge: Catholic Women Reflect on Complementarity, the Feminine Genius, and the Church* (Huntington, IN: Our Sunday Visitor, 2015), 129–54. Subsequent versions improved considerably on that first publication.

22 To be precise, in the original Hebrew, the term used to describe the creation of Eve is "*banach,*" which means "to build." Eve is "built" from Adam's rib.

Now man's relationship to things is clearly a part of God's design. The man is tasked with naming all the things God brings him (including woman); in naming them, he takes dominion over them.[23] He knows them in ways that woman simply does not. This fact—that man's initial horizon includes only "things" and his special knowledge of them—provides a point of departure in Scripture for the well-documented evidence that men seem more naturally oriented toward things than toward persons.[24] This orientation makes him uniquely gifted in the task of declaring what things *are,* what can be attributed to them (or not), and what use they have.[25] And it is man who is put in the garden to "till it" (Genesis 2:15), well before the fall puts him at odds with creation. This is his work. My claim is that this constitutes the "genius" or charism of men and without it, we would still be living in caves, afraid to come out.[26]

23 Indeed, St. Thomas Aquinas argues that Adam received an additional preternatural gift, infused knowledge, in order to be able to name all the animals brought before him. See *Summa Theologiae* I, Q. 94, a. 3.

24 See especially *Mulieris Dignitatem*, sec. 18. Scientific studies have documented that infants and young children display behavior that corresponds to these differences from the very beginning. See Steven E. Rhoads, *Taking Sex Differences Seriously* (San Francisco: Encounter Books, 2004), 22–26; Anne Moir and David Jessel, *Brain Sex: The Real Difference Between Men and Women* (New York: Dell Publishing, 1991), 68–112.

25 Indeed, St. Thomas Aquinas argues that Adam received an additional preternatural gift, infused knowledge, in order to be able to name all the animals brought before him. See *Summa Theologiae* I, Q. 94, a. 3.

26 See Savage, "Adam's Gift," op. cit. Or, as Camille Paglia, declared, "we would still be living in grass huts." See "A Feminist Defense of Masculine Virtues," *Wall Street Journal*, December 28, 2013, http://www.wsj.com/articles/SB10001424052702303997604579240022857012920. But let me point out that this orientation toward things does **not** mean that man is somehow disordered. Man's first contact with reality includes the Lord God. He is, in the first instance, aware of his dependence upon his Creator and he is truly marked by that relationship forever after. It is within this context that he encounters the woman. Until the woman is brought to him, both to name and to love as he can love no other, he has no "other" like himself. Though this will change after the fall, he knows immediately that the woman is *not* a thing, *not an object*; she is a person. Without hesitation he declares that she is "flesh of his flesh, and bone of his bones."

The masculine inclination toward things and their uses is an aspect of the charism of men and accounts in many ways for the building up of human civilization. It has led throughout history to human flourishing and has made and still makes possible the preservation of families and of culture. This "genius" should elicit not our ridicule, but our profound gratitude.

Now to woman. *Because woman comes into existence after man, her first contact with reality is of a horizon that, from the beginning, includes man, that is, it includes persons.*[27] Throughout history, the tradition has assumed that woman was created second and is therefore derivative of Adam and somehow subservient to him. A more honest interpretation of the order of creation described in these Scripture passages reveals that woman is not created *second*; she is actually created *last* and, further, she is created on the way *up.* Man is made from dust—but woman is made from *man*, a creature that already possesses a higher degree of actuality than the matter of which man is made. Indeed, only with the appearance of woman are several things made possible: in recognizing woman as a person like himself ("here at last is bone of my bones, flesh of my flesh") man knows *himself;* the reality of the reciprocal exchange of the gift of self is suddenly manifest; and, for the first time in human history, human community enters the scene.[28]

Further, woman is man's "helper," yes—but the original Hebrew phrase is *"ezer kenegdo."* Both words are important. When used elsewhere in Scripture, *ezer* connotes "Divine Aid." Woman is sent to man,

27 One can imagine Eve, a person also endowed with intellect and free will who, upon seeing Adam, would recognize another like her, an equal, while the other creatures and things around her appear only on the periphery of her gaze. This exegetical insight seems to provide a starting place in Scripture for the equally well documented phenomenon that women seem more naturally oriented toward persons. See Rhoads, *Taking Sex Differences Seriously*, 23–24.

28 For a more comprehensive treatment of this point, see Savage, "Redeeming Woman: A Response to the 'Second Sex Issue' from within the Tradition of Catholic Scriptural Exegesis," *Religions* 11, no. 9 (August 2020). Found in a special issue: *Feminism from the Perspective of Catholic Theology,* ed. Tracey Rowland, https://www.mdpi.com/2077-1444/11/9/474/htm.

by *God,* to help him to live. But she is *ezer **kenegdo;** kenegdo* is a preposition that means "in front of," "before" in the spatial sense. Thus, neither woman nor man are superior to one another. They are, in fact, face-to-face in this account: equal, but different, both possessed of distinct charisms issuing from their place in the order of creation.[29] Their different gifts are a part of God's design, to be used in responding to his command to "fill the earth and subdue it."

In *Mulieris Dignitatem,* John Paul argues that the feminine genius is grounded in the capacity that all women have to be mothers—and this capacity, whether fulfilled in a physical or spiritual sense, orients her toward the other, toward persons. Human experience supports this claim. And in every sense, Eve is certainly the mother of all humankind. But, in addition to her capacity to conceive and nurture human life, indeed *prior to it,* woman's place in the order of creation reveals that—from the beginning—the horizon of all womankind includes persons, includes an awareness of the "other."

The genius of woman is found here. While man's first experience of his own existence is of loneliness, woman's horizon is different. From the first moment of her own reality, woman sees herself in relation to the other. But woman's capacity—to include the other —*is not a lesser quality.* It is not a mere "complication," diverting us from an otherwise clear line of sight to achieving results. Nor does it compromise woman's fundamental intelligence, competence, or ability to get things done.

Now the fall certainly disorders these inclinations. But the punishment visited on man and woman is also differentiated. The effect of the fall manifests itself in ways that are distinct to each. Man will now struggle with creation, woman with relationships. For men, this plays out in an often-disordered relationship toward things; they can tend toward an obsession with them. It is this tendency that has driven and continues to drive our obsession with technological innovation. They begin to treat everything (including persons) as if it were an object.

---

29 A very different word would have been used if the sacred author meant to imply that she was to be man's servant or slave. Woman is sent by God to help man to *live.* But the full text reveals that woman is created *ezer* "*kenegdo*"; *kenegdo* is a preposition meaning "in front of," in the spatial sense.

The consequences of the fall for woman lead her to desire relationship with man, even when she knows he is using her as an object, even though his tendency is to dominate her, to dismiss her concerns or her insights. It has led to an unconscious fear of man and, at least until recently, a reluctance to displease him. It is easy to see this truth playing out in meaningless sexual encounters across college campuses and in social life in general every day. But its most pernicious effect is that it has caused woman to hesitate to make her voice heard.[30]

The effects of Original Sin can complicate the natural impulse for men and women to live out their gifts; it can interfere with their response to the command *given to them both:* to be fruitful and multiply and to exercise dominion over the earth. Even so, each possesses distinct charisms—a "genius" if you will—something unique to each, to be put at the service of that task. Their primary contribution is differentiated, originating in their distinct ways of being in the world; both men and women are necessary to fulfill what is a shared mission. Woman and man remain jointly responsible for returning all things to Christ.[31]

But here we come to the point. Woman's particular genius is to ensure that the existence of living persons, whether in the womb or outside it, is not forgotten as we frantically engage in the tasks of human living. Woman reminds us that *all human activity* must be ordered toward authentic human flourishing. Perhaps this is why the *Compendium* states that since "the feminine genius is needed in all expressions in the life of society therefore the presence of women in the workplace must also be

30 For further treatment of these issues, see Savage, "Reflections on the Revolution," *First Things,* October 2018, https://www.firstthings.com/article/2018/10/reflections-on-the-revolution. See also Savage "Rethinking *Humanae Vitae,*" in *Why Humanae Vitae is Still Right,* ed. Janet Smith (San Francisco: Ignatius Press, 2018) 47–62.

31 Though space does not permit a fuller treatment, it must be noted that, while the masculine and feminine genius can be spoken of on the level of nature, they are in fact both supernatural realities whose full expression cannot be realized without the action of grace. This is clear when one considers John Paul II's claim that Mary is the prototype of the feminine genius. I have argued elsewhere that St. Joseph offers a model for men. See Savage, *The Complementarity of Men and Women,* op. cit.

guaranteed."[32] This statement implies two things. First, that women "belong" everywhere. Second, that women belong everywhere because they bring something to community life that is unique to *female* personhood. Given our analysis so far, this, in turn, implies that the feminine genius is necessary to make the life of society fully human. We will see that women's contribution in achieving that vision includes not only her natural intelligence, competence, and creativity—qualities that characterize all human persons, man and woman alike. I will argue that her specific genius also leads her to insist on the establishment of concretely existing familial structures and social conditions that ensure the needs of persons are met and that all human activity is ordered toward genuine human flourishing. Indeed, in light of our interests here, her mission in the world is to confront the male tendency to turn everything into an object to be dominated and manipulated for profit or advantage. It is woman who must confront the encroachment of technology on human life; that is her responsibility. In what follows I will demonstrate that the realization of the Church's social vision is absolutely dependent upon a fuller expression of woman's genius in the life of society. But first that social vision must be properly articulated.

2. The Socio-Economic Context of the Church's Social Teaching

Pope Emeritus Benedict XVI states in his encyclical, *Caritas in Veritate,* that, "charity is at the heart of the Church's social doctrine." It governs both our "micro-relationships" and our "macro-relationships." It is essential, not only for our personal lives, but also within the context of our social, political, and economic lives.[33] Pope Benedict invokes St. Paul's teaching that while truth needs to be "expressed within the 'economy' of charity," charity must also be practiced within the "light of truth."[34]

And here we come to an essential point: assent to the Church's doctrine concerning the preferential option for the poor must be grounded

32 *Compendium,* sec. 295.
33 Benedict XVI, *Caritas in Veritate* (Vatican City: Libreria Editrice Vaticana, 2009), sec. 2.
34 *Ibid.*

in a proper understanding of poverty and a realistic vision of the socio-economic conditions that will foster human development in general. The Nobel Laureate economist, Amartya Sen, defines poverty as a reality that cannot be reduced to the question of income; it is more properly defined as "capability deprivation," a situation in which human persons are unable to realize their potential to create lives that have meaning for them.[35]

This definition is not only profoundly true, it also points to an important convergence with the social teaching of the Church: John Paul II argues that the source of wealth is man himself, and that in the act of working he not only creates the objective goods and services needed to sustain human life, he also creates himself. Wealth creation is both existential and material; *it is the result of the integral human development the Church has been insisting on for centuries.*[36] And it is both an objective and a subjective reality. Its source is human creativity, a reflection of the nature of man who is made in the image of the God who creates. My contention is that without a full affirmation of the role that human labor and creativity play in achieving prosperity in both its immaterial and material aspects, we will prolong the tragedy of poverty in all its dimensions.

For the hard truth is that before wealth can be shared or (re)distributed *it must first be created*—a fact that must be admitted if we are to create the social conditions that foster human development.

It is human development that serves as the engine of wealth creation. Behind this statement is a dilemma that has confronted humankind since the beginning of recorded history: How do we ensure the just distribution of the goods of creation without compromising the natural right of men and women to retain ownership of the results of their labor? What is the true nature of the socio-economic framework that would allow us to create and sustain conditions that foster human development for all?

35 Amartya Sen, *Development as Freedom* (New York: Alfred Knopf, Inc., 2001), chapter 4.
36 See Savage, "Is Creating Wealth a Virtue?" in *Bridges*. Published in 1998 but now out of print.

In our quest for an answer to these questions, we find our starting place is Pope St. John Paul II's proposal, found in *Centesimus Annus* (1991), that society is comprised of three distinct but interwoven dimensions: the economic, the moral-cultural, and the legal-juridical spheres—three dimensions of community life threaded together by the meaning of human work.[37] Within this context, we will discover the place that women must be called to occupy in the service of human flourishing.

a) Reordering the Principles of Catholic Social Thought: The Central Truth in Centesimus Annus

Since the formal inauguration of the papal social tradition with the promulgation of Pope Leo XIII's landmark encyclical *Rerum Novarum* (1891), the Church has stated unequivocally that she neither offers nor subscribes to any particular economic system.[38] Catholic social teaching maintains a consistently critical stance toward the extreme forms of socialism or communism on the one hand, and unbridled or laissez-faire capitalism on the other.[39] But the dramatic collapse in 1989 of the

---

37   There are clear parallels between this framework and the theory of "democratic capitalism" proposed by Michael Novak in the 1980s and built on ever since by Dr. Novak and his confreres. See Novak, *The Spirit of Democratic Capitalism* (Lanham, Maryland: Madison Books, 1982). He addressed the dangers of crony capitalism and its excesses as well. See Novak, "The Future of Democratic Capitalism," *First Things,* June 2015, found at https://www.firstthings.com/article/2015/06/the-future-of-democratic-capitalism. He makes many of the same arguments found in *Centesimus Annus.* I admire Dr. Novak's work very much and respect his efforts to reconcile the apparent dilemma between a preferential option for the poor and the articulation of a realistic economic framework that could lead to human flourishing. While my argument in this paper does echo many of those themes, my thesis is that the reconciliation we seek will be found in a proper understanding of the real meaning of human work and, further, that this is precisely what St. John Paul II is trying to tell us.

38   John Paul II, *Centesimus Annus* (Vatican City: Libreria Editrice Vaticana, 1991), sec. 43.

39   This argument was made by many in the west, most prominently Margaret

communist-inspired Soviet Union prompted many to argue that capitalism should be considered the "victorious social system" and therefore should be the model and goal for countries, in the aftermath, seeking to define the path to progress.[40]

Writing on the one-hundredth anniversary of Pope Leo's encyclical, John Paul II responds to these new realities in *Centesimus Annus*. His analysis illuminates a complex and important truth: although it plays a critical role in the well-being of human societies, the economic dimension of community life cannot exist autonomously or independently of the legal-juridical or moral-cultural dimensions that both support and govern it. The following passages, in which John Paul II responds directly to questions posed by the "failure of communism," summarize the central insights of the encyclical. Should capitalism be the model we propose to poorer countries seeking the path to true economic and civil progress? The answer, he says, is "obviously complex":

> If by "capitalism" is meant an economic system which recognizes the fundamental and positive role of business, the market, private property and the resulting responsibility for the means of production, as well as free human creativity in the economic sector, then the answer is certainly in the affirmative, even though it would perhaps be more appropriate to speak of a "business economy," "market economy," or simply "free economy." But if by "capitalism" is meant a system in which freedom in the economic sector is not circumscribed within a strong juridical framework which places it at the service of human freedom in its totality, and which sees it as a particular aspect of that freedom, the core of which is ethical and religious, then the reply is certainly negative.[41]

Thatcher in her articulation of the TINA philosophy ("There is no alternative."). See for example: Ulrich Duchrow, "Capitalism will implode," *The Guardian*, November 13, 2009, http://www.theguardian.com/commentis-free/belief/2009/nov/13/1989-capitalism-christianity.

40 John Paul II, *Centesimus Annus*, sec. 42.
41 John Paul II, *Laborem Exercens*, (Vatican City: Libreria Editrice Vaticana, 1981), sec. 3.

John Paul II's answer to the question is indeed complex; the entire encyclical can be thought of as the church's response. The Pope presents a masterfully nuanced account of what has often played out in history as a battle between two radically opposed ideologies: "laissez-faire" capitalism and Marxism. He shows that neither reflects a true understanding of the human person; neither provides an authentic route to fulfillment. For neither grasps the theological and anthropological significance of human work, a reality that John Paul II argues in his first social encyclical, *Laborem Exercens*, is actually the key to the social question itself.[42] His analysis and proposal in *Centesimus Annus* must be seen in light of this previous and arguably radical claim.

In *Centesimus Annus*, the Holy Father points out that God's first gift to man—the earth and all its resources—makes human life and prosperity possible; at the beginning of every human society are two factors—work and the land. And though historically the natural fruitfulness of the earth and its capacity to satisfy human needs has been a primary factor in the creation of wealth, human work itself, in collaboration with others through ever widening circles of cooperation, has increasingly become the source of wealth.[43] That is, "disciplined and creative human work" and essential elements such as "initiative and entrepreneurial ability" are "increasingly evident and decisive" in the ongoing discovery of different ways human needs can be satisfied.[44]

But for John Paul, work is not merely an economic endeavor. Throughout *Centesimus Annus,* he refers to his arguments in *Laborem Exercens* that the call to work—to "be fruitful and multiply"—comes before the fall and so must be seen as a "fundamental dimension of human existence."[45] In fact, we are called to work because we are made in the image of God who creates; in work we reflect that image and cooperate in the ongoing process of creation. Work distinguishes the

42 *Id.*, sec. 31–32.

43 *Id.*, sec. 32.

44 As far as I have been able to determine, there is only one other thing that the Holy Father refers to as "a fundamental dimension of human existence," and that is the call to make of oneself a gift to another. See John Paul II, *Crossing the Threshold of Hope* (PLACE: PUB, YEAR), 11.

45 John Paul II, *Laborem Exercens,* sec. 24.

human person from the rest of creation, for it is only the human person who can be said to work. Through work, he reveals his dominion over himself and over nature. Through work, our lives are sustained, our communities are built, and our nature is realized. The Holy Father even declares that, when it is given the meaning it has in the eyes of God, work "enters into the salvation process on a par with the other ordinary yet particularly important components of its texture."[46] Work is a means by which man joins his suffering to that of Christ on the Cross and "collaborates with the Son of God for the redemption of humanity."[47]

So, what is "work"? Work is not just something we do for pay. It includes any activity we consider work, whether serving a meal, diapering a baby, mowing a lawn, tilling a field, or toiling in the office or factory. It includes the labor of mothers and fathers in the home, volunteers serving soup to the homeless, laborers on a manufacturing line, government employees, politicians, students, and teachers. But for it to be truly and fully human, work cannot be the act of an automaton, a mere functionary. It is or can be an *actus humanus,* or, in John Paul's account, an *actus personae,* the act of a *person.* As such, it *never* takes place outside of a moral context and it *cannot* be thought of as merely an extrinsic activity with only external results. Work forms those who engage in it; work is a factor in our becoming who we are meant to be.

John Paul's argument distinguishes between two dimensions of human work: the objective and the subjective. The objective dimension results from work in the external or material sense, either a product or a service, in either the public or private sphere. This is the dimension we most associate with working—it is what the customer buys, what one may (or may not) get paid to produce; it is the widget, the pizza, the lecture delivered, the meal on the table. The subjective dimension, the primary concern of the encyclical, refers to the person performing the work, that is, the "subject" of work, who, by virtue of his or her very humanity, is called to be a person in the fullest sense of that word. The human person, made in the image of God, reflects God's creative activity in the act of working and is "a person, that is to say, a subjective being capable of acting in a planned and rational way, capable of

46 *Id.*, sec. 27.
47 *Id.*, sec. 6.

deciding about himself and with a tendency to self-realization."[48] In working, the person not only creates some object or provides a service to someone, he also creates himself in the process. John Paul states that work:

> is not only good in the sense that it is useful or something to enjoy; it is also good as being something worthy, that is to say, something that corresponds to man's dignity, that expresses this dignity and increases it. If one wishes to define more clearly the ethical meaning of work, it is this truth that one must particularly keep in mind. Work is a good thing for man—a good thing for his humanity—because through work man not only transforms nature, adapting it to his own needs, but he also achieves fulfillment as a human being and indeed in a sense becomes "more a human being."[49]

The primary basis of the value of work is man himself. This does not mean we cannot rate or quantify the objective value of work; it does mean we must remember that *the value of work is primarily found in the fact that the one doing it is* "a person, a conscious and free subject, that is to say a subject that decides about himself."[50] John Paul points out that "this leads immediately to a very important conclusion of an ethical nature: however true it may be that man is destined for work and called to it, in the first place work is "'for man'—not man 'for work.'"[51]

Parenthetically, it may be obvious, but this analysis absolutely rules out any attempt by the "owners of capital" to pretend that the worker is merely a functionary, another kind of "object" that operates alongside the other tools at their disposal in the effort to generate material goods. It is at this precise point in the process that woman must offer her genius—a gift that can include a specific professional competence and capacity for efficiency—but would also insist on a concern for the

48 *Id.,* sec. 9
49 *Ibid.*
50 *Id.,* sec. 6.
51 Joanna Barsh, "Can Women Save Capitalism?" October 3, 2014, http://www.leathersmilligan.com/can-women-save-capitalism/.

humanity of the worker *qua* person. And, as women have begun to participate more and more in the marketplace, these insights have begun to form the basis of action in economic endeavors, both large and small.[52] We will return to this theme shortly.

But to return to the thread of our analysis, John Paul's conclusions in *Laborem Exercens* provide the lens through which to view his arguments in *Centesimus Annus*. There he affirms that business, the market, and private property represent genuine goods for society. But at its heart, the engine that drives economic prosperity is or ought to be "free human creativity," for "besides the earth, man's principal resource is man himself."[53] This corresponds to the truth about the human person and "it should be viewed carefully and favorably."[54] John Paul argues that the source of material wealth in today's society is the human capacity to foresee the needs of others, and to organize and deploy the productive factors necessary to satisfy those needs. He acknowledges the role that "free bargaining" plays in arriving at a just price for goods and services freely offered.[55] And while John Paul is clear about the risks associated

52 John Paul II, *Centesimus Annus*, sec. 32

53 *Ibid.*

54 *Id.*, sec. 31–32. This also corresponds to something Amartya Sen points out in his book *Development as Freedom*. Sen argues that at the origin of market mechanisms is a fundamental human right, the right to engage in transactions or trade with one another. It as fundamental as the right to have conversations with each other. Unless stopped by regulation or government fiat, they originate in the natural human impulse to exchange "words, goods, or gifts"; they are an aspect of the way human beings in society live and interact with other. See Sen, *Development as Freedom*, 6.

55 In paragraph 2402, the *Catechism of the Catholic Church* states that since "[i]n the beginning God entrusted the earth and its resources to the common stewardship of mankind to take care of them, master them by labor, and enjoy their fruits, [t]he goods of creation are destined for the whole human race." But it goes on to state: "However, the earth is divided up among men to assure the security of their lives, endangered by poverty and threatened by violence. The appropriation of property is legitimate for guaranteeing the freedom and dignity of persons and for helping each of them to meet his basic needs and the needs of those in his charge. It should allow for a natural solidarity to develop between men." The Church is quite intent on preserving both of these principles.

with unfettered "capitalism," he is equally clear in his affirmation of several aspects of the business economy without which human flourishing would be impossible. Though John Paul invokes the principle of the universal destination of goods and the social function of property,[56] he reaffirms the Church's traditional view that the right to private property is "fundamental for the autonomy and development of the person."[57] And though he points out that profit is not the only regulator of the life of a business, he declares that the Church affirms it "as an indication that a business is functioning well."[58] Further, if the business is to experience continued operation and success, it must continue to respect the dignity of its employees, customers, and community. This necessity acts as a natural, though imperfect, check on exploitative business practices.

Aside from the need to generate a profit, the real purpose of a business, says John Paul II, is found in its very existence as a *"community of persons"* whose aim is to satisfy their own basic needs by forming a particular group at the service of the whole of society. The modern business economy, like any other field, is populated by human persons with legitimate needs and governed by the same human and moral factors one finds at work in every human endeavor. It is a place where important virtues are demanded, practiced, and acquired, virtues such as industriousness and diligence, prudence and fidelity, courage and perseverance.[59] It is a place where human freedom can and should be exercised responsibly for the common good of all.[60]

The economic sector has legitimate goals and activities that contribute to human flourishing. Certainly, it provides goods and services and makes possible the material wealth necessary for a stable and orderly human society. But it also provides persons with an opportunity to develop and contribute their talents to the common good. And it permits parents to care for their families and ultimately allows families to be responsible for their own livelihoods by providing means for their own needs.

---

56   *Ibid.*, para. 30. Here quoting both *Rerum Novarum* and *Gaudium et Spes.*
57   John Paul II, *Centesimus Annus*, 35.
58   *Id.*, sec. 32.
59   *Id.*, sec. 29.
60   *Id.*, sec. 36.

However, *Centesimus Annus* also provides a highly integrated vision of the values, institutions, and systems that must be given their place if the economic sector is to be free to realize its own proper ends, without undue control by other forces. These factors ensure that the economic system does not substitute its values for those that lead to authentic human flourishing. The Holy Father notes that, "of itself, an economic system does not possess criteria for correctly distinguishing new and higher forms of satisfying human needs from artificial new needs which [actually] hinder the formation of a mature personality."[61] We should not expect or allow the economic dimension to provide such criteria on its own; its role is to respond to the demands for goods and services that satisfy authentic human needs, many of which cannot be met through market mechanisms anyway.[62] Cultural norms must provide such criteria—cultural norms grounded in a true vision of the human person, the correct ordering of his power of choice, and a grasp of the nature of human freedom.[63] Producers, consumers, as well as those who shape and create public policy, must appropriate these truths so that the economy can be ordered toward human flourishing. Marxism cannot be defeated "on the level of pure materialism" by simply pointing to the effectiveness of the free market to satisfy material human needs. And the free market cannot exclude the spiritual values that exist at the core of its true purpose.[64]

John Paul insists that neither combatant in the historical struggle between the two economic systems (Marxism and laissez-faire capitalism) can be declared the winner. Certainly, we must refuse to affirm an economic model centered on the predominance of capital over labor and which ignores the "free and personal nature of human work." But the counter-proposal is not socialism, itself merely a form of State capitalism. The answer is rather "*a society of free work, of enterprise and of participation.*"[65] His proposal is not directed against the market; the right of persons to trade with one another is basic to human freedom. But the economic dimension

61 *Id.*, sec. 34.
62 *Id.*, sec. 36; sec. 25; sec. 17.
63 *Id.*, sec. 19.
64 *Id.*, sec. 35. Here the Holy Father is quoting *Laborem Exercens,* sec. 7. Emphasis in original.
65 *Ibid.* Here the Holy Father is quoting *Laborem Exercens,* sec. 7.

must be appropriately governed by the forces of society (the moral-cultural dimension) and by the State (the legal-juridical dimension) so as to guarantee that the basic needs of the whole of society are satisfied.[66]

Before turning to the role women should play in the interaction of these forces, let us examine what I believe is the true *telos* of Catholic social teaching. Our analysis so far has several important implications. First, it reveals that the Church's own social tradition confirms that wealth is both existential and material and that both forms of wealth originate in the natural, creative actions of human persons.[67] These actions generate objective goods that can be ordered toward the benefit of the family, kept for one's own consumption, or exchanged for wages or for other goods and services. But also—and more importantly—these actions develop one's own human capabilities, potencies or "talents" given by God and the true provenance of human flourishing. Human persons are naturally ordered toward their own growth. In fact, the gift of life obligates us to become that most excellent person God had in mind when he created us; we must repay our debt to him. Pope John Paul teaches us that this development takes place, at least in part, through our work, something that has theological and moral significance. All work, in every dimension of human activity—whether in the home or in the public arena, is, of necessity, a factor in our movement toward our final end: union with God. This is the foundation of the "right to work"; acknowledging it and insisting on structures that make it possible constitutes a genuine "preferential option for the poor."

Thus is the true devastation of poverty laid bare, for it also is both an existential and material reality. The route to serving the poor and disadvantaged is to remove the obstacles that prevent them from becoming most fully themselves. The Holy Father's concern with capitalism is not its productive capacity; his concern is that the poor and disadvantaged are "marginalized" and have no opportunity to participate in the fruits of human achievement:

66 Deborah Savage, "Is Creating Wealth a Virtue?" *Bridges* vol. 8 (Spring/Summer 2001): 1–32.
67 John Paul II, *Centesimus Annus,* sec. 33.

The fact is that many people, perhaps the majority today, do not have the means which would enable them to take their place in an effective and humanly dignified way within a productive system in which work is truly central. They have no possibility of acquiring the basic knowledge which would enable them to express their creativity and develop their potential. They have no way of entering the network of knowledge and intercommunication which would enable them to see their qualities appreciated and utilized. Thus, if not actually exploited, they are to a great extent marginalized; economic development takes place over their heads, so to speak, when it does not actually reduce the already narrow scope of their old subsistence economies. They are unable to compete against the goods which are produced in ways which are new and which properly respond to needs, needs which they had previously been accustomed to meeting through traditional forms of organization.[68]

John Paul II maintains that this marginalization is not limited to any particular geographical region; it is a global one. And those who control the economic machinery of modern society really must face their responsibility to the poor and the disadvantaged. But we do not serve the poor by simply repeating the exhortation that those who have wealth should give it away. We serve them by acknowledging both *their* dignity and *our* responsibility to help them to develop *their* potential and *their* own capacities to create lives that have meaning *to them*. The poor among us do not need access merely to more consumer goods or even the standard of living that characterizes the West. What the poor really need is access to meaningful work and to the education and training that prepares them to participate in contemporary society. This is more than the simplistic cliché of "teaching a man to fish" rather than just giving him one. If we take the Church's social teaching seriously, we must realize that a man needs to learn more than simply *how* to fish; we must help him to *become* whoever he is meant to be. That could be as a

---

68   Paul VI, *Gaudium et Spes*, sec. 30.

competent fisherman who, with others in his community, goes on to build a fishing *industry*. Or he could discover that he is called to put his gifts to work at some other aspect of a life lived in community. The point is, he may never discover what that is without meaningful, life-sustaining work. The task of serving the poor calls us to help communities in need build for themselves an infrastructure that provides the goods and services necessary to sustain the life of a community of persons "whose aim is to satisfy their own basic needs by forming a particular group at the service of the whole of society." For it is through that effort that integral human development takes place and is sustained.

I have laid out what I believe to be the nature of the economic framework needed for human flourishing. But to honor the fundamental freedoms and rights at stake in this endeavor—and thus find a way for all to benefit from the creative and productive capacity of human persons at the heart of the economic dimension—we must now invoke John Paul II's further argument that the economic dimension does not exist independently of the moral-cultural and legal-juridical spheres which govern it. And here we turn to the specific contributions women are called to make and a consideration of why the authors of the *Compendium* insist that "the feminine genius is needed in all aspects of the life of society."

3. The Contributions of Woman

The Church has consistently affirmed that women occupy a critical place in nurturing the moral and social virtues necessary to a humane social existence—and in advancing the case for their significance in sustaining human life.[69] As the "first teacher of the human being," woman holds a special importance, indeed has a "specific precedence over the man"[70] in the jointly held responsibility to serve as "the molders of a new humanity"[71] that might permit the full flowering of such virtues in society.

---

69 John Paul II, *Mulieris Dignitatem*, sec. 19.
70 Paul VI, *Gaudium et Spes*, sec. 30; *Compendium*, sec. 19.
71 See Pius XII, Address to Catholic Women's Organization (1945); John XXIII, *Pacem in Terris* (Vatican City: Libreria Editrice Vaticana, 1963), sec. 41; Second Vatican Council, Closing Address to Women ((Vatican City: Libreria Editrice

In fact, it is a matter of historical record that, particularly since the latter of half of the twentieth century, the Catholic Church has been calling women, especially women of faith, to a radical exercise of what is most certainly her prophetic voice.[72] Virtually every Pope from Pius XII to St. John Paul II to Pope Francis has called on women to rise to the demands of the times, to speak on behalf of the culture of life, to help humankind resist what has seemed to be a steady and disturbing movement of descent. The Church has made it abundantly clear that women are called in a special way to bear witness to the truth in the here and now.

There may be no more touching statement of this call than that found in the *Closing Address to Women* at the end of the Second Vatican Council. There the Council Fathers express an urgent appeal to women to remember that "at this moment when the human race is under-going so deep a transformation, women impregnated with the spirit of the Gospel *can do so much to aid mankind in not falling*."[73] This statement has become more urgent in recent times; daily news reports bring us face-to-face with the many crises faced by the human family across the globe. The common thread in these crises is a lack of respect for the dignity of human persons—and a frightening refusal to respond to the call to love one another.[74] The response to these crises must begin in the home.

Vaticana, 1965), sec. 1; Paul VI, "Discourse a La Commission d'etude sur la Femme dans las Societe et dans l'Eglise," January 31, 1976; John Paul II, *Mulieris Dignitatem,* especially sec. 31; John Paul II, *Evangelium Vitae*, sec. 99; Benedict XVI, Easter Monday Message (2012), http://www.catholic.org/clife/lent/story.php?id=45627 (audio) http://vaticaninsider.lastampa.it/en/the-vatican/detail/articolo/settimana-santa-holy-week-semana-santa-14170/ (text); Pope Francis, Address to the Participants in the National Congress Sponsored by the Italian Women's Center (January 2014).

72 Second Vatican Council, Closing Address to Women (December 8, 1965), http://w2.vatican.va/content/paul-vi/en/speeches/1965/documents/hf_p-vi_spe_19651208_epilogo-concilio-donne.html. Italics added.

73 I have argued these points more extensively elsewhere. See Deborah Savage, "Woman as Prophet: A Feminism for the 21st Century" in *Woman as Prophet and Servant of Truth: Interdisciplinary Investigations,* ed. Mary Hayden Lemmons (New York: Lexington Books, 2016), pp. 45–64.

74 Angelo Scola, *The Nuptial Mystery* (Grand Rapids, Michigan: Eerdmans Publishing Company, 2005), 242.

Since John Paul II highlighted its significance, the complementarity of man and woman has been the subject of much scholarly reflection and fruitful research. One such scholar, Angelo Cardinal Scola, offers an analysis of this reality, manifested in the tasks of parenthood. Cardinal Scola argues that both parents have an educative task, shaped by the diversity present in the different charisms of the father and the mother. This very diversity reflects both the unity and relationality of the Divine Persons.[75] In Cardinal Scola's account, the father's role is to invite the child to "come out of himself to confront reality" and to initiate the child into "the law of exchange [work] as the law of growth in life." It is this law that reveals to the child that one must work in order to receive something in exchange.[76] The task of the mother is to introduce the child to the "unconditional dimension of being" which allows him to confront all of reality from the certainty of being loved. This is the "law of gratuity" or love. Both laws "exist contemporaneously" within the unity of the Divine Persons and are thus manifest in the nature of human persons. The child must learn both the law of exchange and the law of gratuity in order to grow.[77]

This snapshot from Cardinal Scola's profound analysis reveals the essential contribution of women in forming their children—both sons and daughters—in the home. Both sons and daughters must learn about the law of gratuity; that it is not a secondary element in human living, but is, along with the law of exchange, an essential component for growth, human development, and happiness. Mothers need to be affirmed in their capacity to offer insight into this lawful aspect of human life—and they need to be fearless in insisting that it take its rightful place in the formation of their children. For the home is the first and perhaps the only place that the child will learn about it; unless he or she is schooled in the law of love, love will never find its way into the larger socio-economic context we are seeking to transform. For the family is

75 *Ibid.*
76 *Id.* I can only point to Cardinal Scola's analysis here; further research is needed to unpack its significance for the thesis at work in this paper.
77 John Paul II, *Letter to Families* (Vatican City: Libreria Editrice Vaticana, 1994), sec. 7, http://w2.vatican.va/content/john-paul-ii/en/letters/1994/documents/hf_jp-ii_let_02021994_families.html.

really the first "human society" the children experience.[78] If the law of love has pride of place in the home, it will be seen in the generous way the parents interact both within the family and with the community in which it is nested. If these conditions are met, the children will grow up understanding the need to share their inner resources, talents, and wealth with those who are less fortunate. In this sense, the family is the "way of the Church."[79] The children will thus enter into public life formed in the "law of gratuity," that is, of love, and it will become their task to conform their lives to that law in whatever vocation they seek.

But as we have seen already, woman's task is not limited to her impact in the home. The Church fathers are very explicit that her "genius is needed in every aspect of the life of society," arguing that her presence in public life "must be guaranteed."[80] Woman brings to the tasks of human living a particular genius: to bear witness to the fact that all human activity must be ordered toward authentic human flourishing. But in what sense is the genius of woman the critical element in ensuring the proper ordering of the socio-economic context?

The answer comes into view when we consider that woman does not give up her prerogatives when she enters the workplace or the public arena. Wherever her vocation takes her, woman continues to be tasked with the preservation of the "law of gratuity," to be a prophetic witness to the personal dignity of every person. This witness cannot be reduced to sentimentality or the dangerously flawed notion that women are somehow deficient in reason and tend towards "mere subjectivity" (in contrast to men who are "objective"). Like man, woman is an instantiation of the same substantial form, that is, the rational human soul, and is thus endowed with intellect, will, and freedom.[81] She is not, of necessity, caught

78 *Id.*, sec. 1.

79 *Compendium,* sec. 147

80 For a further exploration of so-called women's "ways of knowing," see *Woman as Knower," The Lonergan Review* 5, no. 1 (2014):109–38. I do argue there that, because of the design of their bodies and natural inclinations, women may be attentive to different things than men and thus receive different phantasms. But her reasoning process must be the equivalent of that of man if we are to maintain that she is human.

81 John Paul II, *Evangelium Vitae,* sec. 3.

in the labyrinth of the subjective; she is an expert on the "personal," which is not the same thing. There is evidence that it may even be true that woman is capable of seeing the "bigger picture" because her vision includes, not only the particulars of the task at hand, but also a sensitivity to the actual existing persons whose job it is to accomplish it.

John Paul II argues that the genius of woman is critical in the transformation of culture. In *Evangelium Vitae* (1995), he highlights the critical role women play in alleviating suffering wherever "life is weak and defenseless"; women are to confront not only "the ancient scourges of poverty, hunger, endemic diseases, violence and war," but also the new threats appearing "on an alarmingly vast scale."[82] He emphasizes that women occupy a "unique and decisive" place in creating conditions that make life more human for all. In fact, he states that such a process *depends* on women taking the necessary steps "to promote a 'new feminism,' which rejects the temptation to imitate models of 'male domination' and instead acknowledges and affirms the true genius of women in every aspect of the life of society, overcoming all discrimination, violence and exploitation." John Paul II argues that this new feminism must "bear witness to the meaning of genuine love, of that gift of self and of that acceptance of others which are present in a special way in the relationship of husband and wife, but which ought also to be at the heart of every other interpersonal relationship."[83] His meaning is clear: Women must not only resist their own oppression, they must also *bring the social order into alignment with Divine love.*

---

82 *Id.*, sec. 99.

83 There are several studies that claim to demonstrate this phenomenon. Perhaps the best place to look is Cindi May, "When Men Are Less Moral than Women?" *Scientific American,* June 19, 2012, http://www.scientificamerican. com/article/whn-men-are-less-moral-than-woman/. May, herself a psychologist, quotes a particular study which analyzes available empirical evidence. See Robert J. Robinson, Roy J. Lewicki, and Eileen M. Donahue, "Extending and Testing a Five Factor Model of Ethical and Unethical Bargaining Tactics: Introducing the SINS Scale." *Journal of Organizational Behavior* 21, no. 6 (2000): 649–64. I would argue that this phenomenon is due to woman's natural orientation toward persons since the *genuine* well-being of persons constitutes at least one of the essential criteria in determining moral action.

Even the secular world and the scientific community are beginning to acknowledge the gift that women bring to public life, though in different language. Numerous studies, by very reputable scholars writing in serious journals, seem to demonstrate that women may behave naturally in ways that can be said to be more moral than that of men.[84] Research suggests that, especially in competitive situations, "men are more likely than women to minimize the consequences of moral misconduct, to adopt ethically questionable tactics in strategic endeavors, and to engage in greater deceit."[85] Management scholars report that large companies now acknowledge that the particular skills women bring to organizational life may be essential for economic success. Women tend to be more committed to creating long-term value for all stakeholders, rather than relentlessly pushing for higher short-term profits. Women are more likely to seek deeper meaning in their work and for their organization, inspiring others by leading with purpose and with the larger aim of achieving personal fulfillment.[86]

But anecdotal evidence also suggests that this phenomenon is not limited to industrialized countries. In fact, the West may simply be slower to recognize what is an accepted fact in cultures throughout the world. Relief workers in Africa tell stories of bringing supplies to areas devastated by drought or famine or disease and giving the supplies to women, refusing to give them to the men. Why? Because men tend to take the supplies and sell them on the black market, but women take them back to the village to feed their children. Or, in a radio interview several years ago on the BBC, we hear the voice of the female Finance

84 *Id.*, May, *Scientific American*.
85 Barsh, "Can Women Save Capitalism?" Indeed, much of this evidence echoes a theory first proposed by Dietrich Von Hildebrand, namely, that if a woman is going to work in an organizational context, unless that organization is ordered toward a purpose larger than itself, something other than the merely pragmatic, there will be no place for gifts and it is "inimical to her nature." See Dietrich Von Hildebrand, *Man and Woman: Love and the Meaning of Intimacy* (New Hampshire: Sophia Institute Press, 1992), 99–100.
86 See her interview: "I keep my ego in my handbag," *The Guardian*, August 1, 2005, http://www.theguardian.com/world/2005/aug/01/gender.uk.

Minister of Nigeria, Ngozi Okonjo-Iweala, responding to a question about the role of women and saying: "Everyone knows here that women are more moral, that women always take the higher moral ground; really everyone knows it."[87] This understanding is a commonplace in other parts of the world, places that remain mostly untouched by the effects of radical feminism. (This situation may change as the forces of "ideological colonialism" make their way across the globe.)[88]

In these examples, we see the tremendous impact that women could have on realizing the socio-economic framework of interest to the Church. In addition to making a professional contribution, women have a natural role to play in concrete situations where the needs of the person must be defended, in identifying and critiquing economic institutions that fail to promote human dignity properly or refuse to acknowledge the legitimate claims of family life on the economic sphere. This critique rightly implicates government bodies and other institutions when they fail to provide adequate structures that respect the unique vocation of women. It includes concerns over family leave policies, equal pay for equal work, access to education, information, and positions of authority and the freedom to exercise her own individuality. Woman's sensitivity to relationships charges her with a special responsibility to ensure not only that the dignity of others is respected, but also that social, political, and cultural institutions pay due attention to the needs of persons, relational and otherwise.

John Paul II argues that woman finds her moral and spiritual strength in the awareness that God has entrusted her with the care of humanity.[89] This role, given to her in the Garden of Eden, is reaffirmed with the birth of every child. Woman's considerable moral force comes from this often-unconscious awareness; it makes her strong, even when she faces social discrimination. The moral authority of woman, displayed in so many

---

87 Future research will investigate the relationship between the role women play in a culture and the general moral standards at work in it. Perhaps we will find that there is a correlation between the level of womanhood and the level of civilization, as Archbishop Fulton Sheen argues.

88 John Paul II, *Mulieris Dignitatem,* sec. 30.

89 It is very interesting to note that, in his entire project, John Paul points to only two things as "fundamental dimensions of human existence": human work and the law of the gift. Herein lies the connection.

human situations, is a gift from God so that she can fulfill her role in creating a just and human social order. Her task is to remind all of us that we cannot make of ourselves a gift to a bottom line or to our work, wherever that takes place, but *only to a person*. That is, in addition to her natural capacity to get things done, wherever woman lives and works, her mission is to keep ever before us the truth that human activity must always be oriented toward the authentic good of persons. There has never been a more critical moment to listen to the prophetic voice of women. Woman's true genius will only become fully visible when both women and men acknowledge its existence and seek truly to complement each other in the great task of creating human history. Perhaps—together—they will find a way "to aid humanity in not falling."

4. Conclusion

Our purpose in this chapter is to shed light on the role that woman is called to play in confronting the encroachment of a dangerous technocratic future. My argument has been that the charisms of woman provide critical leverage in our efforts to reverse the present trends in society and to fight back against what appears to be an unstoppable force. Indeed, woman is essential in the realization of the Church's social vision, articulated so completely in two of St. John Paul II's most profound encyclicals. Namely, that woman was given responsibility for the care of humanity at the moment of her creation. We would be wise to affirm her in her mission, to listen to her wisdom, to invite her more and more into the great task of building a truly human society—and, indeed, human history itself.

Contemplation at Work:
A Theological Conversation Between John Paul II and Josemaría Escrivá

Martin Schlag

1. Introduction

The spirituality of work, as an academic topic, has been the topic of substantial research in business literature, especially in recent years.[1] Specifically, publications have dealt with the general importance of spirituality and religion for business and society,[2] but also with specific topics like mindfulness and meditation,[3] and in a lesser degree with the notion of contemplation in work.[4] Schwanda and Sisemore have rediscovered the

---

1   See Martin Schlag and Domenec Mele, *A Catholic Spirituality for Business: The Logic of Gift* (Washington, D.C.: The Catholic University of America Press, 2019) for further references, especially 1–7.

2   See Suzanna Chan-Serafin, Arthur P. Brief, and Jennifer M. George, "How Does Religion Matter and Why? Religion and the Organizational Sciences," *Organization Science* 24/5 (2013): 1585–1600; Harry J. Van Buren III, Jawad Syed, and Raza Mir, "Religion as a Macro Social Force Affecting Business: Concepts, Questions, and Future Research," *Business and Society* 59/5 (2020): 799–822.

3   See Emma Donaldson, Rachel Lewis, and Joanna Yarker, "What outcomes have mindfulness and meditation interventions for managers and leaders achieved? A Systematic Review," *European Journal of Work and Organizational Psychology* 28/1 (2019): 11–29; Monique Valcour, "A 10-Minute Meditation to help You Solve Conflicts at Work," *Harvard Business Review* (April 27, 2015): 2–5.

4   See Tom Schwanda and Timothy A. Sisemore, "Experiencing God through Head and Heart: The Puritan Practices of Meditation and Contemplation and Their Relevance to Modern Psychology," *Journal of Psychology and*

spiritual, mental, and emotional benefits derived from the Christian Puritan tradition of prayer, meditation, and contemplation. These authors point out that the prevailing literature on meditation and mindfulness generally uses concepts that are of Buddhist origin but has extracted the concept of mindfulness from any religious context. What remains is mindfulness understood as "a peace and acceptance that is without content," with the good intention to "calm and center modern minds."[5] Grandy and Sliwa offer both a conceptual and an empirical study on "contemplative leadership" in the context of various Christian churches. They propose contemplative leadership as a virtuous activity that is a "reflexive, engaged, relational, and embodied practice."[6] The authors combine the eight Cs of contemplative leadership according to Kim Nolan[7] with the ethical approaches of Alasdair MacIntyre and Emmanuel Levinas.

In what follows, I offer a Catholic theological reflection on contemplation in work, in which I set out from Pope John Paul II's encyclical on work *Laborem Exercens*. Then I give an overview of contemplation in general with the aim of focusing on the spiritual message of Josemaría Escrivá, for whom contemplation in the middle of the world was of central importance. I wish to put John Paul II's teaching in conversation with that of Josemaría Escrivá because, as I hope

---

Christianity 39/1 (2020): 40–48; Gina Grandy and Martyna Sliwa, "Contemplative Leadership: The Possibilities for the Ethics of Leadership Theory and Practice," *Journal of Business Ethics* 143 (2017): 423–40. For a Catholic perspective see Michael J. Naughton, *Getting Work Right: Labor and Leisure in a Fragmented World* (Steubenville: Emmaus, 2019); Jim Wishloff, "Work is Love Made Visible: A Meditation on Grace," *The American Journal of Economics and Sociology* 79/4 (2020): 1181–1208.

5   Schwanda and Sisemore, "Experiencing God," 40.

6   Grandy and Sliwa, "Contemplative Leadership," 423.

7   These are *Calling* (clear purpose/meaning); *compassion* (altruism, love); *care for others* (sense of belonging, interconnectedness); *centered communication* (balance between emotion and reason in articulation); *cultivate stillness* (engagement in contemplative practices); *clarity* (wisdom, self and other awareness); *currency of time* (mindfulness); and *contagious joy* (positive energy). Taken from Grandy and Sliwa, "Contemplative Leadership," 426.

to show, they complement each other and highlight different function-
alities of contemplation. John Paul II presupposes union with God when
he calls on Christians to acquire a "contemplative outlook," with which
they behold creation and structure society, especially labor, in a way
that respects human dignity. On the other hand, Josemaría Escrivá
preaches to people who already try to live up to their responsibilities in
the world and strive for social justice. His emphasis is on achieving
personal union with God.

2. The notion of contemplation
in the context of John Paul II's magisterium

When *Laborem Exercens* (henceforth LE) was published, the topic of
spirituality and religion in work was not yet *en vogue*. However, the
encyclical ends with a chapter on "elements for a spirituality of work."
In LE, as in many of his other writings, John Paul II applies the texts
of the Second Vatican Council to contemporary issues—in this case,
the focus is human work.[8] He draws extensively from the Second Vatican Council's Pastoral Constitution, *Gaudium et Spes* (GS). He identifies the spirituality of work with the "vision of human work" as
expressed in GS, n. 35: just as every other human activity, work should
allow individuals to pursue their vocation and find personal fulfillment.
Thus, John Paul II's aim for any spirituality of work is personal flourishing; or, in his own words, "to come closer, through work, to God"
by exercising the threefold mission of Christ as priest, prophet, and
king.[9] As such, Christian workers are to advance true progress, which,
according to GS, is not just any form of growth or increase of posses-
sions. Progress only deserves the name when it is integral to human development: economic growth that fosters justice, unity, and a humane
ordering of social relationships. Therefore, spirituality of work in LE

---

8   LE is the only social encyclical so far (except *Rerum Novarum*) that limits
    itself to explore one theme only, a quality of LE for which readers are cer-
    tainly grateful.
9   John Paul II, Encyclical *Laborem Exercens* (Vatican City: Libreria Editrice
    Vaticana, 1981), n. 24.

is not a mere coping mechanism or a ruse of employers to make their employees labor under unbearable conditions by consoling them with eternal rewards.[10] It is an attitude that requires social change. LE links virtue and spirituality with a constant advocacy for *"the social order of work,* which will enable man [and woman] to become, in work, 'more a human being' and not be degraded by it not only because of the wearing out of his [or her] physical strength (which, at least up to a certain point, is inevitable), but especially through damage to the dignity and subjectivity that are proper to him [and her]."[11]

Shortly after the encyclical's publication, Fr. Hennely observes that in LE's section on spirituality "contemplation and worship are simply not mentioned at all, while the one mention of prayer ('uniting work with prayer') occurs almost as an afterthought at the very end of the encyclical."[12] This, Fr. Hennely explains, is due to the pope's wish to present work and its spirituality from the viewpoint of the acting person: "work in its subjective aspect is always a personal action, an 'actus personae,'...."[13] My conclusion from this methodological decision by John Paul II is that it led him to understand contemplation less in the sense of a prayerful gaze at God and more as a committed participation in secular affairs. Of course, John Paul II is not pushing activism: anyone who has even a superficial knowledge of John Paul II knows that he was a man of deep prayer who spent countless hours in adoration and the recitation of the rosary and the liturgy of the hours. He was by all standards of the word a contemplative person. I myself am witness of his prayerfulness. Nevertheless, in John Paul II's magisterial documents, contemplation means looking at others and the world with the eyes of God, rather than looking at God. Needless to say, such a contemplative glance at the world presupposes union with God in prayer. I will exemplify this characteristic notion of contemplation in John Paul II in the following quotations.

10 See Ikiene Sentime, *"Laborem Exercens* as a Critical Notion of Workplace Spirituality," *Journal of Catholic Social Thought* 12:1 (2015): 143–56 for an underscoring of this fact.
11 LE, n. 9.
12 Alfred T. Hennely, S.J., "A Spirituality of Work," *America*, January 16, 1982, 31–33, 31.
13 LE, n. 24.

In his encyclical on the value and inviolability of human life *Evangelium Vitae*, John Paul II writes of the "contemplative outlook" that we need to understand creation in its true dignity, without a possessive and manipulative attitude:

> Such an outlook arises from faith in the God of life, who has created every individual as a "wonder" (cf. Ps 139:14). It is the outlook of those who see life in its deeper meaning, who grasp its utter gratuitousness, its beauty and its invitation to freedom and responsibility. It is the outlook of those who do not presume to take possession of reality but instead accept it as a gift, discovering in all things the reflection of the Creator and seeing in every person his living image (cf. Gen 1:27; Ps 8:5). This outlook does not give in to discouragement when confronted by those who are sick, suffering, outcast or at death's door. Instead, in all these situations it feels challenged to find meaning, and precisely in these circumstances it is open to perceiving in the face of every person a call to encounter, dialogue and solidarity.[14]

In this paragraph, John Paul II refers the reader to his encyclical *Centesimus Annus*, in which, without using the expression "contemplative outlook," he warns against a poor and narrow outlook that exploits our planet instead of helping us to be its stewards.[15] Contemplation for John Paul II is thus the purified glance of a person who has united himself or herself with God. It is a glance of love and acceptance that lets the other be itself; but at the same time, it is the perception of and struggle against every form of injustice.

In contrast, in the Apostolic Letter *Novo Millennio Ineunte*, John Paul II uses the word contemplation in the classical sense of gazing

---

14 John Paul II, Encyclical *Evangelium Vitae* (Vatican City: Vatican Press, 1995), n. 83. Pope Francis returns to the same theme when he warns against the technocratic paradigm.

15 See John Paul II, Encyclical *Centesimus Annus* (Vatican City: Vatican Press, 1991), n. 37.

at God: our witness to the world as faithful Christians "would be hopelessly inadequate if we ourselves had not first *contemplated his face*."[16] The great legacy of the Jubilee of the year 2000, writes the Pope, was "the *contemplation of the face of Christ.* "[17] However, as if to ensure that he was not misunderstood as promoting a passive notion of contemplation, in a homily of the same year John Paul II reminds his audience that

> to contemplate heaven does not mean to forget the earth. If there were ever the hint of such a temptation, just listen again to the two men in white robes, of the Acts of the Apostles: "Why do you stand looking up to heaven?" (Acts 1,11). Christian contemplation does not take us away from our earthly commitments. The "heaven" into which Jesus was taken up is not his removal into some place far away from us, but the veiling and protection of the presence of One who is always with us until he comes again in glory. The present age is very much the time requiring our witness so that in the name of Christ "repentance and the forgiveness of sins should be preached to all the nations" (cf. Lk 24,47).[18]

John Paul II's concept of contemplation was thus two-directional. One direction leads the Christian to raise his or her mind to God; the other makes the believer engage in the world. This latter understanding was the meaning that John Paul II usually read into the terms contemplation or contemplative outlook, and which already underlay LE's section on the spirituality of work. Thus, contemplation as a contemplative outlook at the world comprises the prophetic dimension of denouncing sin and injustices. In the name of God, a prophet—or a contemplative—gives his or her voice to those who have none or are too weak to raise theirs.

---

16 John Paul II, Apostolic Letter *Novo Millennio Ineunte* (Vatican City: Vatican Press, 2001), n. 16.
17 *Ibid.*, n. 15.
18 John Paul II, Homily, May 24, 2001.

3. Brief overview of contemplation in the Catholic tradition

Contemplation is simultaneously a practice of the spiritual life and an object of theology—the science that studies God and all things in relation to God. The name of the specific branch of theology dedicated to the spiritual life has borne different names.[19] What is beyond debate is that contemplation has been the fulcrum of deep theological thought and controversy.[20] In the New Testament, the Greek word for contemplation (*theoria*) appears only once (Lk 23:48. This passage refers to the spectacle of Christ on the Cross.). The notion of contemplation does not play an important role in Christian literature until Clement of Alexandria and Origen. With these two Christian writers, both flourishing in the third century, contemplation suddenly emerges as a major concern.[21] This is partly due to their utilization of concepts embedded in the cultural and philosophical heritage they had received from Hellenistic philosophy, in which contemplation plays an important role. Neo-Platonism aspires to the contemplation of the One—of truth, goodness, and beauty—as the highest form of life. Platonists were and are aware that this process requires moral purification and elevation. Aristotle, too, affirms the superiority of a contemplative lifestyle over an active one, though more in an intellectual than in a moral sense. Therefore, many Christian thinkers had been educated in a cultural environment in which the contemplative life was highly esteemed and intellectuals were aware of its moral dimension. But the Fathers modify these inherited concepts in two decisive ways: firstly, Christian contemplation is an encounter with the absolutely transcendent mystery of the Triune God which we cannot attain by our

---

19 See Jordan Aumann, *Spiritual Theology* (London-New York: Continuum, 1993 [reprint 2006]), 13.

20 It is impressive that AA.VV., "Contemplation," in *Dictionnaire de Spiritualité* (Paris: Beauchesne, 1953), col. 1643 to 2193 comprises over 500 columns. A mere entry in a dictionary of over 250 pages!

21 See José Luis Illanes, "La contemplazione di Dio nella tradizione cristiana: visione sintetica," in *La contemplazione cristiana: esperienza e dottrina. Atti del IX Simposio della Facoltà di Teologia, Roma, 10–11 marzo 2005*, ed. Laurent Touze (Vatican City: Libreria Editrice Vaticana, 2007), 9–43, 9.

own strength. Contemplation in the Christian sense is thus a gift and God's initiative. José Luis Illanes summarizes the patristic teaching on contemplation as an experience in which we perceive the infinitude, ineffability, and transcendence of God, and thus renounce any attempt to control or dominate him to whom we are united but place ourselves humbly and lovingly before God with trust and love. Secondly, this encounter with God requires the infused virtue of charity for our neighbor. There is no true Christian contemplation without openness to the gift of love for the poor and suffering. And while the Fathers insist on the constant memory of God in all things, they do not reflect on the specific consequences of contemplation for active or ordinary life.[22] Toward the end of the patristic period, Gregory the Great introduces the distinction between contemplative and active life that would have a lasting and profound impact on medieval theology; and lead to an institutional and conceptual separation of the two forms of life.

During the Middle Ages, work and active life were highly appreciated.[23] Nevertheless, for Thomas Aquinas, the universal teacher of the Church, even though work and active life are necessary and willed by God, they are an obstacle for contemplation. Active life hinders contemplative life "in so far as it is impossible for one to be busy with external action, and at the same time give oneself to Divine contemplation."[24] According to Aquinas, active life, with its moral virtues, is necessary in order to quell the interior and exterior passions, but the moral virtues do not pertain to contemplative life. The moral virtues are simply dispositions for contemplative life, not a part of it.[25] However, we can discover an opening of Aquinas toward considering contemplation as configurative of the whole of our existence in his famous adage "*contemplata aliis*

22 See Illanes, "Contemplazione," 19–21.
23 We owe this knowledge in large part to the research of Patricia Ranft. See her chapter in this book.
24 Thomas Aquinas, *Summa Theologica* II-II, q. 182, a. 3.
25 Thomas Aquinas, *Summa Theologica* II-II, q. 180, a. 2. Obviously, this does not mean that members of contemplative life were dispensed from the moral virtues. The moral virtues are the first step toward the contemplation of divine truth, as Thomas reminds his readers in Aquinas, *Summa Theologica* II-II, q. 180, a. 4.

tradere."[26] In contemplation, the human mind has made itself con-natural with the divine truth and is able to communicate it to others. It is "better to give to others the fruits of one's contemplation than merely to contemplate."[27] With these words, Aquinas is defending the superiority of his own Dominican Order over all other religious orders. Nevertheless, the exhortation that giving oneself in preaching was better than mere theory means that even though contemplative life is more excellent than active life, both can be united. Moreover, this implies that the highest form of spiritual life consists of a mixture of both, in which contemplation flows over into action. An example for this union is preaching. Aquinas thus remotely opens theological reflection to the essential unity of active and contemplative life, nodding to the modern conviction that the separation does not make any sense.

Illanes sketches the historical development of the theological understanding of the relationship between contemplation and action in three steps. Each step is associated with a different saint.[28] We have already seen that Thomas Aquinas takes a first step by affirming the goodness of giving to others the fruits of one's contemplation: *contemplata aliis tradere*. Three hundred years later, Ignatius of Loyola encouraged his followers to be "*in actione contemplativus*," contemplatives in action. The expression itself was not coined directly by Ignatius but by Jeronimo Nadal, one of the first Jesuits to express Ignatius's wish to encounter God in all things. If I understand it correctly, what Ignatius had in mind when speaking of action was apostolic, missionary action. He was speaking primarily to priests and religious committed to pastoral service.[29]

Josemaría Escrivá finally proclaims the universal calling of all Christians to be "contemplatives in the middle of the world." He is

26 Aquinas, *Summa Theologica*, II-II, q. 188, a. 6.
27 *Ibid.*
28 See José Luis Illanes, *Existencia cristiana y mundo: jalones para una reflexión teológica sobre el Opus Dei* [Christian Existence and World: Milestones for a Theological Reflection on Opus Dei] (Pamplona: EUNSA, 2003), 301–03.
29 See Ernst Burkhart and Javier Lopez, *Ordinary Life and Holiness in the Teaching of St. Josemaría: A Study in Spiritual Theology*, vol. 1 (New York: Scepter, 2017), 251.

thinking of activities imbedded in work, family, society, science, art, and any other honest secular activity. He speaks to lay people in varying and often difficult and complex socio-economic and familial situations. For Josemaría, normal Christians can attain holiness in and through the honest secular activities in which they are engaged. To be contemplative in the middle of the world is the aim, the ideal, and the sum of the life of prayer to which a Christian is called. To attain this end, it is not necessary to leave the world and enter religious life. It is possible to be contemplative in the world, understood as a theological-spiritual category, not merely as a sociological fact. Work in the world, that is, secular activity, is a tool and instrument of contemplation, not an obstacle.[30]

Before delving into Josemaría Escrivá's teaching, a brief summary might be useful of what the Christian tradition means by the word contemplation. Contemplation is generally considered to be "the summit of prayer life."[31] Various definitions of contemplation from the tradition of Catholic spirituality confirm this affirmation: "Contemplation is when the mind is in some sort lifted up to God and held above itself, so that it tastes the joys of everlasting sweetness";[32] "an infused loving knowledge that both illumines and enamors the soul, elevating it step by step to God, its Creator. For it is only love that unites and joins the soul to God";[33]

---

30 See Manuel Belda, "Contemplativos en medio del mundo" [Contemplatives in the middle of the world], in *Diccionario de San Josemaria Escrivá de Balaguer*, ed. Jose Luis Illanes (Burgos: Instituto Historico San Josemaria Escrivá de Balaguer—Monte Carmelo, 2013), 265–67.

31 Manuel Belda, "Contemplatives in the Midst of the World," *Romana* [Bulletin of the Prelature of the Holy Cross and Opus Dei] 27 (1998), 326–40, 329. Unfortunately this study is not available on the website in English https://en.romana.org/archive/; it is available in Spanish: https://es.romana.org/27/estudio/contemplativos-en-medio-del-mundo-de-manuel-belda/; and in Italian: https://romana.org/27/studio/contemplativi-in-mezzo-al-mondo/.

32 Guigo II, "The Ladder of Monks: A Letter on the Contemplative Life," in *The Ladder of Monks: A Letter on the Contemplative Life and Twelve Meditations*, transl. Edmund Colledge, O.S.A. and James Walsh, S.J. (Kalamazoo: Cistercian Publications, 1981), chapter II, p. 68.

33 St. John of the Cross, "The Dark Night of the Soul," II, 18, 5 in *The Collected Works of St. John of the Cross*, trans. by Kieran Kavanaugh, O.C.D.

"... a single concentrated look at what we love—concentrated reflection that has greater energy, greater power to move the will."[34] The common denominator of these medieval and early modern quotations is that contemplation is "an attentive gaze, marked by simplicity and constancy."[35] Contemplation is often experienced as an Exodus from sin, addictions, and futile pursuits to a life of fullness that leads back to a different perception of the challenges of this world. Thomas Merton expressed this beautifully: "Contemplation, at its highest intensity, becomes a reservoir of spiritual vitality that pours itself out in the most telling social action."[36] The path to contemplation always begins with a period of purification that leads to an illumination and elevation of the human mind, that finally—as if a stream—empties into the great ocean of union with God.

Contemplation is a universal calling, and of that the Church after the Second Vatican Council is convinced,[37] but contemplation does not mean the same for all. For some, contemplation takes on the form of ecstatic raptures that transcend conceptual thinking and elevate the mind into a different mode of experience of God. For others, contemplation brings a special superhuman intensity of love of God. For yet others, contemplation preponderantly is intellectual intuition. These models are not exclusive of each other; they can overlap. There also exist multiple ways to reach contemplation. The meditation on the *vestigia Dei*, the vestiges of God in created things, and His presence in his image, the human person, is one path. Another path stresses the need of ascetical detachment from the creatures and complete surrender to God. Other ways lead the pilgrim wanderer to seek divine adventures of love, to purify his or her interior senses of all detachment, even from images of the senses in their thinking. Meditating on death and the Cross are yet other

and Otilio Rodriguez, O.C.D. (Washington, D.C.: ICS Publications, 1991), 440.

34 St. Francis de Sales, "Treatise on the Love of God," in *Francis de Sales, Introduction to the Devout Life and Treatise on the Love of God*, ed. Wendy M. Wright (New York: Crossroad, 1997), 146.

35 Belda, "Contemplatives," 330.

36 Thomas Merton, *On Christian Contemplation*, ed. Paul M. Pearson (New York: New Directions Publishing Corporation, 2012), 56.

37 We turn to this important question below.

methods.[38] For Josemaría Escrivá the path to contemplation is the humanity of Christ. As we will see, this is based in his wish to imitate Christ in the thirty years of his hidden life in a family and in work. However, before we get there, we need to briefly mention yet another important question that set the course for future theological developement: the mystical question.

The Twentieth century was marked by the theological debate on the "mystical question," which was centered basically on two conundrums. The first question referred to whether contemplation was "acquired" or only "infused"; and the second to whether all Christians or only some were called to be contemplative.[39] Put in simpler and less academic words: the assumption behind the notion of "acquired contemplation" was that a Christian, with the help of God's grace, can remind oneself frequently of God's presence in a such way that over time one acquires the habitual state of contemplating God's presence. There could come a moment in this Christian's life when God intervenes and lifts the soul up to a special experience of God in rapture. However, this would be a completely gratuitous and unforeseeable gift of God. In contrast, those who defended "infused contemplation" were of the conviction that any kind of contemplation is always infused by God's sovereign grace. Josemaría Escrivá must have been aware of the "mystical question" as he writes:

> Asceticism? Mysticism? I don't mind what you call it. Whichever it is, asceticism or mysticism, does not matter. Either way, it is a gift of God's mercy.[40]

His nonchalance reflects the intrinsic vapidity of the mystical question. It simply died from inertia and was left unresolved. Instead, Josemaría

---

38 See the overview in Dietmar Mieth, "Kontemplation," in *Lexikon für Theologie und Kirche*, ed. Walter Kasper, vol. 6 (Freiburg—Basel—Rom—Wien: Herder, 1997; third edition), 326–27.

39 See Illanes, "Contemplazione," 35–40.

40 Josemara Escrivá, Friends of God, n. 308; https://www.escrivaworks.org/book/friends_of_god-point-308.htm.

Escrivá anticipated the universal calling to holiness and to contemplation that we find in the Second Vatican Council and its *Catechism of the Catholic Church*. For Escrivá, contemplation is a supernatural gift not reserved for a few privileged Christians but a grace that belongs to the normal path to holiness. All Christians can be contemplative, and thus holy. In a similar vein, the Second Vatican Council teaches:

> All Christians in any state or walk of life are called to the fullness of Christian life and to the perfection of charity.[41]

The *Catechism* adds:

> Spiritual progress tends toward ever more intimate union with Christ. This union is called "mystical" because it participates in the mystery of Christ through the sacraments—"the holy mysteries"—and, in him, in the mystery of the Holy Trinity. God calls us all to this intimate union with him, even if the special graces or extraordinary signs of this mystical life are granted only to some for the sake of manifesting the gratuitous gift given to all.[42]

Vicente Bosch summarizes the Catechism's teachings on contemplation in four theses:

- Contemplation is God's gratuitous gift;
- Contemplation is union with God;
- This union consists in the intuitive, simple, and loving knowledge of God;
- The universal calling to holiness implies that contemplation is connatural with the Christian vocation. Every Christian by the mere fact of being one is called to be a contemplative.[43]

41 Second Vatican Council, Dogmatic Constitution *Lumen Gentium*, n. 40.
42 *Catechism of the Catholic Church*, n. 2014. The Catechism mentions contemplation in 23 points in all.
43 Vicente Bosch, "La noción de contemplación en el Catecismo de la Iglesia

Considering the poor spiritual state of many Christians, their lack of sacramental and prayer life, such a high calling to contemplation may seem farfetched. Indeed, it is a great ideal. Yet Josemaría Escrivá encourages ordinary Christians to aspire to it in and through their everyday chores and daily work. His definition of contemplation is similar to the ones listed above: "intimacy with God, looking at God without needing rest or feeling tired."[44] By insisting on contemplation in the midst of ordinary activities, he gives the usual concept of contemplation in his time a new frame or horizon. This we will investigate in the following section.

4. Contemplation in the middle of the world

Of course, Josemaría Escrivá was not the only one to recommend contemplation to people in the world. Francis de Sales had done so in the seventeenth century; and spiritual teachers like Thomas Merton[45] and Jacques and Raissa Maritain repeated similar ideas in Escrivá's lifetime. Merton rejects the separation of action and contemplation as "a kind of schizoid split."[46] Action and contemplation, writes Merton, "become two aspects of the same thing. Action is charity looking outward to other men, and contemplation is charity drawn inward to its own divine source. Action is the stream, and contemplation is the spring."[47] The Maritains call for "contemplation on the streets" as the adequate renewal of spirituality in their times.[48] What is unique about Escrivá is

Católica [The Notion of Contemplation in the Catechism of the Catholic Church]," in *La contemplazione cristiana: esperienza e dottrina. Atti del IX Simposio della Facoltà di Teologia, Roma, 10–11 marzo 2005*, ed. Laurent Touze, (Vatican City: Libreria Editrice Vaticana, 2007), 477–92.
44 Josemaría Escrivá, *Friends of God: Homilies* (New Rochelle: Scepter, 1981), n. 296.
45 See Merton's brilliant reflections on "masked contemplation," which so many "hidden contemplatives" in active life were themselves unaware of possessing. Thomas Merton, *The Inner Experience: Notes on Contemplation*, ed. William H. Shannon (New York: HarperCollins, 2003), 64.
46 Merton, *On Christian Contemplation*, 53.
47 *Ibid.*, 56.
48 Quoted from Laurent Touze, "La contemplation dans la vie ordinaire: À propos de Josemaria Escriva," *Esprit et Vie* 67 (2002): 9–14, 9.

that he defines the vocation in Opus Dei, the institution that God had called him to found, as contemplative; *and* that he linked it to secularity, in particular to secular work. This uniqueness is the combination of contemplation and earthly affairs, a uniqueness which is clear as he says,

> My children and I should be, in the world, in the middle of the street, in the midst of our professional work, each one of us in theirs, contemplative souls, souls who continuously are in conversation with the Lord....[49]

And he exhorts his followers again:

> I look at you, my sons...What joy when your turn comes to teach your brothers that the children of God in Opus Dei must be contemplatives, contemplative souls in the middle of the world! You must maintain a life of continuous prayer, from morning to evening, and from evening to morning. From evening to morning? Yes, my son, also asleep.[50]

The Founder could have used many other definitions, e.g., "diligent (or any other virtue) souls in the middle of the world," "poor souls in the middle of the world," "apostolic souls in the middle of the world," etc., but he did not. The only definition by the Founder himself points to contemplation as the essential hallmark of the path to holiness in work.

In the following paragraphs, I do not attempt to present an overview of the spiritual teachings of St. Josemaría. For this, I refer the reader to the bibliography I have already cited in the footnotes. What I attempt to

---

49 Josemaría Escrivá, "Rezar con más urgencia," in *En diálogo con el Señor: Textos de la predicación oral,* ed. Luis Cano and Francesc Castells (Madrid: Rialp, 2017). Josemaría Escrivá de Balaguer Obras Completas V/1, n. 2a, p. 263 (my own translation).

50 Josemaría Escrivá, "Vivir para la gloria de Dios," in *En diálogo con el Señor: Textos de la predicación oral,* ed. Luis Cano and Francesc Castells (Madrid: Rialp, 2017). Josemaría Escrivá de Balaguer Obras Completas V/1, n. 5b, p. 110 (my own translation).

do is to offer my own personal insights and systematic reflections on what I consider the central contributions by Josemaría Escrivá to contemplation and work.

In a homily fittingly titled "Passionately Loving the World," Josemaría Escrivá rejects the separation of active and contemplative life:

> No, my children! We cannot lead a double life. We cannot have a split personality if we want to be Christians.[51]

In his posthumously published collection of thoughts, *The Forge*, he writes:

> I will never share the opinion—though I respect it—of those who separate prayer from active life, as if they were incompatible. We children of God have to be contemplatives: people who, in the midst of the din of the throng, know how to find silence of soul in a lasting conversation with Our Lord, people who know how to look at him as they look at a Father, as they look at a Friend, whom they love madly.

Such an affirmation presupposes that a Christian can consider the world good and perfective, allowing him or her to work towards that end. In all passages in which Escrivá speaks of the sanctification of the world, he reminds the reader that the world is not evil because God created it good; and Christ Redeemer has saved it from slavery to sin. Therefore, once "the Word of God has lived among men, felt hunger and thirst, worked with his hands, experienced friendship and obedience and suffering and death...we cannot say that there are things—good, noble or indifferent—which are exclusively worldly."[52] Escrivá extends his positive view of work as a reality that can be sanctified not only by those callings that have a clear humanitarian and social dimension, as medical,

51 Josemaría Escrivá, *Conversations with Saint Josemaría Escrivá* (New York: Scepter, 2007), n. 114.
52 Josemaria Escriva, *Christ is Passing By: Homilies* (Princeton—New York: Scepter, no year), n. 112. I have inverted the order of the half sentences.

caring, teaching, and helping professions do. He also bears in mind professions that in the Christian tradition might be (falsely) tainted by the impression of being selfish or morally dangerous, such as politics, business, finance, trade, and commerce.[53]

In this context, on a philosophical level, the distinction between the (neo-)Platonic-Augustinian tradition and the Aristotelean-Thomist one is important. The (neo-)Platonic-Augustinian conception of the political, legal, and economic order is that it is basically derived from original sin. That tradition sees the inner-worldly social order as post-lapsarian structures that are necessary to repress evil, but not in themselves perfective elements of God's original plan of creation and salvation. On the other hand, the Aristotelian-Thomist vision considers socio-political and economic realities, if correctly ordered toward God as the final cause of the universe, as in themselves perfective and constitutive elements of human virtuosity and holiness.[54] Thus, Aquinas explicitly recognizes the virtues of Pagans, if their actions in themselves are ordered to the ultimate end of human life (God), as real, albeit imperfect, virtues.[55] Escrivá definitely shares the Thomist vision when he encourages his audience: "Understand this well: there is something holy, something divine hidden in the most ordinary situations, and it is up to each one of you to discover it."[56]

---

53 Thomas Aquinas, e.g., forbade clerics to engage in commercial activities: "Clerics should abstain not only from things that are evil in themselves, but even from those that have an appearance of evil. This happens in trading, both because it is directed to worldly gain, which clerics should despise, and because trading is open to so many vices...." (Summa Theologica II-II, q. 77, a. 4 ad 3). Contemporary Catholic Canon Law requires clerics to seek the permission of their bishop to engage in commercial activity. This regulation has practical reasons and does not imply a condemnation of business activity as such.

54 See George Duke, "The principle of the common good," in *Christianity and Global Law*, ed. Rafael Domingo and John Witte, Jr. (London and New York: Routledge, 2020), 251–66, 253; Paul J. Weithman, "Augustine and Aquinas on Original Sin and the Function of Political Authority," *Journal of the History of Philosophy* 30 (1992): 353–76, 371–72.

55 See Thomas Aquinas, *Summa Theologica*, I-II, q. 23 a 7.

56 Escrivá, *Conversations*, 114.

Each small secular duty, as long as it is not a sinful and unjust imposition, is an occasion to discover God's will and say yes to it. In this way, each of our lives becomes a continuous loving dialogue between a child and our loving parent. Escrivá expressed this in the notion of the "sense of divine filiation." This sense was the foundation of his spirituality:

> Rest and repose in the fact of being children of God. God is a Father who is full of tenderness, of infinite love. Call him "Father" many times a day and tell him—alone, in your heart—that you love him, that you adore him, that you feel proud and strong because you are his son.[57]

Our sense of being children of God stems from our identification with Jesus, the Son of God who dedicated a large part of his life to ordinary work as a carpenter or in some other field of manual artisanship. Therefore, there is no wonder that for Josemaría Escrivá the years in Bethlehem, Egypt, and Nazareth, the hidden or obscure years of Jesus's life on earth, were especially paradigmatic:

> The fact that Jesus grew up and lived just like us shows us that human existence and all the ordinary activity of men have a divine meaning. No matter how much we may have reflected on all this, we should always be surprised when we think of the thirty years of obscurity which made up the greater part of Jesus' life among men. He lived in obscurity, but, for us, that period is full of light. It illuminates our days and fills them with meaning, for we are ordinary Christians who lead an ordinary life, just like millions of other people all over the world.[58]

For this reason, too, Josemaría Escrivá indicated the humanity of Christ as the path to contemplation. Other teachers have suggested other

57 Escrivá, *Friends of God*, n. 150.
58 Escrivá, *Christ*, n. 14.

methods, but many agree with him, that the human nature of Christ, as we know it from the Gospels, is our first book of meditation: "In order to draw close to God we must take the right road, which is the Sacred Humanity of Christ."[59]

On a practical level, this advice translates into a "plan of life," a distribution of pious devotions throughout the day that help us maintain the awareness of God's presence and to be united with him who is the only source of sanctification and grace. For a Christian, God's grace always takes precedence, in the knowledge that we alone can do nothing (see Jn 15:5). Repeatedly, Josemaría Escrivá drove home the fact that prayer not only comes first on a practical level, but that sanctifying work and seeking contemplation through work implies converting work into prayer:

> Let us work. Let us work a lot and work well, without forgetting that prayer is our best weapon. That is why I will never tire of repeating that we have to be contemplative souls in the middle of the world, who try to convert their work into prayer.[60]

Such an idea can seem utopian to people exposed to the hustle and bustle, the constant tensions and interruptions of an average job in the tough economic struggle for survival. Certainly, we should not think that converting work into prayer requires the actual elevation of our mind and thoughts to God in the concentrated silence of a church. Such an attempt would result in frustration and failure. It would also contradict God's will that we be fully concentrated on our tasks. How then can this riddle be solved? In a reflection on the qualities of our minds after the resurrection, Aquinas explains something that Ernst Burkhart and Javier Lopez apply to the question at hand. Aquinas writes:

> When of two things the first is the reason for the second, the attention of the soul to the second does not hinder or lessen its attention to the first...And since God is apprehended by the saints as the reason for all things that will be done or

---

59   Escrivá, *Friends of God*, n. 299.
60   Josemaría Escrivá, *Furrow*, n. 497.

known by them, their efforts in perceiving sensible things or in contemplating or doing anything else will in no way hinder their contemplation of God, nor conversely.[61]

Certainly, Thomas Aquinas is speaking of the saints in heaven after the resurrection of the body, but an analogy may be drawn between the eschaton and this life. When our last and ultimate intention is to love God and our will seeks him—through all the many intermediate aims we might have—as the last reason for our work, then we are united to God even if we are not actually thinking of him. For those who live this way, the fact that they are really united with God will often remain hidden to them because they are absorbed by their present contingent action. Nevertheless, if they refresh and rectify their intention, keep their plan of life, and receive the sacraments regularly, they are contemplatives in their work. Escrivá is reassuringly optimistic in his practical advice:

Rest assured that it is not difficult to convert work into a prayerful dialogue. As soon as you offer it up and then set to work, God is already listening and giving encouragement. We acquire the style of contemplative souls, in the midst of our daily work! Because we become certain that he is watching us, while he asks us to conquer ourselves anew: a little sacrifice here, a smile there for someone who bothers us, beginning the least pleasant but most urgent job first, carefulness in little details of order, perseverance in the fulfillment of our duty when it would be so easy to abandon it, not leaving for tomorrow what should be finished today: and all this, to please him, Our Father God![62]

So far, all quotations have underscored the relationship of the individual Christian in the sense of personal piety. However, we would not

61 Thomas Aquinas, *Summa Theologica*, Suppl, q. 82, a 3 ad 4; the translation follows that in Ernst Burkhart and Javier Lopez, *Ordinary Life and Holiness in the Teaching of St. Josemaria: A Study in Spiritual Theology*, vol. 1, (New York: Scepter, 2017), 249.
62 Escrivá, *Friends of God*, n. 67.

understand Escrivá's teaching on contemplation correctly if we forgot the social consequences of contemplation. Escrivá encouraged Christians to see the world as an altar on which each Christian can celebrate the mass of his or her common priesthood by offering up their work.

> Through baptism all of us have been made priests of our lives, "to offer spiritual sacrifices acceptable to God through Jesus Christ." Everything we do can be an expression of our obedience to God's will and so perpetuate the mission of the God-man.[63]

The sacrifice of our effort at work in perpetuation of Christ's mission on earth entails shaping the world according to the standards of prophetic justice. These are precisely the standards that Jesus set out to proclaim in the synagogue of Nazareth by proclaiming a Jubilee year of liberation and of resetting equality among the people. Thus, contemplation in work means falling into sync with Christ's heartbeat and seeing the world with his eyes: "A man or a society that does not react to suffering and injustice and makes no effort to alleviate them is still distant from the love of Christ's heart."[64]

Josemaría Escrivá taught his followers to be especially attentive to unity of life: it would be a "comfortable" and thus false religiosity to ignore the suffering of so many people and the injustices committed by individuals and systems.

> We do not love justice if we do not wish to see it fulfilled in the lives of others. In the same way, it is wrong to shut oneself up in comfortable religiosity, forgetting the needs of others. The man who wishes to be just in God's eyes also tries to establish the reign of justice among men.[65]

For people working in the middle of the world who depend on the existing structures of economic and political power for their living, it is

63 Escrivá, *Christ*, n. 96, quoting 1 Pt 2:5.
64 *Id.*, n. 167.
65 *Id.*, n. 52.

not at all easy to mount social criticism without becoming ostracized. Building the Kingdom of God implies an uneasy balance between staying part of the system and fighting it—a difficulty that can only be resolved in one's own personal conscience and in collaboration with men and women of good will, independently of their creed.

> It is easy to understand the impatience, anxiety and uneasiness of people whose naturally Christian soul stimulates them to fight the personal and social injustice which the human heart can create. So many centuries of men living side by side and still so much hate, so much destruction, so much fanaticism stored up in eyes that do not want to see and in hearts that do not want to love! The good things of the earth, monopolized by a handful of people; the culture of the world, confined to cliques. And, on the outside, hunger for bread and education. Human lives—holy, because they come from God—treated as mere things, as statistics. I understand and share this impatience. It stirs me to look at Christ, who is continually inviting us to put his new commandment of love into practice.[66]

At this point, we loop back to John Paul II's *Laborem Exercens*. Spirituality at work means exercising the offices of Christ as prophet, who denounces injustice; as king (or queen), who builds a harmonious community and defends his brothers and sisters; and as priest, who mediates between God and creation.[67] It means seeing work, our own and that of others, with the eyes of God.[68] In consequence of this contemplative outlook, a Christian struggles for a humane social order of work, for just and equitable labor laws, and the rights to work and of laborers in work.[69] More than Josemaría Escrivá did, John Paul II underscored the importance of structures and social organization as objects of a contemplative outlook. While Escrivá mentions the pressing issue of social

66 Escrivá, *Christ*, n. 111.
67 See LE, n. 24.
68 *Ibid.*
69 See LE, n. 9.

justice, his accent is on the interior dimension of the relationship with God in prayer and the sense of divine filiation. However, though this does not come to the fore in LE's chapter on the spirituality of work, John Paul II is very much aware of this need of interiority in work. Elsewhere in the document, he explains the primacy of the subjective dimension of work over its objective dimension. The acting human person is central for work: the purpose of work is not the product but the perfection of the human person.[70] The principle of human dignity is demanding also on the subject, the human person in work in relation to him or herself. This is because human dignity also applies to the way we relate to ourselves, seeing ourselves and appreciating ourselves with the eyes of God. God sees us and loves us as his children. We are not his slaves. Therefore, we should perform the work we do as sons and daughters of God; thus, without alienation and with interior freedom. As I write, I am aware that many people are held in modern forms of slavery or forced to labor under unbearable conditions from which they cannot liberate themselves out of their own strength. This is a sin that cries to heaven. However, there are also forms of self-imposed slavery and especially of stress and anxiety in work that contradict the contemplative spirit of a child of God and from which we can free ourselves.

Shortly after World War II, the German philosopher Josef Pieper warned against a world of "total work," in which the human person is absorbed and instrumentalized: in such a world, we live in order to work, rather than, as it should be, working in order to live.[71] Pieper points to the classical notion of leisure, another word for contemplation,[72] as the cure for teleopathy (confusion of aims) at work. Leisure is misunderstood if it is identified with amusement or idleness. Idleness is the opposite of leisure. Idleness is drifting through life without purpose and renouncing the calling to live up to our dignity. Leisure is a mental and spiritual attitude of inward calm and silence. Leisure is "time set aside for remembering the most important things, for rediscovering ourselves and thinking about who we

---

70   See LE, n. 6.

71   Josef Pieper, *Leisure: The Basis of Culture* (San Francisco: Ignatius, 2009), 19–27.

72   See *ibid.*, 41.

ought to be."[73] Bringing leisure into work does not imply working slowly, carelessly, or sloppily. "Leisurely" work means purposeful and mindful work that—precisely because it is aware of its purpose—is all the more energetic, joyful, and dedicated.[74] This is why the Sabbath, the day of the week reserved for contemplation and reorientation of our lives, is an important reservoir of contemplative spirit during the rest of the week. In John Paul II's letter *Dies Domini* on keeping the Lord's Day holy, he states that God himself contemplates his creation and rests with a "*gaze full of joyous delight*. This is a 'contemplative' gaze which does not look to new accomplishments but enjoys the beauty of what has already been achieved."[75] Only once we have sufficiently recognized the value of what God has done through and with us can we have the verve and enthusiasm to keep going.

5. Conclusion

LE leads us to value contemplation and leisure as antidotes to the anxiety that besets much of work in our culture. An important consequence of contemplation is to work not with anxiety but with the serene and relaxed attitude of God's children. Both John Paul II and Josemaría Escrivá point us in that direction. John Paul II emphasizes the contemplative gaze that rests *in* and enjoys in the good that exists and fights to improve it; and Josemaría Escrivá encourages Christians in the middle of the world to abandon themselves trustingly to God wherein he sees a beginning of contemplation.[76] Self-surrender to God's loving providence is a sure path to inner peace and joy. Once we embark on this path, we make an astonishing discovery: that all truly good things in life, including success in business, are a consequence of having put God radically first.[77] Everything is a byproduct of contemplation.

73   Michael Naughton, *Getting Work Right: Labor and Leisure in a Fragmented World* (Steubenville: Emmaus, 2019), 26.
74   Josemaria Escrivá, *The Forge* (London - New York: Scepter, 1987, n. 738.
75   John Paul II, Apostolic Letter *Dies Domini* [1998], n. 11.
76   See Escrivá, *Friends of God*, n. 296.
77   For a powerful testimony, see August Turak, *Business Secrets of the Trappist Monks: One CEO's Quest for Meaning and Authenticity* (New York: Columbia Business School Publishing, 2013).

Laborem Exercens: A Protestant Appreciation

Richard Turnbull

1. Introduction

The very idea of work has long exercised the Christian mind. In antiquity manual work was seen as lacking dignity, contemptuous, and coarse. Christianity rescued work from such negativity by investing the concept of work itself with divine and eternal purpose. Consequently, the worker is endowed with dignity. From these two principles, purpose and dignity, flows the importance with which Christian theology invests work in bringing about the economic and social welfare of humanity.

These matters have concerned both Catholic and Protestant thinkers. Nevertheless, perhaps through the nature of the magisterium, the central body of teaching of the Catholic Church, the prominence given in the formal documents and pronouncements of the Church, not least papal encyclicals, gives the ongoing discussion form and shape.

The link between purpose and dignity gives Christian theology an insight not only into questions of the future of work, its design, and the place of entrepreneurship and enterprise within a market economy, but also into the social questions which emerge. Examples include the problem of lack of work, the rights and protections due to the worker, the opportunities and challenges of technological development, and, indeed, the changing nature of work itself. In addition, at least for Christian reflection, the relationship of work to family and faith is significant.

The period prior to the publication in 1891 of Pope Leo XIII's encyclical *Rerum Novarum*, sub-titled "Rights and Duties of Capital and Labor," was tumultuous even in the context of "industrial revolution" and transformation. Economic depression meant uncertain times, deflation leading to the stagnation of trade and industry with the consequent pressures on labor and wages. One outcome was a period of labor strikes encompassing both Europe and North America, not least the London Dock Strike of 1889 in which Cardinal Manning mediated. It was in this context that Pope Leo spoke.

Perhaps less well known is that the Dutch Calvinist, Abraham Kuyper, delivered an address at the opening of the Christian Social Congress in Amsterdam on November 9, 1891, in which he specifically referred to Pope Leo's encyclical and addressed the problems of poverty, speaking to many of the same themes: the challenge of socialism, the dignity of work, the place of family, the role of the state, and, indeed, the rights of the worker. In doing so, he built upon the teaching of the Protestant tradition from the reformers of the sixteenth century through to the evangelicals of the nineteenth.

Pope John Paul II published his encyclical, *Laborem Exercens* (On human work) on September 14, 1981, to coincide with the ninetieth anniversary of *Rerum Novarum*. In the opening paragraphs, John Paul II refers to work as a basic dimension of human existence that builds up the human person, conveys special dignity, and yet also penetrates deeply into the social questions of our time. John Paul II also places work into the context of new technologies and challenges. Human work, he argues, is the key to the social question.

In his writing, John Paul II reflects many of the common themes of the Christian tradition with regard to work and the economy. This chapter will reflect on those common themes and offer an appreciation of the encyclical from a Protestant perspective, hence drawing upon the themes and resources of the Protestant tradition. The questions of methodology and critique we will leave to the end of the chapter because, important though they are, there is so much more to appreciate in the first place.

Our two main Protestant interlocutors are John Calvin (1509–1564) and Abraham Kuyper (1837–1920).

John Calvin, the sixteenth-century reformer in Geneva, is a representative figure in the historic reformed tradition. This is perhaps primarily due to his magnum opus, *The Institutes of the Christian Religion*, published in numerous editions over the course of nearly 25 years beginning in 1536. Calvin was a prolific writer and the sources for his thought go much wider than the *Institutes*; they include his sermons, letters, documents, and commentaries on both the Old and New Testaments.

Abraham Kuyper is a rather fascinating figure in what might be termed Dutch neo-Calvinism. Kuyper was a pastor, theologian, philosopher, politician, and editor. He founded the Free University of Amsterdam in 1880, a year after establishing his Anti-Revolutionary Party. From 1901–1905, he served as the Prime Minister of the Netherlands. Kuyper's extensive writings in Dutch are increasingly available in translation. Though complex to pigeonhole, he engages with the challenges of a nation-state from a reformed perspective.

As we explore the various elements of *Laborem Exercens* we will consider how these two representative writers from the Protestant tradition handle the themes raised. This will enable us to form a proper assessment of the continuities and discontinuities.

Deployment and Use of Scripture

The encyclical deploys and uses scripture as the essential framework for its discussion of work. This appeal to the common Christian tradition gives work significance and purpose. The encyclical asserts that "the Church's social teaching finds its source in Sacred Scripture, beginning with the Book of Genesis and especially in the Gospel and the writings of the Apostles."[1] Pope John Paul II adds that "the source of the Church's conviction is above all the revealed word of God."[2] Thus, any theological discussion on work must begin with scripture.

The entirety of section IV is dedicated to Genesis. There is an immediate appeal to the first pages of Genesis as the biblical source for understanding work as a fundamental element of human existence. The opening chapters of Genesis place humanity firmly within the mystery of creation. These principles are effective for humanity both before and after the fall:

1   John Paul II, *Laborem Exercens* (Vatican City: Libreria Editrice Vaticana, 1981), sec. 3, https://www.vatican.va/content/john-paul-ii/en/encyclicals/documents/hf_jp-ii_enc_14091981_laborem-exercens.html.

2   *Id.*, sec. 4.

> These truths are decisive for man from the very beginning, and at the same time they trace out the main lines of his earthly existence, both in the state of original justice and also after the breaking, caused by sin, of the Creator's original covenant with creation in man.[3]

The encyclical deploys the argument that God created humanity in his own image, carrying that image as the very essence of what it means to be human, and there follows a mandate, a command, in Genesis 1:28, to be fruitful and to subdue the earth. This not only implies some form of economic activity but also:

> In carrying out this mandate, man, every human being, reflects the very action of the Creator of the Universe.[4]

The encyclical goes on to talk about the discovery and use of the earth's resources—essentially entrepreneurial activity. John Paul is clear about the importance of the creation narrative.

> And so these words, placed at the beginning of the Bible, *never cease to be relevant.*[5]

Later in the encyclical, John Paul II refers to the creation as the first gospel of work. The encyclical goes on to make use of numerous other aspects of Scripture, including a summary of the range of work and professions in the Old Testament, the example of Christ himself, and indeed the teaching in the Pauline epistles. We will return to these paragraphs subsequently.[6]

From the perspective of Protestant teaching and theology, the starting point of scripture illustrates a common Christian adherence to the priority of the Bible. However, the manner in which the papal encyclical

3   *Id.*, sec. 4.
4   *Ibid.*
5   *Ibid.*
6   *Id.*, secs. 25 and 26.

both gives weight to and makes use of the creation narratives in Genesis points also to a deeper resonance with Protestant theology. There remains, however, a rather odd omission, to which we will return presently.

a) Creation Mandates

The notion of the creation mandate is central to any biblical theology of work. Creation mandates establish a number of basic principles around human purpose, creativity, liberty, and dignity. Thus, Catholic and Protestant teaching frequently appeal to the importance of both the divine and human aspects of creation, and especially the fact that work must be done well. Hence the Anglican Dorothy Sayers argues that in respect of an intelligent carpenter, "the very first demand that his religion makes upon him is that he should make good tables";[7] and Josemaría Escrivá, the founder of Opus Dei, that it is not possible to be a good Christian and a bad shoemaker.[8] In his reference to the mandate of dominion, John Paul II reflects this tradition.

Calvin, too, picks up the idea of purpose grounded in the order of creation and its relationship to human work. Ian Hart, in his *Evangelical Quarterly* articles on *The Teaching of Luther and Calvin about Ordinary Work*, grounds his observations in Calvin's understanding of the Genesis mandate.[9] In his *Commentary on Genesis*, 2:15, Hart notes that Calvin writes:

> Here Moses adds that the earth was leased to man, on this condition, that he busies himself cultivating it. It follows from this that men were made to employ themselves doing something and not to be lazy or idle.[10]

7   Dorothy Sayers, *Why Work? An Address Delivered at Eastbourne, April 23rd, 1942* (London: Methuen, 1942), 18.

8   Josemaría Escrivá, *Friends of God* (London: Scepter, 1981), 61, https://www.escrivaworks.org/book/friends_of_god.htm.

9   Ian Hart, "The Teaching of Luther and Calvin about Ordinary Work: 2. John Calvin (1509–1564)," *Evangelical Quarterly* 67, no. 2 (1995): 121–35 [henceforth quoted as "Calvin"].

10   John Calvin, *Commentary on Genesis*, 2:15, quoted in Hart, "Calvin" 121–

He adds, in his *Commentary on the Harmony of the Evangelists*, that we "know that men were created for the express purpose of being employed in labor of various kinds."[11] Martin Luther, in his own commentary on Genesis 2:15, also emphasizes that man "was created not for leisure but for work, even in the state of innocence."[12]

This same principle is also affirmed by the later neo-Calvinist tradition, as exemplified by Kuyper. Calvin, according to Kuyper, articulates a cosmological principle, "the Sovereignty of the Triune God over the whole Cosmos, in all its spheres and kingdoms, visible and invisible." For Kuyper, "the common means of provision are latent in the created order and are discovered by human activity."[13] He goes on:

> The ordinary means are neither our invention nor our fabrication; they are ordinances of God instituted at the time of creation for the sake of his creation. And even there where the means underwent some modification as a consequence of the Fall into sin—like nourishment, since the fruits of paradise were replaced after the Fall by nourishment through bread—the means of nourishment are and remain his divine ordinance.[14]

There is a common Christian appeal to the idea of the creation mandate. In adopting the principle within *Laborem Exercens*, John Paul II not only

22 (author's own translation from the Latin. Hart refers to "Calvinus: in Mosis libros, ad loc, Gn 2:15.")

11 John Calvin, *Commentary on the Harmony of the Evangelists*, vol. 2 (Edinburgh: Calvin Translation Society, 1845), 144, quoted in Hart, "Calvin," 127.

12 Martin Luther, *Commentary on Genesis*, Works of Luther, vol. 1 (Philadelphia: Fortress Press, 1966), 103, quoted in Hart, "The Teaching of Luther and Calvin about Ordinary Work: 1. Martin Luther (1483–1546)," *Evangelical Quarterly* 67, no. 1 (1995): 35–52, 38 [henceforth quoted as "Luther"].

13 Abraham Kuyper, *On Business and Economics*, Abraham Kuyper Collected Works in Public Theology, ed. Peter S. Heslam (Bellingham, Washington and Grand Rapids, Michigan: Lexham Press and Acton Institute, 2021), xlix.

14 Kuyper, *On Business and Economics*, xlix.

stands within that common tradition, but through such a use and deployment of scripture he invites appreciation from his Protestant readers.

There remains one oddity to note. Despite the obvious relevance of the mandate to work in Genesis 2:15, John Paul II makes only passing and fleeting reference to it in his encyclical, replying almost exclusively on the mandate to subdue and have dominion in 1:28. Although this does not discount his appeal to and use of Scripture, it is surprising. However, both Benedict XVI in *Caritas in Veritate* and Francis in *Laudato si'* refer to Genesis 2:15. Perhaps they do so because it is more relevant in contemporary reflections on environmental stewardship and responsibility as a balance to the theme of dominion?

b) Common Grace

The theological teaching of the reformed tradition does, however, extend the discussion beyond the commonly agreed-upon principle of the creation mandate. This is effected by the doctrine of common grace. For a working definition of common grace, we can use that of Louis Berkhof:

> Those operations of the Holy Spirit whereby He, without renewing the heart, exercises such a moral influence on man through his general or special revelation, that sin is restrained, order is maintained in social life, and civil righteousness is promoted.[15]

Common grace is grace at work in the world at large, acting as a restraint on sin and hence permitting human order, law, and culture to flourish. Common grace affirms the continuing value of the order of creation in the Christian dispensation. In his *Commentary on Genesis*, referring to Genesis 4, Calvin says, "the excellent gifts of the Spirit are diffused through the whole human race."[16] The crafts of sculpture and painting,

---

15 Louis Berkhof, *Systematic Theology*, 6th ed. (Edinburgh: The Banner of Truth Trust, 1971), 436.
16 Calvin, *Commentaries* (Philadelphia: Westminster Press: 1958), vol 23, 355, quoted in Hart, "Calvin," 127.

for instance, are gifts of God, given out for his glory and for legitimate use for our good (perhaps the common good?).[17] Kuyper, following Calvin, also teaches that God endows human beings with talent to be used in the workplace, regardless of merit and as part of the natural order; further, that these talents are not the result of special grace. This is exemplified in the raising up of inspired leaders, whom Calvin notes may indeed be flawed in many ways;[18] nonetheless, they are elevated through a common grace that "extends over our entire human life, in all its manifestations." Ultimately, the divinely willed outcome is human flourishing.[19]

We will consider this further in the next section, where we deal with the nature of work and enterprise as set out in both *Laborem Exercens* and the Protestant tradition.

Finally, we should reflect, albeit briefly, on the conception of natural law in the reformed tradition. For Calvin, the restraint from evil that flows from the common grace of God is the natural law, the inward law implanted in each man at his creation. Moreover, the natural law is not only an agent that restrains, but also one that impels each man to seek and pursue the good. This twofold impetus that arises from natural law—to seek good and avoid evil—carries with it a slew of ethical implications. This endorsement of the natural law may be surprising to some, as there has been an historic antipathy towards natural law in much of Protestant thinking. However, it is clear that the reformers accepted the natural law framework, and there has been a more recent resurgence in reformed appreciation of the natural law tradition.[20] Calvin summarizes his own position in a lengthy, though in some ways quite extraordinary quote, where he clearly links natural law, as a gift of God, to common

---

17 John Calvin, *The Institutes of the Christian Religion*, ed. John T. McNeill, trans. Ford Lewis Battles (Philadelphia: The Westminster Press, 1960), I.11.12.

18 Calvin, *Institutes*, II.3.3.

19 Kuyper, *On Business and Economics*, xxvi.

20 For example, see Daryl Charles, *Retrieving the Natural Law* (Grand Rapids: Eerdmans, 2008); Stephen J. Grabill, *Rediscovering the Natural Law in Reformed Theological Ethics* (Grand Rapids: Eerdmans, 2006); and Michael Cromartie (ed.), *A Preserving Grace: Protestants, Catholics and Natural Law* (Grand Rapids: Eerdmans, 1997).

grace, civic order, and the actions of people to act for the common good outside of special revelation.

> Whenever we come upon these matters in secular writers, let that admirable light of truth shining in them teach us that the mind of man, though fallen and perverted from its wholeness, is nevertheless clothed and ornamented with God's excellent gifts.... What then? Shall we deny that the truth shone upon the ancient jurists who established civic order and discipline with such great equity? ... Shall we say that they are insane who developed medicine, devoting their labor to our benefit? What shall we say of all the mathematical sciences? Shall we consider them the ravings of madmen? No, we cannot read the writings of the ancients on these subjects without great admiration. We marvel at them because we are compelled to recognize how pre-eminent they are. But shall we count anything praiseworthy or noble without recognizing at the same time that it comes from God?[21]

This all reinforces the idea that work has meaning and purpose for all, rooted in creation, but expressed in our diverse cultures and societies through natural gifts and skills which lead to entrepreneurial activity.

3. The Nature of Work and Enterprise

As we have already seen, *Laborem Exercens* develops a Christian view of work in the light of the creation principles. The text's appeal to the order of creation grounds the concept of work in natural law, which brings John Paul to not only think about work in the abstract, but also to develop an ethical framework relating to issues of labor.

The encyclical draws a distinction between the objective and subjective dimensions of work. The former sets the framework within which the intrinsic value of work is set, although the encyclical gives more

---

21 Calvin, *Institutes*, II.2.15.

weight to the latter, as it is this dimension which raises ethical questions, although this may be some confusion of category in the sense that the distinction may be somewhat artificial.

a) Work and Enterprise

The objective dimension of work allows Pope John Paul II to affirm the place of enterprise and entrepreneurship as a proper expression of the divine will for all people, not least in respect of the opportunities and challenges of modern technology. This aspect of work emphasises its universality in the concrete goods it produces. Thus, the meaning of work partially lies in "the various epochs of culture and civilization,"[22] instances of great transformation and cultivation that are clearly fulfilments of the creation mandate. Industry and production are the interaction of God-given resources with human work and creativity, whether physical or intellectual. The encyclical notes the transformation and development made possible by the advance of science and technology, a product "that human thought has produced"; further,

> ... technology is undoubtedly man's ally. It facilitates his work, perfects, accelerates and augments it. It leads to an increase in the quantity of things produced by work, and in many cases improves their quality.[23]

John Paul II also recognises the dangers of technology, among which are decreased satisfaction, fewer opportunities for employment, stifled creativity, and a less robust sense of personal responsibility. Nevertheless, there is a relationship between the principle of work as set out in the order of creation and technological advance, "which is the fruit of the work of the human intellect and a historical confirmation of man's dominion over nature."[24] The encyclical is particularly adept at making this connection explicit.

22 John Paul II, *Laborem Exercens*, sec. 5.
23 *Ibid.*
24 *Ibid.*

The encyclical discusses technology in both positive and negative aspects, but, perhaps because of John Paul II's emphasis on the subjective view of work, it does not give weight to ideas of innovation and enterprise in a market economy. These matters are made more explicit in the continuation of the debates around the order of creation in the Protestant tradition. Hence, Calvin sees the gifts which are endowed upon humanity as enabling creativity and innovation:

> Even the artisan with the humblest trade is good at it only because the Spirit of God works in him. For though these gifts are diverse, they all come from the one Spirit; it pleased God to distribute them to each one (1 Cor 12.4). This does not refer only to spiritual gifts, which follow regeneration, but to all the sciences which concern our use of the common life.[25]

In similar fashion, Kuyper, points to the Biblical narrative of Bezalel and Oholiab in Ex 35:30–35. This passage, which deals with the gifts endowed by the Spirit on these individuals tasked with the construction of the tabernacle as the people of Israel wandered in the desert, is the origin of both inspired leadership and entrepreneurship. Citing the principle of common grace, Kuyper argues that "there is a common grace that enriches a nation through inventiveness in enterprise and commerce."[26]

The encyclical would have benefited from a more specific reference to these matters. However, *Laborem Exercens* is not the sum total of Roman Catholic teaching on enterprise, nor even that of John Paul II. There are more explicit references to work and enterprise in other documents and encyclicals.[27] And, of course, *Laborem Exercens* does not

---

25 John Calvin, "Harmony of Ex.–Dt.," (translated from original, Mosis libri V (Harmony of Ex.-Dt.) ad loc Ex. 31:2), quoted in Ian Hart, "Calvin," 127.

26 Kuyper, *On Business and Economics*, xxvi.

27 See, for example Paul VI, *Populorem Progressio* (Vatican City: Libreria Editrice Vaticana, 1967), sec. 25, https://www.vatican.va/content/paul-vi/en/encyclicals/documents/hf_p-vi_enc_26031967_populorum.html; John Paul II, *Centesimus Annus* (Vatican City: Libreria Editrice Vaticana, 1991), sec. 31, https://www.vatican.va/content/john-paul-ii/en/encyclicals/documents/hf_jp-

deny such a connection, but rather seeks to concentrate on the consequences of work and value for the worker, to which we now turn.

b) Work and Value

The encyclical gives more concentrated attention to the subjective dimension of work. The distinction between the object and the subject of
work is helpful in clarifying the principles behind work, production and
markets and action, responsibility, and value in the discharge of work.
However, it is possible that too much is made of the differences. Work
has not only an objective purpose, but also a value intrinsic to the human
person. This value is an essential element of humanity's very being and
nature:

> As a person works, he performs various actions belonging to
> the work process; independently of their objective content,
> these actions must all serve to realize his humanity, to fulfil
> the calling to be a person that is his by reason of his very hu-
> manity.[28]

Since work is carried out by a person made in the image of God, the
conduct and supervision of that work carries ethical consequences. Thus,
there is a direct connection between work and the wider social questions
and dilemmas of humanity. Indeed, Christianity has transformed the nature of the ancient world—which valued work solely according to the
objective dimension of the work—by valuing the person who carries out
the work. The supreme example is that of Christ himself, who "devoted
most of the years of his life on earth to *manual work* at the carpenter's
bench."

ii_enc_01051991_centesimus-annus.html; Benedict, XVI, *Caritas in Veritate*
(Vatican City: Libreria Editrice Vaticana, 2009), sec. 63, https://www.vati-
can.va/content/benedict-xvi/en/encyclicals/documents/hf_ben-
xvi_enc_20090629_caritas-in-veritate.html; Pontifical Council on Justice
and Peace, *Vocation of the Business Leader: A reflection*, 4th ed. (Vatican
City: Pontifical Council on Justice and Peace, 2014), 5.
28 John Paul II, *Laborem Exercens*, sec. 6.

This circumstance constitutes in itself the most eloquent "Gospel of work," showing that the basis for determining the value of human work is not primarily the kind of work being done but the fact that the one who is doing it is a person. The sources of the dignity of work are to be sought primarily in the subjective dimension, not in the objective one.[29]

Perhaps slightly surprisingly given the emphasis on Genesis and creation so far, John Paul II gives pre-eminence to the subjective dimension primarily because work is made for man rather than man for work, which is what one might conclude from a mindset that derives the value of work from the value of its object. In reality, both dimensions belong together, and both have ethical implications.

c) Protestantism and Work

Calvin clearly taught what John Paul II refers to as the objective and subjective value of work, though perhaps he couched it in more explicit biblical terms in linking the subjective value of work more directly to human sin. Calvin emphasizes that the curse brings hardship to work, but that this is at least partially remitted in Christ, allowing the Christian to enjoy work. Ian Hart argues that it is this idea of restoration, a restored dominion and Lordship over the world, which at least in part explains the economic and commercial success of nations shaped by Calvinism.[30]

Calvin also clearly invests ordinary work with the same value as any spiritual work, unsurprising given the Reformers' negativity towards the apparent priority of spiritual work in medieval Catholicism. Calvin writes that no "work will be so mean and sordid as not to have splendour and value in the eyes of God."[31] He notes that agriculture, architecture, shoemaking, and shaving are all lawful ordinances of God.[32] In addition:

29 *Ibid.*
30 See Hart, "Calvin," 123.
31 Calvin, *Institutes*, III.10.6.
32 See *id.*, IV.19.34.

We should also note that there are different kinds of work. Anyone who benefits human society by his industry, either by ruling his family, administering public or private business, giving counsel, teaching, or in any other way, is not to be regarded as having no occupation.[33]

Kuyper reflects this classic reformed position. The general calling to work, including the call to business, is divine in origin, and the choice of one occupation over another derives from this principle of a calling for which the Lord endows the necessary gifts.

There is a real sense of irony that the tables appear to have turned with modern Roman Catholicism adopting the classic Protestant view of call (reflecting, of course, that this concept belongs to our common Christian tradition) whilst significant parts of contemporary Protestantism appear to have reinstituted the pietistic dualism which both Calvin and Kuyper resisted so strongly. David Miller points out that much of modern evangelicalism views lay ministry as increased participation in the church, superior to being in business or the wider world of work. One consequence of this has been that whether "conscious or unintended, the pulpit all too frequently sends the signal that work in the church matters but work in the world does not."[34] Darrell Cosden argues that from "a Christian point of view, all human work (and not just 'religious work' has eternal meaning and value."[35] The Pontifical Council on Justice and Peace is in agreement: "the vocation of the businessperson is a genuine human and Christian calling.... The importance of the businessperson's vocation in the life of the Church and in the world economy can hardly be overstated."[36]

33 Calvin's New Testament Commentaries (Epistles of Paul to the Romans and Thessalonians), trans. R. McKenzie (Grand Rapids: William B. Eerdmans, 1980), ad loc 2 Thess 3:10, quoted in Ian Hart, "Calvin," 128.
34 David W. Miller, *God at Work: The History and Promise of the Faith at Work Movement* (Oxford: Oxford University Press, 2007), 10.
35 Darrell Cosden, *The Heavenly Good of Earthly Work* (Peabody, MA: Hendrickson, 2006), 2.
36 Pontifical Council on Justice and Peace, *Vocation of the Business Leader: A reflection*, 4th ed. (Vatican City: Pontifical Council on Justice and Peace, 2014), 5.

Pope John Paul II then uses his analysis of the subjective understanding of work to contrast a Christian view of work to what he terms as a materialistic and economistic view. This "materialistic economism" makes labor into a commodity or a mere instrument of production, a mistake which he argues is the result of a dominance of the objective view of work over the subjective. With that in mind, he argues for a type of Copernican revolution in the terms that we have historically used in our discussion of capitalism. Capitalism should no longer be understood in the classic terms of capital and labor, as there remains an ever-present danger of treating the individual in merely instrumental terms. In other words, humans have value and worth simply by being humans created in the image of God, not simply by what we do. This, of course, then brings us to the question of human dignity.

All in all, there is a remarkable commonality between the teachings of Catholic and Protestant traditions on the nature of work and enterprise, which is largely reflected in *Laborem Exercens*. The encyclical is particularly helpful in separating the objective and subjective dimensions of work, but the two concepts belong together, not apart. The Protestant tradition is perhaps somewhat more explicit in the affirmation of enterprise, but this is also explicitly affirmed in the wider Catholic tradition. In the nature of work and calling, John Paul II and John Calvin promote the same common Christian teaching and reflection. And as we have noted, some modern Protestant traditions are more lacking in this regard.

4. The Dignity of the Worker

Both the encyclical itself and the common Christian tradition draw the principles considered so far from the idea of an essential human dignity. Human dignity is the basis of the creation mandates, the affirmation of the subjective dimension of work (that work itself conveys dignity and the human subject of work deserves dignity), and the biblical witness. It is a theme we have seen running throughout the analysis of both the encyclical and the Protestant tradition. This human dignity transcends the Fall because it is based in the concept of humanity being created in the image of God, bearing that image and reflecting the character of God himself.

> God's fundamental and original intention with regard to man, whom he created in his image and after his likeness, was not withdrawn or cancelled out, even when man, having broken the original covenant with God, heard the words: "In the sweat of your face you shall eat bread."[37]

The role of work in the human dispensation reflects the fact that, by derivation, both work and worker carry dignity because God himself undertook the work of creation and humanity is created in his image. One consequence of this is that work itself must be meaningful, since, if this were not so, then the implication is that God's creation is meaningless. Thus, Darrell Cosden states, "The person is a worker, not as an accident of nature, but because God first is a worker and persons are created in his image."[38] John Paul II precedes Cosden as he says:

> The knowledge that by means of work man shares in the work of creation constitutes the most profound *motive* for undertaking it.[39]

This sharing in the work of the creator thus endows dignity for the human person as they are created in the divine image. Thus, the value of human work derives not from the particular type of work undertaken, but from its human agency—hence the encyclical's subjective sense of work and the value given to work by Calvin and others. If the dignity of the work comes from the dignity of humanity, then so does the dignity of the worker. This has implications for rights and responsibilities, ethics, the nature of work, remuneration, and other related matters.

---

37 John Paul II, *Laborem Exercens*, sec. 9.
38 Cosden, *Heavenly Good of Earthly Work*, 17.
39 John Paul II, *Laborem Exercens*, sec. 25. Emphasis in original.

a) Rights and Responsibilities

Section IV of the encyclical is entitled "Rights of Workers." This comes immediately after the section dealing with the historic conflict and tension of labor and capital with which *Rerum Novarum* deals. In this section (III) there is an appeal to human rights, to various labor codes, legislative or otherwise, and an appreciation of the work of the International Labor Organization. John Paul II affirms the priority of labor over capital, regarding capital as essentially a mere collection of things, but then goes on to argue that "capital cannot be separated from labor; in no way can labor be opposed to capital or capital to labor."[40] There is some tension in various parts of the encyclical in this regard; do labor and capital belong together or does labor carry a priority? This section of the encyclical is something of a discursus on the changing nature of capital and labor, the place of property rights, and alternative forms of corporate ownership. This approach raises some questions concerning method, to which we will return. However, for our immediate purposes it is the more specific matters of the rights and responsibilities which flow from the endowment of the human person with the dignity that derives from the image of God.

John Paul II acknowledges both sides of the argument. Work is a duty, a moral obligation (not least as the Creator commanded it—a reference to Genesis 2:15 strangely missing in the earlier analysis, as we noted) but carries corresponding rights not least in the relationship, direct and indirect, between employer and worker.[41] The objective rights of the worker must be fully respected by the employer, but the state—as essentially an indirect employer—carries the responsibility for a just labor policy and the creation of rights and expectations within the system of employment. John Paul II talks about the global impact of economic policy, and the impact of multi-national companies suppressing wages in local markets whilst selling for the maximum profit in other markets:

> Finding himself in a system thus conditioned, the direct
> employer fixes working conditions below the objective

40   *Id.*, sec. 13.
41   *Id.*, sec. 16.

requirements of the workers, especially if he himself wishes to obtain the highest possible profits.[42]

John Paul II then analyzes the problem of unemployment, asserting a right to unemployment benefits as a fundamental principle of the moral order. The state—the role of which we will consider in the next section—has responsibilities for planning. John Paul II affirms international organizations, rational planning and organization, just remuneration, the role of unions, and the dignity of the disabled worker, agricultural worker, and migrant.

The encyclical at this point seems at its furthest remove from the biblical and theological analysis which it has so far reflected. There is a degree of superficiality in assessing the impact of globalization and a breadth of coverage that can at times lead to the banal; for instance, John Paul II asserts that "emigration in search of work must in no way become an opportunity for financial or social exploitation"[43]—a point rather difficult for anyone to disagree with.

However, here, perhaps the Protestant and reformed tradition can come to some assistance. This tradition has two strands: first, that work must be for and reflect God's glory; and, secondly, a negativity towards low wages, corrupt business practices, and exploitation.

The significant weight given in the reformed tradition to the majesty, sovereignty, and glory of God in all aspects of life and faith represents a key starting point. Discipleship involves self-denial. Work is done for the Lord, for his glory, and as a result we enjoy the positives and the good of work, as well as a keen awareness of our sins, which requires humility. Every mode of life is under the Lord's sovereignty, including our work. Our diligent application to our calling glorifies God. Male and female, chambermaid and servant, a job well done represents an offering to God. He does not want us to sit idle; but hard work only wins success so far as God blesses the labor. Thus, when we have labored, argues Calvin, we are then to lift our eyes to heaven and thank God for the fruits of our labors.[44]

---

42   *Id.*, sec. 17.
43   *Id.*, sec. 23.
44   Hart, "Calvin," 129.

Kuyper follows Calvin. We conduct our business always in the sight of God and for his glory. For Kuyper, business is a sphere of work in its own right under the sovereignty of God. This, for Kuyper, is the beginning of ethics:

> Wherever man may stand, whatever he may do, to whatever he may apply his hand, in agriculture, in commerce, and in industry, or his mind, in the world of art and science, he is, whatsoever it may be, constantly standing before the face of God, he is employed in the service of God, he has strictly to obey God, and, above all, he has to aim to the glory of God.[45]

Calvin inveighs against corrupt, fraudulent, and exploitative business practices. In this he stands with John Paul II. Unjust gain is effectively theft. The employer should pay proper wages. To offer unfair wages when work is scarce constitutes cruelty and cheating. Profitable employers should improve wages. To charge more than goods are worth is sinful.[46] In this, of course, Calvin is merely reflecting the explicit teaching of the Scriptures. Deuteronomy 24:14–15 deals with timely and unjust wages, and Deuteronomy 25:13–16 with honest weights and measures, an injunction returned to in Amos 8:5–6. In the nineteenth century evangelicals preached against fraud and dishonesty in business dealings. The Quakers sought to be models of business integrity. Neither did Kuyper hold back. In his *The Social Question and the Christian Religion*, he sets out the challenge of the biblical texts on wages and oppression, adding that the "worker, too, must be able to live as a person created in the image of God" and that to "treat the workingman simply as a 'factor of production' is to violate his human dignity."[47]

---

45   Abraham Kuyper, "Lecture 2" in *Calvinism, Six Stone-lectures*, (Amsterdam: Höveker & Wormser: 1899), 63.

46   Hart, "Calvin," 131–32.

47   Kuyper, *On Business and Economics*, 222, quoting Kuyper, *The Social Question and the Christian Religion,* trans. Henry Van Dyke, (Amsterdam: J.A. Wormser: 1891).

Evidently, there is a symmetry between the reformed teaching and *Laborem Exercens*, though the reformed tradition establishes a more explicit theological framework by linking the sinful failures of business and the exploitations of work to a failure to be faithful to the end of work: to give God glory.

b) Work, Vocation, and Family

In *Laborem Exercens*, John Paul II makes a clear claim for the priority of the family, thus echoing our Protestant interlocutors. In paragraph 19 of the encyclical, entitled *Wages and Other Social Benefits*, John Paul II reaffirms the common Christian teaching on the nature and, indeed, priority of the family in respect of both the economic and social order. John Paul II discusses the notion of the just wage, both in terms of participation in goods and also as a marker for the justice of the economic system as whole. He goes on to argue for three things.

First, he argues about the nature of just remuneration for those with dependents:

> Just remuneration for the work of an adult who is responsible for a family means remuneration which will suffice for establishing and maintaining a family and for providing security for its future.[48]

Either through a "family wage" paid to the head of a household or through family allowances, the principle should be to enable mothers to devote "themselves exclusively to their family."[49]

Secondly, John Paul II argues for a social re-evaluation of the role of the mother. There should be, he argues, a proper recognition of the nature of the work involved in raising a family. Women should not be discriminated against for taking care of the family. The recognition "of the need that children have for care, love and affection in order that they may develop into responsible, morally and religiously

48   John Paul II, *Laborem Exercens*, sec. 19.
49   *Ibid.*

mature and psychologically stable persons" is for the good of society.[50]

Thirdly, the labor process must respect the life in the home, which is in accordance with women's own intrinsic nature, and not discriminate against the family, which is for the good of society.

John Paul II goes on to discuss the importance of health care, the right to rest and recreation, the priority of the Sabbath, and, indeed, rights to pensions and insurance for old age. These claims might appear controversial in our contemporary age, but John Paul II can certainly claim the support of the Protestant tradition.

Tellingly, Calvin lists oversight of the family as one of the several kinds of work.[51] This suggests that he views the domestic role as analogous to any other type of vocation or calling. For him, the family was one of the central social features of Genevan society and both civil law and ecclesiastical teaching reflected and reinforced the centrality of the marriage covenant, a reflection of the very order of creation.[52] Kuyper also sees the family as part of God's provision for society and hence the dignity of the individual means that the worker "must be able to fulfil his calling as husband and father."[53] Perhaps reflecting the nature of society and the associated debates around the social question, including those of *Rerum Novarum*, Kuyper extends his analysis further. Both the family and the human person derive their status from the order of creation. So does the idea of Sabbath. Consequently, the worker has a right to rest, "he has a right to a Sabbath," without which he could neither recuperate nor serve God. The worker is also frail and faces old age, accidents, and sickness, and he should also be entitled to sustenance in retirement.[54]

For John Calvin, Abraham Kuyper, and John Paul II, the family unit provides the kinship of ties across generations, a proper place for the

---

50 *Ibid.*

51 Hart, "Calvin," 128.

52 Herman J. Selderhuis (ed.), *The Calvin Handbook* (Grand Rapids, MI: Eerdmans, 2009), 455–65.

53 Kuyper, *On Business and Economics*, 222.

54 *Ibid.*

exercise of vocation and call, and is a key element in any response to the social challenges of the age. Thus, the family is part of a theology of work.

5. The Role of the State

The modern assumption that the state is the answer to every question, perhaps in part due to the significant rise in state spending and involvement since the end of the nineteenth century, results in the tendency to overlook the central role of the church in the voluntary provision of health, education, and welfare in response to "the social question." This tension is reflected in both Catholic and Protestant teaching.

John Paul II in *Laborem Exercens* sees the state as essentially the indirect employer of everyone. Certainly, within the Kuyperian tradition of Protestant teaching this has the potential for confusion between the respective spheres of the state and of business and each's responsibilities to the worker. However, in the first instance, the encyclical must speak for itself:

> The concept of indirect employer is applicable to every society, and in the first place to the State. For it is the State that must conduct a just labor policy.[55]

The Pope proceeds to reflect upon the interdependency between nation states and their involvement in the processes of trade and business. Since the rights of workers are objective rights (for all the theological reasons set out in the encyclical) they must be enforced not merely by the state, but also by international organizations. These ideas of global financial control are not new in Vatican thinking but reflect a certain lack of reality and an over-optimistic view of the state. In paragraph 18, John Paul II invests the state with a degree of responsibility for economic planning, over indeed both the economic and social shape of society and for organizing work in what the encyclical refers to as "a correct and rational way."[56] This rational planning involves discovering the appropriate proportions of work in each sector, which might seem like overreach. This

55 John Paul II, *Laborem Exercens*, sec. 17.
56 *Id.*, 18.

must be matched by a system of instruction and education. The encyclical warns that this cannot be a one-sided centralization and that voluntary groups must be respected, but in this respect the encyclical is a missed opportunity to reaffirm the voluntary principle which lies at the heart of both Catholic and Protestant social teaching. Moreover, *Laborem Exercens* is dangerously close to a view of the state which goes beyond traditional Christian teaching.

All of this, then, raises the question of the proper role of the state.

The classic Protestant view of the state is that the role is a negative one, essentially to prevent sin and evil though defense and good order. Although Calvin reflects this emphasis, we also see in his teaching and writing a more nuanced and positive view of the role of the state. Calvin argues that man by his very nature will seek to cherish and preserve society, though of course we should be somewhat wary of identifying society simply with the state. In his *Commentary on Romans*, Calvin advances both the positive and negative reasons for civil government: "to provide for the tranquillity of the good and to restrain the waywardness of the wicked."[57] Calvin expands his thinking in Chapter 20 of Book IV of the *Institutes of the Christian Religion*, the last chapter of his work, where, alongside a role in maintaining doctrine and worship, he argues that the role of civil government is also "to adapt our conduct to human society, to form our manners to civil justice, to conciliate us to each other, to cherish common peace and tranquillity."[58] Calvin's Geneva also reflected some elements of central planning in the social welfare provision, which was overseen by the "hospital." Calvin's approach is more nuanced than either a rejection of the role of the state (that, in Calvin's view, was the error of the anabaptists) or a deification of the state as the provider of social welfare and benefits, which would almost certainly obscure personal responsibility and accountability before God.

57 *Calvin's New Testament Commentaries*, eds. T. F. Torrance and D. W. Torrance, The epistles of Paul the apostle to the Romans and Thessalonians (Edinburgh: Oliver & Boyd: 1961), ad. loc. Romans 13:3, quoted in William R Stevenson, "Calvin and Political Issues," in *The Cambridge Companion to John Calvin*, ed: Donald K. McKim (Cambridge: Cambridge University Press, 2004), 174.
58 Calvin, *Institutes*, IV.20.2.

Kuyper's understanding of the role of the state is closely linked with his ideas around sphere sovereignty, developed in his inaugural address at the founding of the Free University of Amsterdam in 1880 and in his *Lectures on Calvinism* in 1898. He views the world as divided into spheres, each of which is independent and has its own rights and pre-rogatives, each sphere being under the sovereignty of God. Hence each sphere is to be honored in its own right. Business is one such sphere:

> ...we understand hereby, that the family, the business, science, art and so forth are all social spheres, which do not owe their existence to the state, and which do not derive the law of their life from the superiority of the state, but obey a high authority within their own bosom; an authority which rules, by the grace of God, just as the sovereignty of the State does.[59]

He regards the state as a consequence of the Fall and hence its prime reason for existence is the negative reason given by Calvin; that is, to restrain sin. So, Kuyper argues, "God has instituted magistrates, by reason of sin."[60] Kuyper understands society as composed of many different elements, from the arts to business to the family. Each of these elements has "sovereignty in the individual social spheres and these different developments of social life have nothing above themselves but God, and the state cannot intrude here."[61] Essentially, Kuyper sees the state as one of the spheres which exists under the sovereignty of God with its own rights, prerogatives, and responsibilities. The state should not intrude upon the prerogatives of the other spheres. Indeed, the danger of this is that the state would grow and crowd out the other elements of society. Society is organic, government is mechanistic, according to Kuyper. The role of the state is to avoid social conflict (by preserving the sovereignty of each sphere), defend the weak, and maintain the overall unity of society.

59   Abraham Kuyper, "Lecture 3" in *Calvinism, Six Stone-lectures*, (Amsterdam: Höveker & Wormser: 1899), 116.
60   *Id.*, 81.
61   *Id.*, 91.

Kuyper displays some ambiguity in discussing the state and society. Although his rationale for the state is primarily negative, he does seem to allow for some more positive view of the state in a fallen world but does not develop it. Common good is primarily the responsibility of the sphere of civil society but the role of the state cannot be excluded; however, it is nonetheless limited.

The consequence of this is the priority given within the Protestant tradition, though also of course within Catholicism, to the voluntary principle. To be precise it is recognizing the proper, though limited role of the state, but also seeing the vitality and centrality of family, voluntary associations, and societies in the achievement of social good. Likewise, Thomas Chalmers (1780–1847) argues that "we cannot translate beneficence into the statute-book of law, without expunging it from the statute-book of the heart."[62] Chalmers is relatively negative towards the role of the state and sees the central importance of locality and personal relationships, which are characteristics of the voluntary principle. Lord Shaftesbury is, of course, an example, *par exemplar*, of a public leader who sought a balanced path between the state as both a restrainer of evil (legislation against child labor, for example) but also the voluntary principle in education, welfare, training, and employment.[63]

The encyclical would have benefited from more nuance in this area, and an appreciation of the teaching of the Protestant tradition could, in this instance, have enriched John Paul's reflections, which, of course, also have a rich history within Catholicism.

6. Spirituality of Work

Part V of the Encyclical, "Elements for a Spirituality of Work" is an original and dynamic reflection building on the biblical and theological work which preceded it and which, indeed, could have been given a

---

62 Thomas Chalmers, "On Natural Theology," vol 2.4.4.6, in *The Collected Works of Thomas Chalmers*, vol. 2 (Glasgow: William Collins: 1836–42), 128.

63 See Richard Turnbull, *Shaftesbury, the Great Reformer* (Oxford: Lion Hudson, 2010).

greater degree of prominence earlier in the publication—a point I will return to in discussing the methodology of the encyclical in the next section.

John Paul II points out that the living word of God is directed towards the whole person, body, mind, and spirit, and that work, manual or intellectual, is part of that. The church, he says, has

> ... a particular duty *to form a spirituality of work* which will help all people to come closer, through work, to God, the Creator and Redeemer, to participate in his salvific plan for man and the world and to deepen their friendship with Christ.[64]

Neither John Calvin, nor Abraham Kuyper, nor any other representative of the Protestant tradition could have worded it better. In reality, neither of our Protestant representatives established such a spirituality of work with such an explicit framework. In that respect, Pope John Paul II should be congratulated.

The encyclical continues by reasserting the basic framework which has been previously discussed: that human work is a sharing in the divine work of creation. This work should glorify God as the original creation and also necessitates the rest of the Sabbath. This, says, John Paul II, is the most profound motive for undertaking work.

> The word of God's revelation is profoundly marked by the fundamental truth that *man,* created in the image of God, *shares by his work in the activity of the Creator* and that, within the limits of his own human capabilities, man in a sense continues to develop that activity, and perfects it as he advances further and further in the discovery of the resources and values contained in the whole of creation.[65]

The Pope here gets the closest in the encyclical to setting out the ideas of development, education, innovation, and creativity—perhaps

---

64   John Paul II, *Laborem Exercens*, sec. 24.
65   *Id.*, sec. 25.

entrepreneurship—which are the true source of human enterprise, human ingenuity, and acting for the good of all in society. It is this principle which endows ordinary human work with divine empowerment, and it is refreshing how Pope John Paul II marshals his theological resources in that way, for instance, in how he quotes *Lumen Gentium* (1964), one of the documents of the Second Vatican Council.

> Therefore, by their competence in secular fields and by their personal activity, elevated from within by the grace of Christ, let them work vigorously so that by human labor, technical skill, and civil culture created goods may be perfected according to the design of the Creator and the light of his Word.[66]

This is a further reminder that *Laborem Exercens* stands strongly within a tradition of Catholic teaching.

In paragraph 26, John Paul II relates all of this to the person of Christ. Jesus, of course, was the carpenter; but also, says, John Paul II, the Lord sees in human work a particular facet of humanity's likeness with God, as a bearer of his image. He then lists all the occupations listed in the pages of the Old Testament from craftsman to builder, sower to merchant, artist, musician, doctor. Reflecting on the writing of the apostle Paul, the Pope refers to both "if anyone will not work, let him not eat," and "whatever your task, work heartily, as serving the Lord," reflecting a sense of both responsibilities and rights, as well as the concept of glorifying God in our work, echoed in the Protestant tradition and surely a key starting-point for ethics.

> The teachings of the Apostle of the Gentiles obviously have key importance for the morality and spirituality of human work. They are an important complement to the great though

---

66   *Ibid.*, quoting Second Vatican Council, Dogmatic Constitution *Lumen Gentium*, sec. 36. Note that the text of *Lumen Gentium* in the internal citation by *Laborem Exercens* is not identical with the text of *Lumen Gentium* on www.vatican.va.

discreet gospel of work that we find in the life and parables of Christ, in what Jesus "did and taught."[67]

In the final section, paragraph 27, John Paul II brings all of this together in accordance with the common Christian tradition, and again in a way which is exemplified by the Protestant writers. The impact of sin and the Fall can only be redeemed in the cross and resurrection. When John Paul says that "The Christian finds in human work a small part of the Cross of Christ and accepts it in the same spirit of redemption in which Christ accepted his Cross for us,"[68] he is saying exactly the same as evangelicals who argue that work is a place of discipleship.

The cross is indispensable to a spirituality of work which, with the resurrection, represents restoration, with the promise of a new heaven and a new earth, a new creation. All of this has echoes in the Protestant tradition, perhaps, in theological terms, far more than might be thought likely. Perhaps if Pope John Paul II had written his entire encyclical with this framework of spirituality, those resonances would have been even stronger; that, however, is a methodological question to which we must now turn.

7. Methodological Reflections

We have only a little space to reflect upon the methodological approaches used by John Paul II. The range and comprehensiveness of the encyclical is both its strength and weakness. The encyclical establishes a framework but then seeks to leave no stone unturned. The comprehensiveness is exhaustive, and indeed, exhausting. The consequence is a rather labored narrative in some places as every potential topic under the sun is touched upon, sometimes with a regrettable degree of superficiality. This also causes a greater distance from the biblical narratives as the encyclical moves increasingly into policy and political prescriptions. That distance from the common biblical and Christian narrative would be a matter of some regret for Kuyper and Calvin.

67 *Id.*, sec. 26.
68 *Id.*, sec. 27.

8. Conclusion

Catholic and Protestant writers alike, whether John Paul II, John Calvin, or Abraham Kuyper, are agreed that work has purpose, meaning, and conveys dignity upon the human person, which is in line with their common theological tradition. Work, hence, is a theological concept which has enormous implications for society.

From a Protestant perspective, particular thanks are due to Pope John Paul II for establishing a framework within which to discuss these important themes, frankly in a manner for which Protestants really do not have the resources. This is an enormous contribution to our common tradition. Protestantism will also appreciate the extent to which the order of creation, the biblical narratives, and the person and work of Jesus all form a significant part of that framework.

There are two regrets, both essentially methodological. First, the distance that is created from the biblical narrative in the middle sections of the encyclical could result in the criticism that the encyclical's prescriptions are more political than biblical. Secondly, this matter could have been avoided if the encyclical had used the framework of a spirituality of work for its entire discussion rather than only in conclusion. This would have transformed the form and format of the work and resulted in even more resonance with the Protestant tradition. The *reality is* that most Protestant writers would theologically, spiritually, and practically agree wholeheartedly with the encyclical's spirituality of work. It could have been very fruitful indeed to frame the encyclical around this theme. The fact remains, however, that Protestantism has not and cannot produce such an authoritative framework. Protestantism can, however, offer wisdom and insight to the common Christian tradition which John Paul II can affirm and draw upon. Indeed, concepts such as sphere sovereignty could be of great assistance in delineating the proper role of the state in society.

Calvin and Kuyper would both have appreciated the encyclical. The greater the extent to which we can together draw upon the resources of our respective traditions for the enrichment of our common Christian tradition, the greater will be our insight and impact in the world which God created for work, for family, for purpose, for dignity, and for faith in Jesus Christ.

Good Work:
Insights from the Subjective
Dimension of Work

Michael Naughton

Of all the social encyclicals in the Catholic Church, St. John Paul II's *Laborem Exercens* (1981) has had the most profound impact on me, both personally and professionally. Its influence began in the early 1980s when I was asked to teach the course on social justice at the Catholic high school at which I was employed. However, I found the textbook that was historically used for the course to be inadequate. Like many high school textbooks, it failed to spur students to intellectually form a vision of the good that drew on the moral imagination of the Catholic tradition. So I reached for the most recent social document the Church issued, which at the time was *Laborem Excercens*.

For me, it was love at first sight; although, not so much for my students. Despite their difficulty in reading the document, John Paul II's words nontheless explained to them and to me the experience of work. He opened us up to reality. In particular, John Paul II illuminated for us what he calls the "subjective dimension of work." This dimension of work helps us to see that when we act, we not only affect and change objects outside of ourselves, but more profoundly, we change our very selves. The highest reward or punishment "for man's toil is not what he gets from it, but what he becomes by it."[1] The grandeur of one's work transforms not only the face of the earth, but his or her own face and all that goes on beneath that face.

---

1 This quote is said to be from John Ruskin, but I have not been able to find the source.

John Paul II's insights into the subjective dimension of work did not only reveal for me a way to engage students in the deeper insights on the meaning of work. It also allowed me to enter into a conversation with professionals from the perspective of Catholic social teaching, a conversation which has continued to this day. To grasp these insights, I structure my comments in this paper in five levels on which the insights of the subjective dimension of work can be expressed. These five levels capture an integrated view of work and the role work plays in our lives.

The first level is the phenomenological. What is work? At its basic level, work changes objects and at the same time it changes the one who does the work, the subject. John Paul's distinction between the so-called "subjective" and "objective" dimensions of work brings us to the second level of work: the moral. Questions about the morality of work follow upon the subjective-objective distinction, since it implies the changes in the subject of work that are inherently moral (our thoughts, words, habits, character, destiny) and also leads us to how the objective and subjective dimensions are ordered to each other (namely, in the priority of labor over capital). Thirdly, moral insights into the subjective dimension raise philosophical and especially theological questions rooting the subjective dimension of work within a moral order grounded in a created reality. John Paul II calls this a spirituality of work, which serves as the central core to understanding the subjective dimension of work. It is this level that serves as a deeper theological root system to the subjective dimension of work. Fourthly, since most work happens within institutions, and since there is a moral and spiritual orientation to work, what are the institutional implications of the subjective dimension? Finally, the fifth level provides a case study of how the subjective dimension of work is lived, including the tensions and disorders that can come from it.

1. Phenomenological Description: What Is Work?

When we act, we affect and change *objects* outside or beyond ourselves (this is what John Paul II terms "transitive" change).[2] This is most

---

2   John Paul II, *Laborem Exercens* (Vatican City: Libreria Editrice Vaticana, 1981), sec. 4.

evident in our work. We are by nature a *homo faber,* a "builder of the world and maker of things."[3] This process of making is what the Greeks called *techne*, which is about the means (skills, techniques, tools, instruments, etc.) necessary to build things. And the ability of people to build demonstrates our rational capacity to see and anticipate opportunities and to change the world. As Robert Kennedy puts it, "It is a development of the mind's ability to bring into being objectively what it can conceive in the imagination."[4] John Paul II considers all of this part of the objective dimension of work.[5]

Professional leaders are often practiced in this objective dimension of work. They have developed a whole series of metrics, scorecards, and incentives to measure and achieve the goals of the objective dimensions of work, such as output related to product quality, plant efficiency, return on investment, inventory turns, etc. Such metrics tell us something about how well we are doing in creating goods and services (good goods) and how much wealth we are creating (good wealth). People are hired, evaluated, rewarded, and fired based on how they perform according to the standards of the objective dimension of work.

Yet, when a manager, a teacher, a technician, a lawyer, or a plumber works, he or she also affects the inner landscape of his or her life. If one changes this landscape for the better, then one is engaged in good work (the immanent change).[6] The key insight into the subjective dimension

3   Hannah Arendt, *The Human Condition* (Chicago: University of Chicago Press, 1958), 160.
4   Robert Kennedy, "The Professionalization of Work," in *Work as Key to the Social Question* (Citta del Vaticano: Libreria Editrice Vaticana, 2002), 107. Jacques Maritain explains that this desire to make things, to be creative, is a response to a very obvious truth of the created order, namely that "[t]he whole order of human life is not ready-made in nature and in things; it is an order of freedom; it has not just to be discovered and accepted: it has also to be made." See Jacques Maritain, *Freedom in the World,* in *The Collected Works of Jacques Maritain*, ed. Otto Bird (Notre Dame: University of Notre Dame Press, 1996), 43.
5   See John Paul II, *Laborem Exercens*, sec. 4–5.
6   To appreciate the philosophical depth of this subjective dimension of work and human activity, John Paul II (Karol Wojtyła), before he was pope, wrote an important book called *The Acting Person*. In it he states: "Every

of work is not only that we are changed by our work, but also that it is crucial how we are changed. We see the fact of subjective change quite clearly in the physical changes of the blacksmith. As he forms the metal with his hammer, the very activity he performs imbues a certain form in him: the growth of his muscles, the calluses of his hands, the possible burn scar on his arm. This dynamic, while obvious on one level, is quite striking on another, especially when we take into consideration not only the physical aspects of work, but also the intellectual, emotional, social, and spiritual. When people work, they not only make a choice about what they work on, that is, the objective dimension of work. They also simultaneously make a choice about themselves, that is, the subjective dimension of work. Human work remains in the person and "determines the subject's immanent quality or value."[7] In many respects, the

act of self-determination makes real the subjectivity of self-governance and self-possession: in each of these interpersonal structural relations there is given to the person as the subject—as he who governs and possesses— the person as the object—as he who is governed and possessed.... This objectification means that in every actual act of self-determination—in every "I will"—the self is the object, indeed the primary and nearest object." See Karol Wojtyla , *The Acting Person,* trans. Andrzcj Potocki (Dordrecht, Holland: D. Reidel Publishing Co., 1979), 108–09. The aspect of self-determination is crucial to properly human action and is linked to the potential of the person for self-governance. In acting, one experiences a moment of "efficacy," of "making a difference," whereas in experiencing something "happening" in oneself, one experiences one's passivity. The experience of passivity is genuinely human, and is certainly not purely negative, but what usually needs to be emphasized with regard to work is the importance, for the development of the human person, that he or she is able to act purposefully. In acting, one exercises one's will, which is both moved (motivated) by external objects and refers to one's knowledge of practical truths. That is, one responds to motives in accord both with one's sense of what is morally right and in accord with one's sense of what is technically or artistically correct; one is not "determined" by external motivation. See also Angela Franks' chapter in this volume.

7   Samuel Gregg and Gordon Preece, *Christianity and Entrepreneurship: Protestant and Catholic Thoughts* (St. Leonards, NSW, Australia: The Centre for Independent Studies Limited, 1999), 74. Gregg and Gordon go on to write "In his *Quaestiones Disputatae de Veritate* (q.8, a.6c), Aquinas ex-

subjective change may last longer than some of the objective changes he or she has initiated.

While the recognition of the subjective dimension is obvious in the abstract, it is easily marginalized and ignored in practice. The objective accomplishments of our work can overwhelm us. Our collective progress in communications, computerization, construction, manufacturing, finance, and transportation can blind us to the changes work is having on us. Because so much of our time and energy is devoted to the development of metrics and techniques to perfect the objective dimensions of work, the necessary time and space to consider the subjective dimension of work is too often overlooked. It looks as if the work done in organizations only involves people merely busy with objects. But this conceals rather than reveals reality. As Bernard Lonergan S.J. explained, "it appears that deeds, decisions, discoveries affect the subject more deeply than they affect the objects with which they are concerned. They accumulate as dispositions and habits of the subject; they determine him; they make him what he is and what he is to be."[8] Or as the Russian novelist Leo Tolstoy reminded us, "everyone thinks of changing the world, but no one thinks of changing himself."[9] This blindness or agnosticism to the subjective dimension of work is precisely what John Paul II is concerned about, which is why he emphasizes its importance at the beginning of his encyclical letter.

plained this distinction in the following manner: 'Action is of two sorts: one sort—action [*action*] in a strict sense—issues from the agent into something external to change it ... the other sort—properly called activity [*operatio*]—does not issue into something external but remains within the agent itself perfecting it" (74). Simply put there, human action has both an outer effect upon the world [objective dimension] and an inner effect within its author [subjective dimension].

8   Bernard Lonergan, S.J., *Philosophical and Theological Papers 1965–1980*, 2nd ed., eds. Robert Doran and Robert Croken, Collected Works of Bernard Lonergan (Toronto: University of Toronto Press, 2004), 315.

9   Quoted in Mark A. Bryan, Julia Cameron, and Catherine A. Allen, *The Artist's Way at Work: Riding the Dragon* (New York: William Morrow, 1999), 160.

2. Moral Orientation: What Is Good Work?

Not only is it clear that there is a subjective dimension, but also that the nature of the subjective change has profound implications for our personal development. With regard to this latter point, it is clear that the subjective dimension of work has both a descriptive and a normative aspect. It is descriptive in that it describes work as a phenomenon. But it transcends the merely descriptive. It has built within it the normative, namely, prescriptions of how work can be *good* work. The normative understanding of the subjective dimension of work can be grasped in at least two ways.

The first way we come to this normative and inherently moral character of the subjective is from "the fact that the one who carries it [the work] out is a person, a conscious and free subject, that is to say, a subject that decides about himself."[10] For John Paul II, the impact of work on the subject "conditions" our moral development. These moral conditions can be captured in various ways, but I find the following quote illuminative in bringing out the moral nature of our activity and work:

> Watch your thoughts, they become words.
> Watch your words, they become actions.
> Watch your actions, they become habits.
> Watch your habits, they become your character.
> Watch your character, it becomes your destiny.[11]

The quote expresses the moral ecology operating within the subjective dimension of work. The *actions* of our work are never merely neutral. They are conditioned and formed by the intentions of our *thoughts* and *words*, and the actions of work move into *habits* that form *character*, taking us to a particular *destination*. Precisely because work is carried out by persons, it is never simply technical but always deeply human. These interdependent aspects of the human act—thoughts, words,

---

10 John Paul II, *Laborem Exercens*, sec. 6.
11 The source for this quote is unknown. It appears to be Lao Tzu, but we could not locate the source.

actions, habits, and destiny—are part of a whole that forms the moral ecology of our work. As John Paul II puts it, "Work is a good thing for man—a good thing for his humanity—because through work man not only transforms nature, adapting it to his own needs, but he also achieves fulfillment as a human being and indeed, in a sense, becomes 'more a human being.'"[12]

The insights of this moral ecology of work are often best expressed in its breach. Lee Iacocca, who famously engineered one of the most significant turnarounds in American business when he took the Chrysler Corporation out of bankruptcy in the 1980s, provides a case in point. In the early 90s, Iaccoca retired. Three years later, he was on the cover of the *Fortune* magazine with the caption, "How I Flunked Retirement." This icon of American industry, who rescued a major auto company, explained that his three years of retirement were more stressful than his forty-seven years in the auto business. His destination at the end of his career was found to be wanting. While he was seemingly an economic giant at work, he was spiritually small in his retirement. He supposedly knew who he was at work, but outside of the corporation he was simply at sea. No amount of achievement in the objective dimension of work can justify a broken soul found in its subjective dimension. Nonetheless, one can only admire Iacocca for being so honest about it to the public.

To help understand where Iacocca's work landed him, the Jewish theologian Abraham Joshua Heschel wrote about how the objective dimensions of work can turn on and disorder the subject, the person:

> How proud we often are of our victories in the war with nature, proud of the multitude of instruments we have succeeded in inventing, of the abundance of commodities we have been able to produce. Yet our victories have come to resemble defeats. In spite of our objective triumphs and achievements, we have fallen victims to the work of our hands; it is as if the forces we had conquered have conquered us.[13]

12   John Paul II, *Laborem Exercens*, sec. 9.
13   Abraham Joshua Heschel, The Sabbath: Its Meaning for Modern Man (New York: Noonday, 1951), 27.

Our "triumphs and achievements" in the objective dimension can too easily become forces that deplete the subjective soul. Rather than being conquerors, we have become conquered by our own objective achievements. When Iacocca speaks of flunking retirement, he is expressing a certain lack in the subjective dimension that was not developed, most likely because all his attention was fixated on objective achievements.

The subjective dimension of work is like a door to a vista—you start to see things you could not see before. Our work is deeply informed by our thoughts and words, which is so connected to the spiritual life. And our work creates habits in us that form character and land us in a place, a destiny. Our work activities are not discrete, arbitrary acts without consequences; they mold our character and they are the prime indicators of our destiny.[14] It is precisely the destiny question, including its origins, that directs us to the spiritual implications of work, which we will address in the next section.

The second moral condition of the subject of work should persuade us that human work is never reduced to a simply material reality such as financial or productive goals, or some overarching purpose such as the maximization of shareholder wealth. The maximization—or prioritization—of wealth necessarily means that wealth is valorized above other factors in the productive process. Indeed, profits and shareholder wealth are necessary for an organization; without them the institution dies. However, they are things, and we should never prioritize things over people. Precisely because work, in its subjective dimension, affects personal character and the human soul, the ethos of organizations should be the priority of persons and labor over things and capital. It is this moral principle that derives from the subjective dimension of work.

Alasdair MacIntyre gives us an example of fishing to see how the subjective dimension of work brings out the inherent moral insights of the priority of labor over capital. He argues that the end of fishing, farming, architecture, engineering, construction, and any kind of work, "when they are in good order, is never only to catch fish, or to produce beef or milk, or to build houses. It is to do so in a manner consonant with the excellences of the craft, so that not only is there a good product, but the

14   John F. Kavanaugh, S.J., "Last Words," *America: The Jesuit Review*, January 21, 2002, 23.

craftsperson is perfected through and in her or his activity.... It is from this that the sense of a craft's dignity derives."[15] Of course the fisherman who fails to catch fish is no longer a fisherman; he is broke. But his work is never fully or essentially explained by the fish caught or the profit earned. In other words, to explain the phenomenon of the fisherman only by his product of fish (a good good) or his compensation (good wealth), is to fail to grasp the complete reality of what is actually happening in terms of the subjective dimension of work (which necessitates the pursuit of good work). The same could be said about any kind of work whether it is law, engineering, the trades, medicine, journalism, or business. As John Paul II put it human actions, such as work, do not vanish once they are performed; "they leave their moral value, which constitutes an objective reality intrinsically cohesive with the person, and thus a reality profoundly subjective."[16] And so he explains that "[t]he sources of the dignity of work are to be sought primarily in the subjective dimension, not in the objective one."[17]

3. Spirituality of Work: What Is the Created Order of Work?

So far, our inquiry into the subjective dimension of work has been largely on the natural level, but it has already raised some interesting theological questions that point us to a spiritual and created reality. Why does work have a subjective and an objective dimension? Why does the developing character and soul of the person cause work to have a moral dimension? Is there something about work that reflects a universal order of things?

Albert Einstein wrote that "the most incomprehensible thing about the universe is that it is comprehensible."[18] The moral ecology of the

---

15 Alasdair MacIntyre, "A Partial Response to my Critics," in J. Horton and S. Mendus (eds.), *After MacIntyre: Critical Perspectives on the Work of Alasdair MacIntyre* (University of Notre Dame Press, Notre Dame, 1994), 284.

16 Karol Wojtyła (John Paul II) *The Acting Person,* trans. Andrzej Potocki (Dordrecht, Holland: D. Reidel Publishing Co., 1979), 151.

17 John Paul II, *Laborem Exercens*, sec. 6.

18 Albert Einstein, "Physics and Reality," *Journal of the Franklin Institute* 221, no. 3 (March 1936): 349–82.

subjective dimension of work points us to a point of contact between human nature and the whole of reality—a reality explains our origin and our destination. As human nature begs for a habit of mind to see things in relation to each other, we necessarily wonder what it is about the world and ourselves that makes work what it is. Considering the phenomenological insights of the subjective and objective dimensions of work that move into the moral ecology of work, John Paul II points us to a created order of reality that he calls spiritual. He explains that "[s]ince work in its subjective aspect is always a personal action, an *actus personae*, it follows that the whole person, body and spirit, participates in it, whether it is manual or intellectual work."[19]

For John Paul II, the phenomenological and moral character of the subjective dimension of work is only fully comprehended and realized through the spiritual and theological illumination of a doctrine of creation. He draws from the Bible and in particular the book of Genesis to ground his insights. Humanity's ability to create things is not an accidental reality but a created one. People are called to this reality. John Paul II writes:

> Man has to subdue the earth and dominate it, because as the "image of God" he is a person, that is to say, a subjective being capable of acting in a planned and rational way, capable of deciding about himself, and with a tendency to self-realization. As a person, man is therefore the subject of work. As a person he works, he performs various actions belonging to the work process; independently of their objective content, these actions must all serve to realize his humanity, to fulfill the calling to be a person that is his by reason of his very humanity.[20]

This connection between the subjective dimension of work and the biblical creation account gets to "the most profound motive" for our work.[21]

19 John Paul II, *Laborem Exercens*, sec. 24.
20 *Id.*, sec. 6.
21 *Id.*, sec. 25.

It tells us something about our origins as well as our destination. We have a created DNA to work. God created us in His image that reflects the creative nature of God. We have been given a mandate to subdue and have dominion over the earth. John Paul II explains that in "carrying out this mandate, man, every human being, reflects the *very action* of the Creator of the universe."[22] Our work has a transcendent character that is largely inexhaustible, but it is simultaneously pregnant with meaning that can be ever deepened over a lifetime.

Some readers may find this spiritual and theological insertion as unnecessary to understanding the subjective dimenion of work. The modern mind is in the habit of bracketing the theological and the spiritual. And while it is true that human reason can grasp the phenomenological and moral dimensions of human work, life grinds away too hard for such a naturalistic account to hold over a lifetime, especially in workplaces. Lee Iacocca is a case in point. We are spiritual beings, and when we constantly bracket our spiritual nature, we create views of the world that are too small for the human spirit. When we jettison the theological and spiritual in our accounts of work, in the words of C. S. Lewis, we create "men without chests."[23] We have removed the spiritual organ of humanity, yet naively still expect people of virtue. Particularly in the West, we too often believe that we can escape the deepest convictions of our humanity, which are fundamentally spiritual and religious, and still remain ethical. The absence of the spiritual and theological will do damage to the natural. Grace perfects nature, and nature devoid of grace is prone to disorder.

What a spiritual and theological vision brings to work is a theological root system that gives our ethical commitments more grounding than the mere cover of a utilitarian logic that instrumentalizes everything that it touches. Especially in the realm of productive work that is constantly tempted to reduce everything to a metric, to a utility, to profit, our work needs a deeper source than a human ethic can give. Work needs to participate in and be grounded in an understanding of reality that recognizes

22 *Id.*, sec. 4.
23 C. S. Lewis, *The Abolition of Man* (New York: HarperOne, 2001), 26.

its created source. For John Paul II, this is why our work "is a participation in" God's creative activity.[24]

This spiritual vision of reality as a created order orients us to the fact that not everything is a *possession,* a utility to be manipulated for our own ends. Rather, in its deepest and most profound reality, our work is a *participation* in the "inexhaustible" reality of a created cosmos, which we did not create. A spirituality of work fosters a disposition of receptivity, of receiving creation as a gift and then giving such a gift in a way that it was received. It is precisely this receptive orientation where the subjective dimension of work will have the deepest soil for people to develop and become who they were created to be.

4. Institutional Form: What Does the Subjective Dimension of Work Look Like Institutionally?

For John Paul II, the foregoing phenomenological, moral, and spiritual insights into the subjective dimension of work reveal a participatory structure within the subject—namely, that persons are ordered to overall personal flourishing and that our acts ought to reflect that structure. In fact, John Paul II's fundamental criterion concerning the fulfillment of human acts (which includes the act of work) is whether they are conducive to the participatory structure of the human person. In turn, the existence of this structure has implications for how institutions are structured. He asks:

> do [acts] create conditions for the development of participation, do they make it easier for a human being to experience a human being and other human beings as the "other I," and, through that, allow also a fuller experience of one's own humanity, or do they, on the contrary, impede it, destroying that basic fabric of human existence and activity?[25]

24 John Paul II, *Laborem Exercens*, sec. 25.
25 Karol Wojtyła , "Participation and Alienation," in *The Self and the Other,* ed. Anna Teresa Rymieiecka (Boston: D. Riedel Publishing Co., 1977), vol. VI: 72–73.

This criterion of participation is critical to how institutions are structured.[26] Since human acts are self-determining, and since work is a human act, the workplace must be structured in light of the impact such work will have on the subjective dimension of the worker. This is the argument on which the priority of labor rests. Those who structure institutions have an obligation of justice to respect the participatory structure of the human person. Just as Pope Leo XIII argued that the wage structure must conform to the needs of the person, that is, wages must be living wages, so John Paul II argues that the structure of work institutions must conform to the subjective dimension of the person.

For John Paul II, the workplace must implement within its design an effective participatory strategy for its workers. The idea of worker participation has been an integral part of the Catholic social tradition.[27] In 1931, Pope Pius XI wrote that "It is a scandal when dead matter comes forth from the factory ennobled, while men there are corrupted and degraded."[28] Employees are not mere "human resources" or "human capital." In the encyclical *Mater et Magistra*, St. John XXIII states:

> If the whole structure and organization of an economic system is such as to compromise human dignity, to lessen a man's sense of responsibility or rob him of opportunity for exercising personal initiative, then such a system, We maintain, is altogether unjust—no matter how much wealth it produces, or how justly and equitably such wealth is distributed.[29]

Every employer, manager, and administrator should strive to facilitate their employees to grow and develop within the opportunities and

---

26 See John Paul II, *Redemptor Hominis,* sec. 15–16, where he outlines criteria for judging social, economic, and political systems.

27 See Pius XI, *Quadragesimo Anno,* sec. 65; John XXIII, *Mater et Magistra,* sec. 82–96; Paul VI, *Gaudium et Spes,* sec. 68; Paul VI, *Popularum Progressio,* sec. 28.

28 Pius XI, *Quadragesimo Anno* (Citta del Vaticano: Libreria Editrice Vaticana, 1931), sec. 135.

29 John XXIII, *Mater et Magistra* (Citta del Vaticano: Libreria Editrice Vaticana, 1961), sec. 83.

constraints of the organization. The subjective dimension of work and its corresponding phenomenological, moral, and spiritual implications point to three responsibilites of institutions and their leaders: job design, training and development, and delegation and trust.[30]

Job design: One of the most signficant responsibilities for leaders of organizations related to the subjective dimension of work is job design. How can we design jobs that both benefit the organization and foster the growth of employees by providing opportunities for them to exercise their talents and skills? If work affects the subjective dimension of people, then certainly the design of work will influence whether this is positive or negative. The challenge is to design work such that it taps into the gifts, talents, and skills of employees, while at the same time keeping the organization competitive in the marketplace by improving efficiency, quality, and profitability. These two qualities are not always easy to get right.

Howard Rosenbrock, a manufacturing engineer, has pointed out that engineers often design work that requires only a fraction of a person's talents, skills, and knowledge. If they were to "consider people as though they were robots," he wryly commented, they would "provide them with less trivial and more human work."[31] Most engineers would not design a machine and use only ten percent of its capacity, but they too often design jobs that only use a fraction of human talent. Such mechanistic and technocratic attitudes can prevent them from seeing the gifts, abilities, and talents of their employees. However, if work is designed humanely but fails to compete in the industry, the result is not good work but bankruptcy.

The paradox here is striking: engineers and managers often feel no such need to make better use of the available talents, skills, and abilities of the human worker. Indeed, human workers are often woefully

---

30 See Michael Naughton, *Getting Work Right* (Steubenville: Emmaus Road Publishing, 2019), chapter 5, "Good Work: Gift Recognition and Coordination."

31 Howard H. Rosenbrock, "Engineers and the Work That People Do," in *The Experience of Work*, ed. Craig R. Littler (Aldershot, UK: Gower in association with The Open University, 1985), 161–71, http://ieeecss.org/CSM/library/1981/sept/w04-8.pdf.

underutilized and actively de-skilled in order to minimize the compensation they might be due. The subjective dimension of work requires leaders to take seriously the task of drawing the full talent, knowledge, abilities, and skills out of workers by creating a culture that invites initiative, innovation, creativity, and a sense of shared responsibility.

Training and Development: Second, good institutional leadership should teach, develop and appropriately equip employees, making sure they have the right tools, training, and experience to carry out their tasks. To define one's work broadly, but not to provide the education and skills to competently carry out such work, is a recipe for failure both personally and organizationally. The general rule of thumb here is that those closest to the work often know the most about the work, especially when well-educated and equipped. When people bring their skills and knowledge into an organization and have this intelligence enhanced through training and development, the institution adds to its "collective intelligence." This collective intelligence does not just grow of its own accord. Leaders need to strengthen their subordinates through effective education, training, mentoring, counsel, and evaluation so that their gifts and talents are effectively coordinated within the company's overall project.

Delegation:[32] Third, good leaders establish strong and deeply trusting relationships with their employees when they delegate. When leaders take upon themselves, in full trust, the risks of delegating decision-making to lower levels, they are conferring a significant authority upon the employee. In return, when employees exercise this authority in freedom, responsibility, and competence, bonds of trust are formed, thereby strengthening the relations between them. Taking on the risk of the decisions is what can transform delegation from a mere technique of management to delegation as part of the virtue of trust, which contributes to strengthening the bonds of connection. One who merely delegates to maximize efficiency is one who will take back authority at any time, often at times of highest stress, which is precisely the crucible where the deepest trust can be earned.

---

32 Many of the insights on delegation come from Jeanne Buckeye and Pierre Lecocq. For future discussion see Michael Naughton, Jeanne Buckeye, Ken Goodpaster and Dean Mains, *Respect in Action: Applying Subsidiarity in Business* (Saint Paul, MN: University of St. Thomas, 2015).

When business leaders accept responsibility for developing employees, delegation becomes a mini-classroom for both leaders and employees. They test performance with increasing levels of risk and trust: from carrying out orders, to independent choices where the costs of failure are low, to consultation and feedback (early stages of trust), to full participation with leaders in decision making (advanced stages of trust), and finally to independent problem solving (full trust).[33]

While these three institutional structures are not only places where the subjective dimension of work can be expressed, they are obvious places where the subjective insight comes into play. In the next section, I focus on these three areas in a company called Reell Precision Manufacturing.

5. Case Study: A Lived Reality

So what does the subjective dimension of work concretely look like in an organization? What are its opportunities as well as its tensions and temptations? I currently serve as the board chair for Reell Precision Manufacturing. The company specializes in engineering solutions in torque, motion, and positioning mechanisms with offices and operations in the US, Netherlands, and China. Like many other entrepeneurial companies in Minnesota, Reell Precision Manufacturing was started by three former employees from the 3M Coporation. These three founders of the company were engineers and Protestant Christians.

In the early 1990s, I came in contact with the company meeting the founders. They knew nothing about the concept of the subjective dimension of work or Catholic social teaching. Later, however, one of the founders, Bob Wahlstedt, began to read about the principles of Catholic social teaching, and in particular the subjective dimenison of work. It broke open for him something that he could only intuit. Learning about the subjective dimension of work was a powerful intellectual experience for him since it helped him to articulate more clearly what his commitment to coworkers entailed. This intellectual conviction gave him the confidence that his intuition was on to something.

33   This insight particularly comes from Jeanne Buckeye.

178

In particular, the subjective dimension of work helped Bob Wahlsted understand the deeper roots of some of the problems the company was facing, such as issues they encountered on the assembly line. As a manufacturing company, Reell does a lot of custom design and so they have to change the product on the line on a regular basis. This entails a quality controller doing an independent evaluation of samples after each setup was complete and before the job was run. The problem with this model was in dealing with the necessary time required for the setup to be approved by the quality controller. The setup person would submit samples to quality control, but would usually have to wait several hours until the inspector was available to evaluate. By that time, the setup person had usually gone on to the next job. This meant that if the samples were not satisfactory, it would take even more time before adjustments could be made. In some cases, the process needed to be repeated several times before the job was approved. Operations found this frustrating because they would find themselves setting up jobs and not being able to run them for several days.

Someone asked the question, "What if we taught the setup people to do their own inspection and trusted them to do it right?" While the person who asked this question had never heard about the subjective dimension of work, he was putting the insight into practice by removing the frustration from the work and allowing employees to more fully participate in the work they were doing. After restructuring the work process such that it tapped into the skills and talents of the assembly workers, many benefits ensued. The employees decreased setup times for new products, reduced the need for quality inspection, increased overall quality, and required less supervision. By reducing these costs, the company not only created more humane work giving expression to the subjective dimension of work, but also became more profitable and was able to increase its wage rates.[34]

What is interesting about this case is its inductive character. It started with a problem that needed to be solved and led to the redesigning of work, demanding greater education and equipping of employees, and a

34 See Michael Naughton and David Specht, *Leading Wisely in Difficult Times: Three Cases of Faith and Business* (New York: Paulist Press, 2011).

deeper trust in coworkers. Yet, while it started off as a practical problem, it ended with a new philosophy of work that Reell calls Teach-Equip-Trust. Reell, like most manufacturing companies, traditionally designed its assembly line on what can be called a "Command-Direct-Control" style of management, in which managers and engineers made all the decisions concerning the assembly area. As the set-up times sputtered with inefficiencies and frustrations, a new way to work emerged in which employees were taught inspection procedures, equipped with quality instruments, and trusted to do things right on their own assembly lines.[35] The company did not come to this change by a deductive moral argument, but rather because they faced a practical problem that needed to be solved. The change was transformative in leading to greater productivity, better quality products, the growth of coworkers, and a better overall company culture.

For Bob Wahlstedt, however, he came to realize that something more than a technical problem was at issue. The subjective dimension of work helped him to understand the moral and spiritual ecology of what was happening. The change in the work process was not only a technical and productive improvement, but it was also a moral and spiritual participation in the subjective dimension of work. Reell's move to a Teach-Equip-Trust philosophy of work created better production processes, improved the nature of work, and helped workers excercise their God-given gifts and talents.

As powerful as this new way of working was at Reell, as time went on in the company, its understanding and promise became disordered. The Teach-Equip-Trust philosophy began to be perceived as a form of autonomy among coworkers and any expression of accountablity from management was interpreted by coworkers as a lack of trust. In other words, a shadow was cast. The shadow of the subjective dimension of work is that it can lose touch with its "objective dimensions." Reell's strong culture and conviction in the growth of its coworkers unintentially created a creeping sense of entitlement. This led to a weak and at times non-existent employee evaluation system. It also focused coworkers on

---

35　Parts of this case are taken from Naughton, *Getting Work Right,* chapter 5 "Good Work: Gift Recognition and Coordination."

their rights and less on their duties to financial and productive discipline and customer service. Both the 2001 recession and especially the 2009 financial crisis resulted in a wake-up call to everyone in the company. Reell needed to strengthen its objecive dimensions of work and more effectively manage performance, and build in accountability in order to remain financially viable.

Yet, despite Reell's experience of the shadow side, Reell's leaders are grounded in the phenomenological, moral, and spiritual insights of the subjective dimenion of work. While never perfect and always prone to disorder, they tend to take on certain positive characteristics. For one, they expect their employees to work independently and to take prudent risks in what they do. The prudence is framed around the shared vision of the company. For another, they admit their own failures and model what it means to learn and grow from one's mistakes. A third characteristic is their good knowledge of their employees. They are not distant from their employees; they know them and their work. They often work beside them on certain projects and they take an interest in what they are doing. They spend time observing, coaching, counseling, and evaluating their employees, getting to know their strengths and weaknesses. They know the families of their coworkers, the sports their children are involved in, the challenges they are having. They talk with them meaningfully and with respect. They are aware of how much progress their people have made and what responsibilities they are ready to shoulder, and they have taken the time to craft customized development plans for them.

6. Conclusion

On this occasion of the fortieth anniversary of *Laborem Exercens*, let me conclude with an experience I had on its twentieth anniversary at an academic conference I had helped to organize in Rome. It occured on September 12, 2001. The day before, on September 11, was that infamous day when the Twin Towers in New York City were destroyed by terrorists. That event changed the tone and approach to our conference. When the conference started on September 12, the US was at rest, a forced leisure. All air travel stopped, most institutions were closed, and a silence hushed the most productive and industrious country in the world.

As one of the principal conference organizers, I gave the opening address. What struck me at the time was the paradox that as we were in Rome talking about work, the US was at leisure. When we face moments of leisure, and unfortunately they are usually forced moments of sickness, death, imprisonment, pandemic, tradegy, failure, etc., they can open up for us a much larger world. St. Augustine puts it best in the *Confessions* when he writes, "The house of my soul is too small for you to come to it. May it be enlarged by you."[36] Our temptation is to create small places of work. We either lose sight of the subjective dimension of work, reducing all work to its objective dimensions, or we fixate on the subjective dimension of work, creating an entitlement culture. This is why the spiritual core to the subjective dimension of work is so important. It places work on "the widest possible conceptual map."[37] John Paul II's theological account of a created order which includes the subjective dimension of work prevents work from being reduced to its instrumental tendencies, which are all too often dominated by power or self-absorption blinded by entitlement. Moreover, this spiritual source comes not from work itself, but from a profound receptivity found in a grace that can only be received and not acheived. It is precisely in the spiritual core of the subjective dimension of work that gives the worker the self-awareness to see how work is changing his or her character and the conviction to create institutions where other coworkers can grow and develop.

36   Saint Augustine, *Confessions* (Oxford: Oxford University Press, 1991), 6.
37   Augustine Di Noia, "Faith Liberates Reason From Its Blind Spots," (address, Pontifical Academy of Social Science, Vatican City, May 5, 2007), https://www.ewtn.com/catholicism/library/on-deus-caritas-est-and-international-charity-3266.

Subjects and Objects in Meaningful Work

Christopher Michaelson

Are people the subjects or objects of work? Of course, we are both and more. As working subjects, we engage in the practice of work to make the products of work; as working objects, we are a piece of the production process; and as consumers, we are also the beneficiaries of production. Work can matter morally in all these senses—as a satisfying (or unsatisfying) personal experience; as a referendum on workplace conditions; and as a measure of social contribution.

In the encyclical, *Laborem Exercens*, Pope John Paul II claims that "work is 'for man' [*sic*] and not man 'for work,'" and he therefore argues for the "pre-eminence of the subjective meaning of work over the objective one." "In fact, in the final analysis," he concludes, "it is always man who is *the purpose of the work*"—that the working subject is the end for which work matters.[1]

In this chapter, I will explain the importance of the subjective meaning of work in relation to what makes work meaningful—that is, why it matters in a moral sense. However, I will also challenge it by suggesting that positioning the subject as the sole purpose of work entails consequences that we may not want to accept about meaningful work. In doing so, I will also introduce and attempt to clear up potential terminological confusion and limitations relating to the use of "objective" and "subjective" in scholarship about work and meaningfulness.

In distinguishing between "work in the objective sense" and "work

---

1   John Paul II, *Laborem Exercens* (Vatican City: Libreria Editrice Vaticana, 1981), sec. 6. Emphasis mine. (Henceforth referred to as *LE*.) In several passages that I quote verbatim, *LE* refers to "man," which I render as "human being" or "person" when not quoting directly.

in the subjective sense,"[2] *LE* first introduces the former in the context of the evolution of industrial technology. Originally, the person was a "factor of production" and then became the supervisor of machines intended to make us work faster and better.[3] However, in a prescient observation several decades before the so-called Fourth Industrial Revolution, *LE* foresees how "technology can cease to be man's ally and become almost his enemy," when it "supplants" the human worker or "reduces" us "to the status of a slave."[4]

In the sense in which "objective" is used by *LE*, then, the person is the means to the end of production. This is a moral concern in that it renders us vulnerable to use and abuse by employers who may treat us as—and even replace us with—machines. When we are working objects, we may be deprived of the autonomy to decide, among other things, what work to do, what to do it for, how we do it, and how much we do.

But we are clearly more than machines. *LE* introduces "man as the subject of work" in relation to our aptitude for "acting in a planned and rational way, capable of deciding about himself and with a tendency to self-realization."[5] In this subjective sense, then, the working subject—not the work itself nor the consumer who benefits—is the moral end of work. *LE* goes on to say that, subjectively, "human work has an ethical value of its own" to "a conscious and free subject...[who] decides about himself."[6]

The way *LE* distinguishes between objective and subjective senses of work aligns with the scholarship of many ethicists who study meaningful work. For example, Ciulla says "the objective element of meaningful work consists of the moral conditions of the job itself" (such as being "treated with dignity and respect" in the workplace). The "subjective elements," she says, "consist of the outlooks and attitudes that people bring with them into the workplace." These have to do with the

2   *Id.*, secs. 5–6.
3   *Id.*, sec. 5.
4   *Ibid.*
5   *Id.*, sec. 6.
6   *Ibid.*

"things we value," which may include work "in which people directly help others or create products that make life better for people."[7]

Particular attention among ethicists who study meaningful work has been paid to organizing work in the objective sense in a way that preserves workers' autonomy to choose what is meaningful to them. Schwartz laments the lack of autonomy afforded to assembly line workers who are "in effect paid for blindly pursuing ends that others have chosen."[8] All six of Bowie's "characteristics of meaningful work" (freedom of entry, autonomy, rational development, sufficient wages, moral development, and non-paternalism) prescribe objective conditions of work to preserve the subjective capacity of the worker to choose their work.[9] Yeoman conceptualizes meaningful work as a "fundamental human need" that society ought to be arranged to enable.[10]

Meanwhile, organizational scientists who study meaningful work have tended to examine what workers with autonomy to choose experience as subjectively meaningful.[11] This research reveals that meaningfulness means different things to different people and so may come from a variety of sources—"the self, other persons, the work context, and spiritual life."[12] In general, subjective perspectives on meaningful work can be classified in terms of "realization" (work that enables "self-actualization") and "justification" (why work is "worthy or valuable").[13]

---

7   Joanne Ciulla, *The working life: The promise and betrayal of modern work* (New York: Three Rivers Press, 2000), 225.

8   Adina Schwartz, "Meaningful work," *Ethics* 92(4) (1982): 635.

9   Norman E. Bowie, "A Kantian theory of meaningful work," *Journal of Business Ethics* 17 (1998): 1083.

10 Ruth Yeoman, "Conceptualizing meaningful work as a fundamental human need," *Journal of Business Ethics* 125 (2014): 235.

11 Christopher Michaelson, Michael G. Pratt, Adam M. Grant, and Craig P. Dunn, "Meaningful work: Connecting business ethics and organization studies," *Journal of Business Ethics* 121 (2014): 77–90.

12 Brent D. Rosso, Kathyrn H. Dekas, and Amy Wrzesniewski, "On the meaning of work: A theoretical integration and review," *Research in Organizational Behavior* 30 (2010): 95.

13 Douglas A. Lepisto and Michael G. Pratt, "Meaningful work as realization and justification: Toward a dual conceptualization," *Organizational Psychology Review* 7 (2017): 104, 106.

From a moral perspective, ethicists and social scientists agree that meaningful work is a good worth individually pursuing in a subjective sense and, to an extent, a good that organizations may be obligated to provide in an objective sense. Moreover, they suggest that, despite the distinction between subjective and objective, they are inseparable in so far as objective conditions influence subjective experiences. Furthermore, they are aligned with the moral claim in *LE* that work in an objective sense is the means to the end of work in a subjective sense, especially in a capitalist context that too often treats workers as objects.[14]

Although *LE* contends that the subjective dimension "conditions *the very ethical nature* of work," pertaining to "a subject that decides about himself,"[15] there are good reasons to doubt whether work that is subjectively meaningful is always objectively moral. For one thing, a working subject may value self-aggrandizing fame and fortune over substantive service to others. For another, a worker may support nefarious political movements through work, even licensing unethical conduct in furthering such causes. In short, if meaningful work is morally praiseworthy, the term should not apply to work that is simultaneously subjectively meaningful yet objectively bad.[16]

Conversely, work that makes a useful contribution to society may not be valued in the eyes of the worker or society. So called "dirty work," such as trash collecting and hauling, is necessary to social functioning. Further, many stereotypically meaningful jobs, including teaching and social work, are conventionally undervalued by the free market. In this sense, there may be a gap between experienced meaningfulness and normative meaningfulness, or what ought to be experienced as meaningful.[17]

In the immediately foregoing section, I have subtly but intentionally introduced a very different sense of objectivity than the one used in *LE*. An objective sense of work in *LE* has to do with the treatment of the

14   See note 1.
15   *LE*, sec. 6.
16   Christopher Michaelson, "A normative meaning of meaningful work," *Journal of Business Ethics* 170 (2020): 413–28.
17   *Ibid.*

worker amid the moral conditions of the workplace. By contrast, an objective perspective on meaningful work (as I have used it) concerns the moral perspective from which we judge work's meaningfulness. The former is descriptive, and the latter is evaluative.

From an evaluative perspective, objective considerations can cast doubt on whether an individual's subjective appraisal of meaningful work warrants the moral approbation that meaningfulness confers. Meanwhile, although not all ethicists agree that there are objective moral principles that are universally binding, they largely agree that subjective moral judgment can be mistaken. So, for example, an objective perspective on meaningful work can adjudicate between whether it is more meaningful to pursue work that enables self-realization or service to others when they are not perfectly aligned.[18]

Moreover, characterizing meaningful work as more than the worker's subjective experience raises the possibility that meaningful work might be measured in terms of its value to society. This, in turn, may influence the worker's own experience of meaningfulness to the extent that making a social contribution is subjectively satisfying.

One might expect there to be numerous examples in the scholarly literature in which writers have confused these two different senses of objectivity about work and meaningfulness, especially when they share a sense of subjectivity. However, I have not found that to be the case.

Rather, as I have suggested above, social scientists who study meaningful work have tended to focus only on subjective experience, especially those who come from the "dominant" realization perspective. Yet, to the extent that the justification perspective on meaningful work is "underdeveloped,"[19] it would be useful in social scientific research to anchor those justification characteristics—which purport to articulate why meaningful work has value—in objective criteria.

Meanwhile, most ethicists have focused primarily on objective conditions of work rather than objective criteria for meaningful work. This has had the effect, however, of impoverishing ethicists' accounts of meaningful work. For example, Schwartz's, Bowie's, and Yeoman's

18 Norman S. Care, "Career choice," *Ethics* 94 (1984): 283–302.
19 Lepisto and Pratt, "Meaningful work," 101.

accounts of meaningful work say more about what conditions prevent meaningful work than they say about criteria enabling it.[20] As we should expect, however, some ethicists admit that work that is "morally worthy" is more meaningful than that which is not.[21] Others, including Yeoman,[22] draw on Wolf's famous characterization of meaningfulness as "when subjective attraction meets objective attractiveness"—meaning that which is subjectively meaningful demands that which is objectively worth valuing.[23]

In conclusion, *LE* has done the meaningful work of defining a distinction between two senses of work that influence the human potential to experience meaningful work. In particular, it has placed a necessary emphasis on the person as a morally worthy end of work, not merely the means by which work gets done. In addition, it has presciently articulated moral concerns that ever-advancing technological industrialization brings to the experience of and access to work.

In focusing its concern on the welfare of the worker, however, *LE* has done more to protect the worker from being used as a working object than it has done to promote the moral potential for the worker to contribute to society as a working subject. It has placed less emphasis on the person as a morally worthy end of work in another sense, namely, as a consumer—and the possibility that the worker can experience meaningfulness by making a social contribution. The second sense of objectivity with which this chapter is concerned opens the possibility of meaningful work as a path to human flourishing, not just prevention of workplace abuse.

20   Schwartz, "Meaningful work"; Bowie, "A Kantian theory"; Yeoman, "Conceptualizing meaningful work."
21   Ciulla, *The working life*, 225.
22   Yeoman, "Conceptualizing meaningful work."
23   Susan Wolf, *Meaning in Life and Why it Matters* (Princeton: Princeton University Press, 2010), 26.

The Worker and the Transistor:
The Dignity of Work and Business Ethics
in Global Corporate Practices

Javier Ignacio Pinto Garay and Alvaro Pezoa Bissieres

1. The place of CST in Business Ethics Theory

Among other philosophical approaches to business ethics theory, virtue-based business ethics theory has introduced an original conceptual framework. This development is grounded in both neo-Aristotelian virtue ethics[1] and New Natural Law theory, which is a legacy of Thomistic and Scholastic economic thought with particular emphasis on the common good.[2] These two philosophical traditions of virtue and common good—both traditions deeply related with the principles of Catholic Social

---

1   Alejo José G. Sison and Ignacio Ferrero, "How Different Is Neo-Aristotelian Virtue from Positive Organizational Virtuousness?" *Business ethics (Oxford, England)* 24, no. S2 (2015): S78–S98.

2   Domènec Melé, "Scholastic Thought and Business Ethics: An Overview," in *Handbook of the Philosophical Foundations of Business Ethics*, ed. C. Luetge (Dordrecht: Springer, 2013), 133–58; Juan Manuel Elegido, "The Just Price: Three Insights from the Salamanca School," *Journal of Business Ethics* 90, no. 29 (2009): 29–46; Javier Pinto-Garay, Ignacio Ferrero, and Germán Scalzo, "Pricing for a Common Good: beyond Ethical Minimalism in Commercial Practices," *Philosophy of Management* (2021): 1–21; Surendra Arjoon, "Reconciling Situational Social Psychology with Virtue Ethics," *International Journal of Management Reviews: IJMR* 10, no. 3 (2008): 221–43; Surendra Arjoon, "An Aristotelian-Thomistic approach to management practice," *Philosophy of Management*, 9(2) (2010): 47–64.

Teaching (CST henceforth)— have allowed commentators to develop a more concrete conceptual foundation of a CST business ethics theory needed to understand business practices and modern corporations.[3]

This project is not simply the introduction of the Gospel into business ethics theory, nor is it a redundant repetition, in different terms, of virtue ethics in economic affairs. On the contrary, CST brings a whole host of original wisdom to business ethics. Indeed, a business ethics informed by CST is distinctive in two respects: (i) its conceptual novelty based on the concept of human dignity; and (ii) its doctrinal status. The former refers to the value of CST as a source for an original conceptual framework applied to modern corporations and economic institutions according to which business practices must remain consonant with the principles of subsidiarity, solidarity, common good, participation, and, in particular, the dignity of work.[4] All of these principles are grounded in the principle of human dignity, which is the seminal component of what CST has to offer in the realm of business ethics; indeed, human dignity is the ground of the tradition's doctrines of virtue, common good, and even justice. Accordingly, Pope John XXIII referred to human dignity as the "one basic principle" of CST:[5]

3   Claus Dierksmeier and Anthony Celano, "Thomas Aquinas on Justice as a Global Virtue in Business," *Business Ethics Quarterly* 22(2) (2012): 247–72; Domènec Melé, "Integrating Personalism into Virtue-Based Business Ethics: The Personalist and the Common Good Principles," *Journal of Business Ethics* 88(1) (2009): 227–44; Martijn Cremers, "What Corporate Governance Can Learn from Catholic Social Teaching," *Journal of Business Ethics* 145(4) (2017): 711–24; Helen Alford and Michael Naughton, *Managing as if Faith Mattered* (Notre Dame, IN: University of Notre Dame Press, 2001); Alejo José G. Sison, Ignacio Ferrero, and Gregorio Guitián, "Human Dignity and The Dignity of Work: Insights from Catholic Social Teaching," *Business Ethics Quarterly* 26(4) (2016): 503–28; Michael Naughton and Jeffrey Cornwall, "The Virtue of Courage in Entrepreneurship: Engaging the Catholic Social Tradition and the Life-Cycle of the Business," *Business Ethics Quarterly* 16(1) (2006): 69–93.

4   Congregation for the Doctrine of the Faith, "Instruction on Christian freedom and liberation *Libertatis Conscientia*," accessed October 1, 2015, http://www.vatican.va/roman_curia/congregations/cfaith/documents/rc_con_cfaith_do_19860322_freedomliberation_en.html.

5   John XXIII, *Mater et Magistra* (Vatican City: Libreria Editrice Vaticana, 1961).

"individual human beings are the foundation, the cause and the end of every social institution."[6] Hence, a business ethics theory based on CST is essentially a call to respect human dignity in every facet of one's business life. Further, this principle is the basis of the well-known personalism of John Paul II and others,[7] which some researchers have applied to business ethics and to which we will refer presently.[8]

As for its doctrinal status, CST is much more a teaching than a theory, meaning that the main authors of the CST corpus—the popes—are not firstly motivated by academic goals, but by the need to teach Catholics and non-Catholics a precise understanding of the Gospel's relationship to currents of change in society, institutions, environment, and culture.[9] Accordingly, even when some principles have a perennial value, the changing tides in society and new forms of economic systems demand the Church's reflection on how productive and social life can be lived in accord with human dignity. And evidently, this profound responsibility has been seen by popes. For they have developed the bedrock principles of CST to respond to the changing reality of society, as seen in *Quadragesimo Anno* and *Centesimus Annus*. Clearly, this is a reflection in which human work has a prominent and even essential role.[10]

That said, a business ethics theory inspired by CST has special concern for new forms of work, especially when they are affected by digital technology (artificial intelligence (AI), big data, automation, robotics, 5G, the Internet of things (IoT), blockchains, neuroscience, genetic

6   Sison, Ferrero, and Guitián, "Human Dignity."
7   Catholic Church, *Catechism of the Catholic Church*, 2nd ed. (Washington, D.C.: United States Conference of Catholic Bishops, 2000).
8   Domènec Melé and Cesar González Cantón, *Human Foundations of Management* (New York: Palgrave Macmillan, 2014).
9   Matthias P. Hühn, "Why Catholic Social Thought is not a Theory (and How that Has Preserved Scholarly Debate)," *Philosophy of Management* (2021). This trend of development of the Church's teaching and commitment in the social question exactly corresponds to the objective recognition of the state of affairs. While in the past the "class" question was especially highlighted as the center of this issue, in more recent times it is the "world" question that is emphasized. See John Paul II, *Laborem Exercens* (Vatican City: Libreria Editrice Vaticana, 1981), 4; *LE* henceforth.
10 *LE*, 3.

engineering) and the globalization of markets that have contributed to unforeseen negative consequences for today's labor force. John Paul II's *Laborem Excercens* has precisely such a concern. Even though it was written forty years ago, it still carries a swath of insights into the way the technology-work relationship can be understood by integrating the role of international corporation into global markets.

2. Technology for Good, Not Simply Good Technology

John Paul II's reflection on work starts with the principle of the primacy of the worker over the material, financial, and technological resources used in productive organizations, that is, the primacy of man over things.[11]

> This truth, which is part of the abiding heritage of the Church's teaching, must always be emphasized with reference to the question of the labor system and with regard to the whole socioeconomic system. We must emphasize and give prominence to the primacy of man in the production process, the primacy of man over things. Everything contained in the concept of capital in the strict sense is only a collection of things. Man, as the *subject* of work, and independently of the work that he does—man alone is a person. This truth has important and decisive consequences.[12]

It is here that the Pope's distinction between the objective and subjective dimensions of work, largely indebted to his personalistic approach, asserts itself with special importance:

> The development of industry and of the various sectors connected with it, even the most modern electronics technology, especially in the fields of miniaturization, communications

11 *Id.*, 12.
12 *Ibid.*, emphasis mine.

and telecommunications and so forth, shows how vast is the role of technology, that ally of work that human thought has produced, in the interaction between the subject and object of work (in the widest sense of the word).[13]

But in light of the subjective-objective distinction, technology can only be considered an "ally" of work inasmuch as the objective features of activity—the efficiency of our productive output, aided by the advent of modern technology—is subordinated to the subjective dimension of action. The impressiveness of technological advancement can never overshadow the supreme sovereignty and dignity of the human person at work. The danger of this is evident by what the Pope defines as acceleration processes[14]—which, to be fair, can work to the benefit of human labor, not only its detriment. Clearly, new products and innovation have had an impact on society, culture, and civilization, both for good and for bad.[15] Hence the clear "social problem" raised by work and technology:

> ... the fact that human work is a key, probably the essential key, to the whole social question, if we try to see that question really from the point of view of man's good. And if the solution—or rather the gradual solution—of the social question, which keeps coming up and becomes ever more complex, must be sought in the direction of "making life more human,"

13 *Id.*, 5.
14 *Ibid.* "While people sometimes speak of periods of 'acceleration' in the economic life and civilization of humanity or of individual nations, linking these periods to the progress of science and technology and especially to discoveries which are decisive for social and economic life, at the same time it can be said that none of these phenomena of 'acceleration' exceeds the essential content of what was said in that most ancient of biblical texts."
15 See *LE*, 1: "While it is true that man eats the bread produced by the work of his hands and this means not only the daily bread by which his body keeps alive but also the bread of science and progress, civilization and culture"; and *LE*, 6: "Work understood as a 'transitive' activity, that is to say an activity beginning in the human subject."

then the key, namely human work, acquires fundamental and decisive importance.[16]

Moreover, changing technology has also profoundly changed the way in which work is performed. This is a relationship that can be defined as the "organizational problem" of work and technology; meaning by "organizations" all the economic institutions in which human labor is performed, such as firms, industries, businesses.[17] In addressing this organizational problem, John Paul II places special attention on the kind of technology that he describes as computers, microprocessor technology, miniaturization, telecommunication, etc.[18] The problem, therefore, is not technology in general terms, but a specific kind of technology that we identify as digital, which is, as we will explain, an important factor in the globalization of work.

Indeed, advances in digital technology have been massive, seeing as they include all the advances made since the invention of the transistor: silicon-made devices, which are miniature electronic components that can work either as amplifiers or controlling switches. Transistors are the basic component of computer chips, which can contain billions of them. As amplifiers, a transistor is used in electronic devices such as speakers, microphones, phones, etc., having an important impact on communication, internet, georeferenced devices, etc. By replacing the old vacuum tube technology, transistors made possible three main working technologies: digital communication, digital data, and especially the software technology. However, the transistor technology that gave place to digitalization started as a revolution before John Paul II's *Laborem Exercens* was even published. The first transistor was invented by William Shockley, John Bardeen, and Walter Brattain in December of 1947 after ten years of work.[19] It ultimately caused the digital revolution

---

16 *LE*, 3.
17 *Id.*, 18.
18 *Id.*, 5.
19 William F. Brinkman, Douglas E. Haggan, and William W. Troutman, "A History of the Invention of the Transistor and Where It Will Lead Us," *IEEE Journal of Solid-State Circuits* 32(12) (1997): 1858–65.

that led to AI developments based on software technology which have been on the scene since 1957.[20]

As the Pope took in these technological breakthroughs, he came to see that they need to be situated within a wider framework that seeks human flourishing. All the achievements of modern technology, taken alone, are simply manifestations of good technology, but not necessarily technology for good; the Pope was insistent that we must value and use technological devices only insofar as they improve human life.

Accordingly, John Paul II contends that every form of technology used at work, no matter the complexity, must be used correctly—or in his own words—as an "ally" to personal work, meaning that a positive alliance between work and technology takes place when the capacity and aptitude for work is safeguarded by the worker him or herself.[21] If technology, on the contrary, is used in such a way that the worker does not preserve his own initiative during the process of work because of the technological resources, then technology becomes the "enemy" of work. At its limit, this mechanization of production passes through the

20 Niklaus Wirth, "A Brief History of Software Engineering," *IEEE Annals of the History of Computing* 30(3) (2008): 32–39. It is worth mentioning that IBM developments were based on the idea and work of a Jesuit priest, Father Roberto Busa, who was working on an *Index Verborum* of all the words in the works of St. Thomas Aquinas; a list totaling some 11 million words of medieval Latin. Father Busa imagined a machine that might be able to help him and, having heard of computers, he visited Thomas J. Watson at IBM in the United States. The company provided help and the entire texts were gradually transferred to punched cards that gave way to the first programing cards ever used in computer science. See Steven E. Jones, *Roberto Busa, S.J., and the Emergence of Humanities Computing: The Priest and the Punched Cards* (New York: Routledge, 2016).

21 See *LE*, 12: "All the means of production, from the most primitive to the ultramodern ones—it is man that has gradually developed them: man's experience and intellect. In this way there have appeared not only the simplest instruments for cultivating the earth but also, through adequate progress in science and technology, the more modern and complex ones: machines, factories, laboratories, and computers. Thus everything that is at the service of work, everything that in the present state of technology constitutes its ever more highly perfected 'instrument,' is the result of work."

suspension of autonomy to a total replacement of workers by machines.[22]

However, *Laborem Excercens* asserts that technology does not *a priori* imply a negative relationship with human work. Rather, technology in itself is neutral until its powers are actualized by the persons truly conducting the work. Since technology is not good on its own, but as an instrument and as result of good human work,[23] we can say that the possibility for technology to be marshalled as an ally of human work derives from the very nature of personal work and can thus be an extension of it. Truly, great technology is a manifestation of the subjective dimension of work inasmuch as it is an outcropping of human rationality and consciousness; thus, in the event that technology is utilized properly, it has a unique capacity to show the ontic status of work as derived from its subjective dimension. But, as the Pope insists, this requires a conscientious engagement with the tools that lie before us:

> At the present stage of technological advance, when man, who is the subject of work, wishes to make use of this collection of modern instruments, the means of production, he must first assimilate cognitively the result of the work of the people who invented those instruments.[24]

And this is not only the case as regards work. It is something of a rule for all human action. Even before his papacy, Karol Wojtyła's writings show a deep concern for a subjective dimension of personal living, a dimension of action through which every person can act as himself, that is, in self-possession:

> The interpretation of man on the basis of "experience lived through" demands introducing the aspects of consciousness into

22 *LE,* 5.
23 See *id.,* 5: "It facilitates his work, perfects, accelerates and augments it. It leads to an increase in the quantity of things produced by work, and in many cases improves their quality."
24 *Id.,* 12.

the analysis of the human being. Man is thus given to us not only as a being specifically defined, but as a concrete "I," as a subject "living himself" (*qui se vit lui même*).... The experience lived through reveals not only the acts and experiences of man in their profoundest dependence on his own "I"; it also reveals the whole personal structure of self-determination in which man discovers his own "I" as the one who possesses himself and dominates himself.... While experiencing self-possession and self-domination man experiences the fact that he is a person and that he is a subject. Each of us experiences the structure of self-possession and self-domination as being essential to the personal.[25]

But if a man is himself—acting in accord with his unique person-hood—only by developing self-mastery over the different dimensions of his personality, then we can say that anything that is personal is only so in the measure that it is subjected to the acting human agent. If this principle is applied to human work, it forces us to acknowledge that work is only personal inasmuch as the tools of that work are properly subjugated to the "I" which is performing the work, meaning a mastery of technological resources, an integral form of objective-subjective possession that is defined as "dominion":

... "dominion" spoken of in the biblical text being meditated upon here refers not only to the objective dimension of work but at the same time introduces us to an understanding of its subjective dimension.... This dominion, in a certain sense, refers to the subjective dimension even more than to the objective one: this dimension conditions the very ethical nature of work. In fact there is no doubt that human work has an ethical value of its own, which clearly and directly remain linked to the fact that the one who carries it out is a person, a conscious and free subject, that is to say a subject that decides about himself.[26]

25   Karol Wojtyła, "Subjectivity and the Irreducible in Man," *Analecta Husserliana* 7 (1978): 107–14.
26   *LE*, 6.

Thus, according to John Paul II's subjective-objective paradigm, the value of personal work is only actively recognized when the worker achieves mastery over technology.[27] And as we have seen, mastering technology is possible only because workers' subjective dimension of action is the source and purpose of personal labor. That is, man must maintain dominion in both the initiative and meaning of his own work; otherwise, work loses humanity.

> … work means any activity by man, whether manual or in-tellectual, whatever its nature or circumstances; it means any human activity that can and must be recognized as work, in the midst of all the many activities of which man is capable and to which he is predisposed by his very nature, by virtue of humanity itself.[28]

To put it another way, the feature of having "humanity" (i.e., an activity "by man") means that a person is acting on his own. For this reason, John Paul II sustains that only man is capable of working, not the instruments or any other form of technology that might be used in productive processes:

> As a person [man] works, he performs various actions belonging to the work process; independently of their objective content, these actions must all serve to realize his humanity, to fulfil the calling to be a person that is his by reason of his very humanity.[29]

Accordingly, an autonomous process performed by machines or modern robots is nothing but a mechanic activity, not human work. In fact, referring to digital devices or AI as 'working' is only a matter of speaking, because they are only said to 'act on their own' in an analog-

---

27 *Ibid.* The sources of the dignity of work are to be sought primarily in the subjective dimension, not in the objective one.
28 *Ibid.*, Blessing.
29 *Id.*, 6.

ical manner, that is, in reference to human work. Thus, the Pope explains that work has the mark of man and of humanity, that is, of a person operating within a community of persons.[30] No form of technology, therefore, has the capacity to be an authentic source of initiative and originality of action. Technology is operative only as an extension of human work.

In a similar way, technology is incapable of having and introducing original purposes into action. As John Paul II has it, "... the primary basis of the value of work is man himself, who is its subject."[31] In this sense, recognizing the goal of AI, algorithms, or modern robots is, in fact, the capacity to find in that artifact the original purpose of its maker, not a purpose conceived by the technological artifact itself. This is evident because technological "work" does not bear a subjective dimension but is purely objective: there is no "digital conscience" or "mechanic purpose." On the contrary, only the interiority proper to the human person bears a subjective dimension of action, giving man the privilege of being able to introduce meaning and purpose into the technological world.

Now, the content of such meaning and purpose is, according to the Pope, not just the worker's capacity to understand the reason why some tasks are being performed in one way or another. While this is indeed a component of the meaning of work, it also derives from the human capacity—and moral responsibility—to contribute to the common good. For John Paul II, the subjective dimension of work is essentially associated with a sense of the common good, according to which every worker combines his human identity with a membership in a society, which occurs insofar as work contributes to the general heritage of the community.[32] Work, therefore, is not solely a matter of individual dominion over technology, but also of service; otherwise, it is impossible to connect the value of work and technology with a real understanding of human progress: "A person is more precious for what he is than for what he has. Similarly, all that people do to obtain greater justice, wider brotherhood,

30 *Id.*, Blessing.
31 *Id.*, 6.
32 *Id.*, 10.

and a more humane ordering of social relationships has greater worth than technical advances. For these advances can supply the material for human progress, but of themselves alone they can never actually bring it about."[33] In this sense, mastering technology means not only original-ity, but making technology a resource that provides the possibility for all others to thrive, i.e., a common good in society and in the community of work itself.[34]

3. Work and International Corporations

John Paul II understood that the negative impact of technology on work is not simply the result of the nature of new technological devices. Rather, it is the social and moral circumstances that have given rise to a degenerate understanding and culture of work. In particular, the Pope's concerns are mostly the social character of the internationalization process that we, nowadays, would define as globalization. In this sense, the problem is not essentially a matter of a new industrial revolution, but of social change, even though both technological and global features have played a major role:

> The recent stage of human history, especially that of certain societies, brings a correct affirmation of technology as a basic coefficient of economic progress; but, at the same time, this affirmation has been accompanied by and con-tinues to be accompanied by the raising of essential ques-tions concerning human work in relationship to its subject, which is man. These questions are particularly charged

33   Second Vatican Council, *Gaudium et Spes* (Vatican City: Libreria Editrice Vaticana, 1965), 35.
34   See *LE*, 13: "Working at any workbench, whether a relatively primitive or an ultramodern one, a man can easily see that through his work he enters into two inheritances: the inheritance of what is given to the whole of hu-manity in the resources of nature, and the inheritance of what others have already developed on the basis of those resources, primarily by developing technology, that is to say, by producing a whole collection of increasingly perfect instruments for work."

with content and tension of an ethical and social character.[35]

To illustrate what the Pope is saying above, let us take the example of the transistor once more. Modern transistors are the result of an exponential optimization process of innovation. And even though the science used for their improvements has made revolutionary advances from Newton to quantum physics, they are still transistors. The revolution is evidently scientific, but not necessarily technological. The latest technology has been available for use in processes of production for quite some time. The issue is not the technology itself. In fact, considering only the technological aspect of work to assess the moral quality of modern employment is closer to a Marxist approach, a technological determinism,[36] rather than an approach informed by CST. Simply maintaining that John Paul II associated the problem of work with technology alone is a much more Marxist interpretation of the Pope's ideas, not to mention that it is simply incorrect. It is here that the "globalization factor" interposes itself as the key dimension of the problem.

One might suppose that globalization is irrelevant since it is not explicitly addressed by John Paul II's encyclicals. But as Samuel Gregg has pointed out, CST must consider the fact that global change has introduced a number of complex processes of concern to the Church: namely, new phenomena of socialization, subsidiarity, and common good, which have been catalyzed by the growth of multinational corporations and the proliferation of non-governmental organizations and public agencies, international law, and courts of justice.[37] Further, international corporations have managed to produce and sell complex technology to the low-income population worldwide. Based on an economies of scale strategy combined with new forms of telecommunication and, more important, the

---

35 *LE,* 5.

36 Sally Wyatt, "Technological Determinism Is Dead; Long Live Technological Determinism," *The Handbook of Science & Technology Studies* 7 (2008): 165–81.

37 Samuel Gregg, "Globalization and the Insights of Catholic Social Teaching," *Journal of Markets & Morality* 4, no. 1 (Spring 2001): 1–13.

incorporation of cheap labor from poor countries, corporations have been able to use and produce complex technology with low costs of production and distribution.

This modern scenario is much more prevalent today than when *LE* was written. John Paul II, therefore, did not witness this major change in industrial and commercial practices of modern global markets, nor its contemporary impact on human work. Nevertheless, he foresaw the risk of it in the burgeoning internationalization of corporations:

> Because fresh questions and problems are always arising, there are always fresh hopes, but also fresh fears and threats, connected with this basic dimension of human existence: man's life is built up every day from work, from work it derives its specific dignity but at the same time work contains the unceasing measure of human toil and suffering, and also of the harm and injustice which penetrate deeply into social life within individual nations and on the international level.[38]

In particular, the Pope foresaw the possibility of a negative evolution of globalization, and this from the fact that work was turning in a commodity or a "merchandise," meaning an impersonal "force" needed for production. This is to say that the negative impact of modern technology on work has stemmed from a culture of mercantilization that has increased the problems of labor associated with internationalization; these are ethical and social problems in which modern corporations have an important responsibility.

According to John Paul II, a culture of work based solely on the value of merchandise derives from a materialistic philosophy in which the economic success depends on the fact that work is valued only in the same economic terms and, consequently, managed only in its objective dimension.[39] This idea of work as a merchandise —i.e., an asset—

38   *LE*, 1.
39   *Id.,* 13: "… resources of creation, and also on other human beings, those to whose work and initiative we owe the perfected and increased possibilities of our own work.

has its roots in the liberal interpretation of work and in primitive capitalism,[40] according to which the activity of labor is "something" that workers sell to those who have the capital to acquire it. This interpretation of working conditions often leads to treating human labor as a "merchandise," meaning an impersonal "force" needed for production. This is, in fact, associated with the classification of work as workforce,

> "All that we can say of everything in the production process which constitutes a whole collection of 'things,' the instruments, the capital, is that it conditions man's work; we cannot assert that it constitutes as it were an impersonal 'subject' putting man and man's work into a position of dependence.
>
> This consistent image, in which the principle of the primacy of person over things is strictly preserved, was broken up in human thought, sometimes after a long period of incubation in practical living. The break occurred in such a way that labor was separated from capital and set in opposition to it, and capital was set in opposition to labor, as though they were two impersonal forces, two production factors juxtaposed in the same 'economistic' perspective. This way of stating the issue contained a fundamental error, what we can call the error of economism, that of considering human labor solely according to its economic purpose. This fundamental error of thought can and must be called an error of materialism, in that economism directly or indirectly includes a conviction of the primacy and superiority of the material, and directly or indirectly places the spiritual and the personal (man's activity, moral values and such matters) in a position of subordination to material reality. This is still not theoretical materialism in the full sense of the term, but it is certainly practical materialism, a materialism judged capable of satisfying man's needs, not so much on the grounds of premises derived from materialist theory, as on the grounds of a particular way of evaluating things, and so on the grounds of a certain hierarchy of goods based on the greater immediate attractiveness of what is material."

40 *Id.*, 9: "But in the light of the analysis of the fundamental reality of the whole economic process first and foremost of the production structure that work is—it should be recognized that the error of early capitalism can be repeated wherever man is in a way treated on the same level as the whole complex of the material means of production, as an instrument and not in accordance with the true dignity of his work—that is to say, where he is not treated as subject and maker, and for this very reason as the true purpose of the whole process of production."

manpower, or human resources; which are acceptable concepts only under the premises of materialistic economism,[41] a moral philosophy totally inimical to Church teaching.[42]

As we have shown, the Pope concurs that globalization has encouraged this materialistic approach to work by means of promoting and facilitating large international companies which employ non-local workforces, which are "bought" from contractors who manage cheap manpower in third-world economies.[43] This is the case in Asia, and especially in China, where there are industrial facilities for rich countries because of the "comparative advantages" of a workforce acclimated to

41   *LE*, 7.
42   Additionally, John Paul II associates to the international mercantilization of work a new form of alienation in terms of the common good: "... the loss of a subject of work, whose efforts of mind and body could contribute to the common good of his own country, but these efforts, this contribution, are instead offered to another society which in a sense has less right to them than the person's country of origin." See *id.*, 23. The problem was not so much the inability for workers to understand and value the result of their work, but now the incapacity to see in which sense their work is contributing to their own community. "Economies of scale, especially in the agricultural sector, end up forcing smallholders to sell their land or to abandon their traditional crops. Their attempts to move to other, more diversified, means of production prove fruitless because of the difficulty of linkage with regional and global markets, or because the infrastructure for sales and transport is geared to larger businesses." See Francis, *Laudato Si'* (Vatican City: Libreria Editrice Vaticana, 2013), 129.
43   *LE*, 11: "Throughout this period, which is by no means yet over, the issue of work has of course been posed on the basis of the great conflict that in the age of, and together with, industrial development emerged between 'capital' and 'labor,' that is to say between the small but highly influential group of entrepreneurs, owners or holders of the means of production, and the broader multitude of people who lacked these means and who shared in the process of production solely by their labor. The conflict originated in the fact that the workers put their powers at the disposal of the entrepreneurs, and these, following the principle of maximum profit, tried to establish the lowest possible wages for the work done by the employees. In addition there were other elements of exploitation, connected with the lack of safety at work and of safeguards regarding the health and living conditions of the workers and their families."

low salaries, bad working conditions, and almost nonexistent labor regulation. In fact, this international system becomes what the Pope would classify as international exploitation:

> For instance the highly industrialized countries, and even more the businesses that direct on a large scale the means of industrial production (the companies referred to as multinational or transnational), fix the highest possible prices for their products, while trying at the same time to fix the lowest possible prices for raw materials or semi-manufactured goods. This is one of the causes of an ever-increasing disproportion between national incomes. The gap between most of the richest countries and the poorest ones is not diminishing or being stabilized but is increasing more and more, to the detriment, obviously, of the poor countries. Evidently this must have an effect on local labor policy and on the worker's situation in the economically disadvantaged societies. Finding himself in a system thus conditioned, the direct employer fixes working conditions below the objective requirements of the workers, especially if he himself wishes to obtain the highest possible profits from the business which he runs (or from the businesses which he runs, in the case of a situation of "socialized" ownership of the means of production).[44]

Moreover, global markets and international corporations—once they have normalized the use of cheap labor in foreign countries and the materialistic approach to employment—are one step away from automatization and substitution, that is, the introduction of technology into the industrial process in a way that is inconsistent with the inherent dignity of human work. As we have explained, both processes of automatization and labor substitution are possible because of an economic system of production based on the same materialistic understanding of globalization, not simply because technology is available.

44 *Id.*, 17.

4. From Automatization and Substitution
to Participation and Opportunity

We are led to wonder precisely how this regnant materialism in global production can be overcome. To answer this question, we need to consider how the primacy of workers over technology demands two forms of working policies, namely, participation and labor opportunity; both features are opposed to automatization and labor substitution:

> ... the principle of the substantial and real priority of labor, of the subjectivity of human labor and its effective participation in the whole production process, independently of the nature of the services provided by the worker.[45]

Automatization is an organizational strategy in which technological resources are operated by employees with an ever-decreasing amount of participation by the employees themselves. The role of workers becomes much more the activity of an operator, whose activity is prescribed by the way a machine is to be operated, thus jettisoning the role of rational judgment in human work. Historically speaking, automatization derives from the original proposal for organizational central planning supported by Taylor's scientific management theory published in 1911. Taylorism, indeed, became a major theory of work management (or the planning of tasks) according to which employees function in a mechanistic system of assigned tasks designed to improve efficiency.[46] Taylorism and its issue, Fordism, were the central ideas in the American industrial revolution before the great wars. Nevertheless, the original purpose of Taylorism was not simply the optimization of production, but to raise overall profits and thereby increase workers' salaries. This goal was justified by Taylor because he was concerned to find a way to increase the living standards of workers.[47] A few decades later, after Taylor's ideas became essential

---

45 *Id.*, 13.
46 Beverly Burris, "Technocratic Organization and Control," *Organization Studies* 10(1) (1989): 1–22.
47 Peter Drucker, *Post-Capitalist Society* (New York: Routledge, 2012).

to Western industries, new digital technologies made possible the path from mechanization to automatization, that is, the introduction of better technology in which employees were even more limited in their autonomy, albeit with better standards of productivity.[48] However, according to John Paul II's perspective, automatization is in fact highly inconsistent with promoting the dignity of work. For it means a mechanization of employment that finally supplants workers by taking away personal satisfaction, creativity, and responsibility.[49] Accordingly, Taylor's arguments in favor of mechanization and central planning of tasks—even when well-meant—are reductive; and this is not only so because it culminates in the replacement of human workers, but also because the value of work is not only recognized in a salary:

> ... the person who works desires not only due remuneration for his work; he also wishes that, within the production process, provision be made for him to be able to know that in his work, even on something that is owned in common, he is working "for himself." This awareness is extinguished within him in a system of excessive bureaucratic centralization, which makes the worker feel that he is just a cog in a huge machine moved from above, that he is for more reasons than one a mere production instrument rather than a true subject of work with an initiative of his own. If it is to be rational and fruitful, any socialization of the means of production must take this argument into consideration.[50]

---

48 Jacopo Staccioli and Maria Enrica Virgillito, "Back to the past: the historical roots of labor-saving automation," Eurasian *Business Review* 11(1) (2021): 27–57.

49 *LE*, 5.

50 *LE*, 15. It is worth mentioning that automatization brought many problems to employees. For Brenkert, employees should have autonomy because their identities and self-esteem are linked to the firm. Similarly, Hsieh argues that the same can be said in relation to employees' self-respect. Organizations must empower workers by giving them more autonomy. Having greater control helps them to avoid the psychological experience of alienation, which results in a cognitive separation from their job, frus-

Substitution, as referenced above, refers to the process of totally replacing employees by technology or, in other cases, building new factory facilities and productive systems without major human participation. Sophisticated technological devices can do certain jobs faster, more efficiently, and at a lower cost than human beings. Moreover, automatization avoids the innumerable complexities of work performed by human beings. Subsequently, there are numerous reasons to think that there will be large sectors of unemployment in certain regions of the world and reduced global economic activity performed by humans. That said, there are those who argue that the creation of new, heretofore unknown tasks will compensate for and even overcome the disappearance of many other tasks existing today. There is a lack of consensus on the matter; expert analyses make a wide range of predictions ranging from the frankly pessimistic to the enthusiastically optimistic. On this point, it is relevant to determine what a realistic final scenario might be in terms of the outcome of the addition and subtraction of jobs, and thereby come up with a plausible approximation of how long the concomitant period of adjustment might be before a certain state of equilibrium is reached (or at least a final state that is not worse than the initial one). An estimated duration of a few years verses several decades, for example, are quite distinct matters. The corresponding individual, familial, social, and global impacts will be radically different depending on the way in which the two variables—the quantity and timing of changes in employment—are worked out in practice. What is more, it should be noted that once aggregate numbers are calculated, it will nonetheless be necessary to complement these with specific geographical predictions based on regions and countries on the one hand, and by areas of economic activity on the other. Herein, it is highly possible that different realities will evidence significant inequalities. The underlying concerns, in any case, are as

tration, apathy, stress, anxiety, and a variety of illnesses (Kanungo). See George Brenkert, "Freedom, Participation and Corporations: The Issue of Corporate (Economic) Democracy," *Business Ethics Quarterly* 2(3) (1992): 251–69; Nien-hê Hsieh, "Survey Article: Justice in Production," *Journal of Political Philosophy,* 16(1) (2008): 72–100; and Rabindra N. Kanungo, "Alienation and empowerment: Some ethical imperatives in business," *Journal of Business Ethics* 11 (1992): 413–22.

follows: what will happen to people who lose their source of employment due to these changes? and how will their families as well as society at large be affected?

As explained by Marengo, the technological advancement since the First Industrial Revolution has caused what Keynes describes as technological unemployment. This phenomenon, nevertheless, has been observed optimistically in terms of a temporary frictional situation that comes to an end when the unemployed workforce, once they have been reskilled, can be hired in new industries that arise in a changing economic system. The problem, Marengo continues, is the real capacity of operators to be reintegrated into a productive system that demands high qualification. Therefore, a pessimistic view sees that, at this point in history, new technologies are out of reach for unskilled workers, making the technological unemployment a structural phenomenon of global economies.[51]

However, the temporary situation of unemployment is still a harm that needs to be avoided, especially when substitution is caused only because of economic purposes and competitive advantages without any concern for employees:

> They cannot be possessed against labor, they cannot even be possessed for possession's sake, because the only legitimate title to their possession— whether in the form of private ownership or in the form of public or collective ownership—is that they should serve labor, and thus, by serving labor, that they should make possible the achievement of the first principle of this order, namely, the universal destination of goods and the right to common use of them.[52]

Again, the primacy of workers over technology impels us to guard against care for the unwilling consequences the unemployed circumstances

---

51 Luigi Marengo, "Is this time different? A note on automation and labour in the fourth industrial revolution," *Economia e Politica Industriale: Journal of Industrial and Business Economics* 46(3), no. 2 (2019): 323–31.

52 *LE*, 14.

of living. For the Pope, indeed, an exclusion of workers from industries can mean an unjust distribution of work, even in regard to skilled employees,[53] only for the sake of profit.

> The opposite of a just and right situation in this field is unemployment, that is to say the lack of work for those who are capable of it. It can be a question of general unemployment or of unemployment in certain sectors of work.

> It is particularly painful when it especially affects young people, who after appropriate cultural, technical and professional preparation fail to find work, and see their sincere wish to work and their readiness to take on their own responsibility for the economic and social development of the community sadly frustrated.[54]

In a different manner, Church teaching has shown that people engaged in business leadership "are called to engage with the contemporary economic and financial world in light of the principles of human dignity and the common good."[55] Business is a noble vocation, directed to producing wealth and improving our world. It can be a fruitful source of prosperity for the areas in which it operates, especially if it sees the creation of jobs as an essential part of its service to the common good.[56] Accordingly, the problem of unemployment can often be the result of a lack of opportunities provided by employers; to proactively provide opportunities in society is a responsibility of business leaders, not just a deterministic outcome of the productive process.

53 *Id.*, 1.
54 *Id.*, 18.
55 Peter K. A. Turkson, "Foreword to the 2018 English Edition," in *Vocation of the Business Leader: A Reflection* (Vatican City: Dicastery for Promoting Integral Human Development; St. Paul, MN: John A. Ryan Institute for Catholic Social Thought of The Center for Catholic Studies, University St. Thomas, 2018), 1.
56 Francis, *Laudato Si'*, 129.

5. Conclusions

It is very clear that we are living in an age of globalization and technological acceleration, and modern corporations have not only participated in the process, but they have also increased the extension and the complexity of global markets and the integration of technology into modern work. Facing such industrial and economic circumstances, a business ethics theory based on CST, with special attention to John Paul II's *Laborem Exercens*, demands for highly technological business practices to organize and promote human work based on the principle of dignity, that is, facilitating workers' participation in their own tasks by means of personal deliberation and with a special sense of common good. Regardless of the nature of the technology utilized, workers must experience a personal domain and mastery over their own tasks. Hence, the dignity of work is not only a matter of just salaries, but of work design. Accordingly, business policies are responsible for making the necessary adjustments and innovations needed to offer job positions that, while remaining efficient, are also dignifying. Hence, the incapacity of international and local firms to avoid labor substitution and restrict job opportunities is a moral failure, no matter the profitability of those business models. Thus, businesspersons, CEOs, and managers have a great responsibility in terms of being both economically and morally excellent, especially in terms of the organization of human work.

Finally, a business ethics theory based on John Paul II's work does not fixate on the features of modern technology as the main source of moral assessment to modern corporations, as in a Marxist perspective, but it focuses upon the responsibility of economic institutions to use that technology in accordance with personal dignity and the common good. This means that international and local firms are called to facilitate workers' mastery, no matter their tasks, for them to receive moral development, self-possession, meaning, and freedom through their work. And without understanding what it means to provide dignifying work in modern organizations, such a call will go unheeded—even as we continue to deepen our understanding of the transistor.

The Real Work:
Making the Encyclical
Laborem Exercens Operational

Gonzalo Flores-Castro Lingán

1. Introduction

2021 marks forty years since the publication of Pope St. John Paul II's encyclical *Laborem Exercens*, an occasion to reflect upon the wisdom that it still has to offer. However, in this chapter, we are not going to do so merely at the level of philosophical or theological principle, but with the aim of making the principles of *Laborem Exercens* operational; to do so, we will bring the encyclical into conversation with Professor Juan Antonio Pérez López's theory of action.[1] And while Pérez López comments about the encyclical in a 1987 article,[2] there remains much more for his theory of action to elucidate.

We are inspired by the following statement made by Sertillanges back in the thirties: "Every truth is practical; the most apparently abstract, the loftiest, it is also the most practical. Every truth is life, direction, a way leading to the end of man. And therefore Jesus Christ made this unique assertion: 'I am the Way, the Truth, and the

---

[1] Juan Antonio Pérez López, *Teoría de La Acción Humana En Las Organizaciones: La Acción Personal* (Madrid: Rialp, 1991); Juan Antonio Pérez López, *Fundamentos de La Dirección de Empresas*, 6th ed. (Madrid: Rialp, 2006).

[2] Juan Antonio Pérez López, "La Laborem Exercens y La Visión Científica de La Acción Humana," in *Estudios sobre la Encíclica "Laborem Exercens,"* ed. F. Fernández (Madrid: BAC, 1987), 267–94.

Life.'"[3] We think that the principles that *Laborem Exercens* (LE) lays out, and more precisely, the principle that is "the guiding thread"[4] of the document, is the most practical and valuable of all for management theory; moreover, we think that it can be a point of contact between the Church's Social Teaching and management theory. The principle can be stated as follows: "[There is] the primacy of the human person over things, the primacy of the worker over the work (in the objective sense), the primacy of work (in the subjective sense) over capital."[5]

This emphasis on the importance of the person in work is the primacy of what John Paul II would call the subject of work.[6] It relates to a sense of the dignity of the human person, his social nature, and even the principle of the common good. But even if true at the level of principle, there is a gap to be filled by the acting agent. The gap is the distance between principle and practice. To teach the worker only principles and let him discover how they can help him in the exercise of his profession is to leave him, in most cases, faced with the most challenging part of the matter.[7] Moreover, to do so is dangerous because it can reinforce the alleged separation between the principles of morality and economic-management theory.[8]

Our goal is twofold: first, to operationalize the principles in *Laborem Exercens* through the theory of Pérez López, thereby realizing their

3   Antonine Dalmace Sertillanges, *The Intellectual Life* (Washington: The Newman Press, 1960).

4   John Paul II, *Laborem Exercens* (Vaticano: Libreria Editrice Vaticana, 1981), sec. 12.

5   Gerald E. Schotte, "The Social Teaching of the Church: Laborem Exercens, a New Challenge," *Review of Social Economy* 40, no. 3 (1982): 349.

6   Michael J. White, "Homo Laborans: Work in Modern Catholic Social Thought," *Villanova Law Review* 58, no. 3 (2013).

7   Juan Antonio Pérez López and Ramón San Román, *Enseñanza de Economía a Profesionales No Economistas* (Madrid: Confederación Española de Cajas de Ahorros, 1973).

8   Domenec Melè and César G. Cantón, *Fundamentos Antropológicos de La Dirección de Empresas* (Pamplona: Eunsa, 2015).

normative character;[9] and, in a way analogous to the role of *praeambula fidei* ("the discourse meant to dispose one to the grace of faith")[10] in evangelization, the action theory of Pérez López could serve to open minds to the Social Teaching of the Church.

Firstly, we are going to develop part of the action theory of Juan Antonio Pérez López. Then we are going to expose the principal thesis in *Laborem Exercens* about the subjective and objective dimensions of work. Thirdly, we will explicitly compare the aforementioned thesis of *Laborem Exercens* with the action theory of Pérez López. And finally, we will conclude that the categories of Pérez López can be used in managerial science to operationalize the principles of (1) the subjective and objective dimensions of work and (2) human dignity as developed in the Catholic Social Teaching.

2. Action Theory and Decision-Making Criteria

The action theory of Pérez López has been developed in other places and for different reasons.[11] For our present purposes, we will develop

9   Alejo José G. Sison, Ignacio Ferrero, and Gregorio Guitián, "Human Dignity and The Dignity of Work: Insights from Catholic Social Teaching," *Business Ethics Quarterly* 26, no. 4 (2016): 503–28.

10   Ralph McInerny, *Praeambula Fidei: Thomism and the God of the Philosophers* (Washington: The Caholic University of America Press, 2006), 35.

11   Rafael Andreu, Josep Riverola, Josep M. Rosanas, and Rafael de Santiago, "Capability Building and Learning: An Emergent Behavior Approach," *International Journal of Management and Economics* 44, no. 1 (2015): 7–38; Antonio Argandoña, "Fostering Values in Organizations," *Journal of Business Ethics* 45, nos. 1–2 (2003): 15–28; Antonio Argandoña, "Integrating Ethics into Action Theory and Organizational Theory," *Journal of Business Ethics* 78, no. 3 (2008): 435–46; Antonio Argandoña, "Beyond Contracts: Love in Firms," *Journal of Business Ethics* 99, no. 1 (2011): 77–85; Domènec Melé, M. Nuria Chinchilla, and Marta López-Jurado, "The 'Freely Adaptive System'. Application of This Cybernetic Model to an Organization Formed by Two Dynamic Human Systems," *Philosophy of Management* 18, no. 1 (2019): 89–106; Josep M. Rosanas, "Beyond Economic Criteria: A Humanistic Approach to Organizational Survival," *Journal of Business Ethics* 78, no. 3 (2008): 447–62; Gonzalo Flores-Castro,

only the structure of the theory at the level of decision-making criteria, and not at the level of the constructs necessary to achieve those criteria.

First, we must conceptualize the interaction (action-reaction) between two people, for it is the minimum scheme that can be used to analyze an organization. We depict such an interaction as follows:

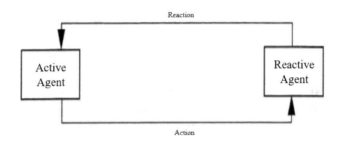

Figure 1. Basic system model[12]

When the active agent has a problem—that is, he realizes that "there is a situation that is not completely pleasant for a person [himself or another person], or when it is suspected that there are more pleasant situations than the current ones"[13]—which he cannot solve alone; he executes an action with another agent (reactive agent), hoping that the action of that agent (the reaction) will solve his problem.

If we briefly analyze this interaction, we realize that we have at least three evaluations that we must carry out to try to know *a priori* the *effectiveness* of the active agent's action. First, we must analyze the action

"Modelo teórico para la integración de las emociones en el campo del comportamiento organizacional," *Illustro* 10 (2019): 5–20; Gonzalo Flores-Castro, "¿Qué hace a una decisión buena? Criterios de toma de decisiones desde el management cibernético," *Revista De Psicología* 9, no. 3 (2020): 107–22; Roberto García-Castro and Miguel Ángel Ariño, *Wonderful Decisions* (Leipzig: Independently published, 2019).

12 Original from Pérez López, *Teoría de La Acción Humana En Las Organizaciones,* 25.

13 Miguel Ángel Ariño, *Toma de Decisiones y Gobierno de Organizaciones* (Barcelona: Deusto, 2005), 19.

plan, the "action-reaction" dyad; that is, evaluate the *validity* of this plan, which is nothing more than "the extent to which the action and the reaction solve the problem that was intended to be solved."[14] Secondly, we must evaluate whether the internal state of the active agent is such that it allows him to execute the action plan; that is, whether it is feasible or *operational* for him to execute it. Finally, we must assess whether the internal state of the reactive agent is such that he can carry out the reaction; that is, whether it is operative or *instrumental* for that agent to execute the action (the reaction).

This brief consideration of a concrete action is only a static evaluation. In the everyday operation of organizations, there are a plethora of interactions among various agents, whether between managers and collaborators, collaborators with other collaborators, salespeople with customers, etc. Now, what would happen if the internal states of any of these agents changed due to past interactions? This question in particular is vital to perform a complete analysis. Experience shows that this change not only occurs, but deeply influences future interactions, even at the neuronal level.[15] Failing to consider the possible change in the internal states of such agents would be an "incomplete abstraction."[16] In that sense, the possible change produced in the active agent is a change in the *efficiency* of an action—the future feasibility or operationality of the active agent—and the possible change produced in the reactive agent is a change in the *consistency* of the action—the future instrumentality of the reactive agent.

Now, the change to which we refer is not any type of change, but a "change that occurs in the agents as a result of the interaction process execution, as long as such change is significant for the explanation of future interactions."[17] To distinguish this type of change from more general internal changes, we will use the term *learning*, which is much more precise. Learning may be positive, that is to say, it may allow interactions

---

14 *Id.*, 30.
15 Cf. Robert M. Sapolsky, *Behave: The Biology of Humans at Our Best and Worst* (New York: Penguin Books, 2017), 459–60.
16 Pérez López, *Teoría de La Acción Humana En Las Organizaciones.*
17 *Id.*, 28.

to continue to take place in the future (or even facilitate future interactions); or negative, which means a kind of learning that makes future interactions difficult or even impossible. Thus, we have the minimum complete evaluation of the interaction: a static analysis—effectiveness of the action plan—and dynamic analysis—an action plan's efficiency and consistency.

3. Structural Relationship, Operational Relationship, and Types of Learning

Furthermore, given the previous analysis, we can deduce two types of relationships between agents. The first relationship is supposed and necessary for the other. The first type of relationship provides the conditions for the possibility of interaction (action-reaction): namely, the conditions are such that the internal states of the agents—operationality and instrumentality—allow the interaction. In other words, there has to be a minimum of operationality and instrumentality that makes the interaction possible. This underlying relationship is called the *structural relationship* and is illustrated by "the degrees of confidence that may exist between two people."[18] Assuming the existence of this structural relationship (which requires, among other things, a minimum of trust), the relationship takes another form, called the *operational relationship*, which concerns those actions and reactions that in fact solve the problems of the active and reactive agents. Note that both the structural and operational relationships are only abstractions from the real relationship or real organization. Suppose there is to be a real relationship. In that case, the agents must: a) be in a situation that allows them to interact with each other (minimum of operationality and instrumentality), b) they must also be able to solve each other's problems (validity of their action plans), which is the effectiveness of the interaction; however, if they wish to continue the relationship in time, c) their decisions must take into account the criteria of efficiency and consistency; that is, ensuring that the future internal states of the agents guarantee the possibility of future interaction.

18   Pérez López, *Fundamentos de La Dirección de Empresas*, 156.

A person who only considers the operational relationship will learn to create effective action plans to a certain extent (positive operational learning). However, if he also considers the efficiency and consistency of his actions—the structural relationship—he will learn to solve his and others' problems both now and in the future (positive structural learning). But if a person evaluates effectiveness and not efficiency and consistency (the person learns operationally but not structurally), there will be a dynamic contradiction in the system. While problems are solved in the immediate, they will not be solved in the future. This contradiction is what Pérez López calls *negative learning*.

4. *Laborem Exercens:*
The Objective and Subjective Sense of Work

At the beginning of this chapter, we state that our aim is not to philosophically or theologically analyze *Laborem Exercens*, but to make its principles operational; that is, to bring them closer to practice, to real work. We also profess to start from the guiding principle of the encyclical,[19] reformulated in Schotte's words as follows:

> [There is] the primacy of the human person over things, the primacy of the worker over the work (in the objective sense), the primacy of work (in the subjective sense) over capital.[20]

The encyclical refers to work's objective dimension when it references man's dominion over the earth: "... man's dominion over the earth is achieved in and by means of work. There thus emerges the meaning of *work in an objective sense....*"[21] We dominate the earth, for example, by domesticating animals, raising them, and obtaining from them the food and clothing we need. In its most total sense, objective work is the transformation of nature, adapting it to our needs. In other words, it is the way we solve our problems, performing certain actions and expecting certain

19 See note 4.
20 Schotte, "The Social Teaching of the Church," 349.
21 John Paul II, *Laborem Exercens,* sec. 5.

reactions from our environment (which includes other people) to attend to those problems.

Our appreciation of work's objective dimension has grown significantly since the industrial revolution, which has enormously increased our ability to transform nature.[22] However, it remains true that, despite living in a post-industrial era, "the proper subject of work continues to be man."[23] Interestingly, the pervasive focus on the object of work was inherited in management theory from the end of the nineteenth century until the 1970's.[24] Apparently, the industrialization of work and an accompanying "naive empiricism"[25] painted the worker as a production machine devoid of subjectivity. On that model, only the object of work, the goods produced by man's toil, is valuable.

The encyclical elucidates the subjective meaning of work as follows. It is grounded in the fact that the human being, as a person, is a "subjective being capable of acting in a planned and rational way, capable of deciding about himself, and with a tendency to self-realization."[26] The encyclical then adds, "as a person he works, he performs various actions belonging to the work process; independently of their objective content, these actions must all serve to realize his humanity, to fulfill the calling to be a person that is his by reason of his very humanity."[27] Thus, the value of work is given not by the external result of the work, but by the human worker: *"the primary basis of the value of work is man himself."*[28] This fact has an important ethical consequence: "work is 'for man' and not man 'for work'" and, therefore, the person cannot be used as a mere "instrument of work."[29] In other words, the dignity of work comes from the dignity of its subject.

22 *Ibid.*

23 *Ibid.*

24 Miguel Alfonso Martínez-Echevarría, "Teorías de La Empresa y Crisis de La Modernidad," *Cuadernos de Empresa y Humanismo* 83 (2001): 4–84.

25 Alan F. Chalmers, *¿Qué Es Esa Cosa Llamada Ciencia?*, 7th ed. (Madrid: Siglo XXI de España, 1988).

26 John Paul II, *Laborem Exercens*, sec. 6.

27 *Ibid.*

28 *Ibid.*

29 *Ibid.*

This prioritization of the subject of work is a clear criticism of the economistic thought[30] still prevailing in management theories and practice.[31] However, applying theoretical principles to solve real problems is no easy task, nor something that can be taken for granted once the principles are known. Therefore, with the help of the proposed action theory, we can see how the primacy of work's subject over its object in *Laborem Exercens* can be realized in real work.

5. Action Theory and *Laborem Exercens*

With the help of Pérez López's theory of action, we have seen that the "action-reaction" dyad of agents depends on their internal states, both present and future. That is, it depends on the consideration of the operability and instrumentality of the agents—present structural relationship—and on the efficacy and consistency of an action plan—future structural relationship. The "action-reaction"—or operative relationship—is the extrinsic result of the interaction of the agents, that is, the "objective work." Therefore, the operative relation—the "extrinsic result" or "objective work"—presupposes and needs an adequate present and future structural relationship, which means that the "action-reaction"—the objective dimension of work—is intrinsically dependent on the subjective dimension of work.

As we have said, a decision that is effective but inefficient and inconsistent (negative learning) is a dynamic contradiction. What does this mean? Simply that the instrumentalization of any agent (as if it were a machine) will discourage a future operational relationship. Any organization whose agents cause negative learning, *ceteris paribus*, will invariably break down; it is condemned to real, not merely theoretical, failure. Hence, the consideration of the subjective dimension of work

30 *Id.*, sec. 7.
31 Fabrizio Ferraro, Jeffrey Pfeffer, and Robert I. Sutton, "Economics Language and Assumptions: How Theories Can Become Self-Fulfilling," *Academy of Management Review* 30, no. 1 (2005): 8–24; Jeffrey Pfeffer, "Why Do Bad Management Theories Persist? A Comment on Ghoshal," *Article in Academy of Management Learning and Education* 4, no. 1 (2005): 96–100.

over the objective, as the encyclical maintains, is not only an ethical issue; therein lies the very economic success of an organization. It should be noted that this is not a slogan like "good ethics is good business"; instead, it recognizes the economic implications of principles of *LE* given our proposed action theory.

Moreover, the distinction between operational and structural learning forces us to consider the ethical criteria of decision-making. First, making consistent decisions implies having a minimum of consideration for the subjectivity of the reactive agent. This means that the active agent must think explicitly about the other agent: what will happen to the reactive agent when the active agent implements this concrete plan of action? As the active agent does not know with certainty the internal state of the reactive agent (neither present nor future), he can make a reflexive simulation: if the reactive agent were to implement with him—the active agent—the same action plan that he intends to implement with the reactive agent, and with the same intentions that he has, would the active agent want to collaborate with him?[32] If the answer is negative, we would be facing a contradictory version of the system, and it therefore should be avoided (at least if we want to continue with the relationship). In turn, this formulation is none other than "the golden rule," the well-known ethical principle of universal value.[33] So, we can say that the evaluation includes an ethical assessment in its assumptions.

But the ethical implications go beyond the golden rule. To value what will happen to another person in the interaction, that is, to consider him explicitly in the decision, is to act in such a way that the active agent treats the reactive agent (or vice versa) always as an end and never simply as a means. This formulation is none other than that of Kant's second categorical imperative, which "is the most important [moral] principle to govern the relations of persons in the firm as the community of

---

32 Ariño, *Toma de Decisiones y Gobierno de Organizaciones.*

33 Domènec Melé, *Business Ethics in Action: Seeking Human Excellence in Organizations* (London: Palgrave Macmillan, 2009); Domènec Melé, "Integrating Personalism into Virtue-Based Business Ethics: The Personalist and the Common Good Principles," *Journal of Business Ethics* 88, no. 1 (2009): 227–44.

persons that it is."[34] This principle was taken up by Wojtyła and trans-formed into the "personalist principle."[35] This principle can be formu-lated positively—unlike the negative Kantian formulation—as follows: "people should be treated not only with respect, but with benevolence and care."[36] This provides a framework for ethical goodness in the de-cisional criteria we are analyzing.

Further, it is significant that both "operational and structural learning are the two types of internal results that are produced in a person *by the mere fact of having acted*, regardless of what comes from the outside or what happens to the people with whom he or she interacts";[37] these can be positive and negative learning. The notion of learning allows us to introduce another ethical tradition, Aristotelianism, through the notion of virtue. This is the path that Alasdair MacIntyre[38] has rediscovered and that Pérez López explicitly recognizes: "To speak of ethics without men-tioning the moral virtues is like speaking of mechanics without men-tioning gravitation: one would be making a more or less poetic discourse, but nothing that can resemble a rigorous analysis."[39] In the words of *La-borem Exercens*: "Work is a good thing for man—a good thing for his humanity—because through work man not only transforms nature, adapting it to his own needs, but he also *achieves fulfilment* as a human being and indeed, in a sense, becomes 'more a human being.'"[40]

This brief consideration brings the principles of subjective and ob-jective work closer to the manager's decision-making process. In other words, the only way to dignify work is to consider the internal states of

34 Carlos Llano, *Dilemas Éticos de La Empresa Contemporánea* (México D.F.: Fondo de Cultura Económica, 2015), 98.

35 Melé, "Integrating Personalism"; Karol Wojtyła, *Amor y Responsabilidad* (Madrid: Palabra, 2013).

36 Melé, *Business Ethics in Action*, 81.

37 Pablo Ferreiro and Manuel Alcázar, *Gobierno de Personas En La Empresa* (Lima: Planeta, 2012), 62.

38 Alasdair Macintyre, *After Virtue: A Study in Moral Theory*, 3rd ed. (In-diana: University of Notre Dame Press, 2007).

39 Juan Antonio Pérez López, *Liderazgo y Ética En La Dirección de Empresas* (Bilbao: Deusto, 1998), 26.

40 John Paul II, *Laborem Exercens*, sec. 9.

people involved in decisions, both now and in the future. A decision that is evaluated from the criteria of effectiveness, efficiency, and consistency implicitly considers the principles of *Laborem Exercens*.

6. Conclusion

As we have developed it throughout this chapter, Pérez López's theory of action allows us to bring the principles of *Laborem Exercens* closer to the real decisions of people in an organization by applying the three criteria of effectiveness, efficiency, and consistency. These criteria make it possible to put into practice the principles of work, in both its objective and subjective dimensions, as well as implicitly recognizing the principle of the dignity of the human person, which is the foundation of all Catholic Social Teaching.

The effectiveness of the decision, taken in its broadest sense, lies in the actions and reactions that transform reality and solve our problems—objective work. On the other hand, the efficiency and consistency of the decision allow us to take into account the subject of the work, the human person. Such consideration presupposes treating people not only as means but as ends in themselves, respecting their dignity. The repetition and success of these interactions will have an internal effect on the agents that, in the end, will allow better interactions with other people. This internal effect is operative improvement in the acting agent, which is what Catholic Social Teaching, following the Aristotelian tradition, has called virtue. These considerations allow us to conclude that using Pérez López's theory of action can bring the teachings of *Laborem Exercens* closer to the reality of organizational work by introducing criteria that make those teachings operational.

Laborem Exercens and the Subjective Dimension of Work in Economics and Finance

Geoffrey C. Friesen

Introduction

Most models in economics and finance treat work according to its objective characteristics: the objective dimension of work involves the person acting on external objects, creating goods and services via the well-known processes of economic production. Absent in these models, and nearly invisible to many in economics and finance, is the subjective dimension of work, which involves the "creative process" of work operating on the person performing the work.

Because persons tend toward self-realization, and because meaningful work is an integral part of the process of self-realization, the person is therefore also the proper subject of work. In the encyclical *Laborem Exercens*, John Paul II argues that the subjective dimension of work is primary and that the primary basis of the value of work is the person—the subject of work. This teaching lends itself to misinterpretation. Some have argued that this statement is consistent with certain forms of communism or socialism, where workers are paid according to need and not ability. My thesis is that this interpretation is incorrect. John Paul II does not mean that the *economic value* of work is independent of the work performed. He also does not mean that the compensation paid to the worker cannot or should not be in proportion to the marginal product or value of the work. I argue that the meaning is actually much deeper.

John Paul II states that the primary value of work is *not economic at all* since the wage itself represents a secondary value. He directly challenges the standard economic assumption that the wage is the sole motive for human action at work. By identifying the historical roots of this error, John Paul II also identifies the starting point for economists who seek to re-integrate the subjective dimension of work into economic and financial theory.

The fact/value dichotomy emphasized by the social sciences during the first part of the twentieth century is relevant: this broader division between fact and value facilitated the dichotomy between the objective and subjective dimensions of work in economics and finance. The movement towards a "value-free" economic science, championed by Pareto, Robbins, Fisher, and others, led to the elimination of the subjective dimension of work from economic and financial models. The resulting "objective-only" models rely exclusively upon the "logic of costly effort" in which work is viewed purely as a means to an end, with no inherent value or meaning itself.

Yet meaningful work is an integral part of being human. Meaningful work and the subjective dimension of work find support in biblical wisdom and modern science. This paper summarizes the subjective dimension of work as presented in *Laborem Exercens*; highlights modern scientific evidence that supports the legitimacy of the subjective dimension of work; presents a framework that integrates the subjective and objective dimensions of human work; and highlights the changes to our financial logic when this subjective dimension is given its proper place in economic and financial models.

Section 1: The Objective (Transitive) Dimension of Work

The transcendent nature of human work is a key idea introduced in the encyclical *Laborem Exercens*. John Paul II notes that even within the realm of our earthly existence, humans have a higher purpose that is rooted in our eternal nature and the transcendent destiny given to us by God. Speaking of the person, John Paul II describes

... the *eternal designs and transcendent destiny* which the living God, the Creator and Redeemer, has linked with him.[1]

In addition, because work is a fundamental part of our earthly existence, and because this earthly existence has a transcendent nature, work by its very nature contains transcendent characteristics:

> The Church finds in the very first pages of the Book of Genesis the source of her conviction that *work is a fundamental dimension of human existence on earth.* An analysis of these texts makes us aware that they express—sometimes in an archaic way of manifesting thought—the fundamental truths about man, in the context of the mystery of creation itself. These truths are decisive for man from the very beginning, and at the same time they trace out the main lines of his earthly existence, both in the state of original justice and also after the breaking, caused by sin, of the Creator's original covenant with creation in man.[2]

Before examining the transcendent nature of work, however, John Paul II begins with a description of the more familiar "transitive" aspects of work.

A. The Transitive Nature of Work

Work has several fundamentally different dimensions within this transcendent reality. The first, and the one most commonly associated with work in the modern economy, is the *objective,* or "transitive" nature of work, which is described in Sections 4 and 5 of *Laborem Exercens*:

> Work understood as a "transitive" activity, that is to say an activity beginning in the human subject and directed towards

1 John Paul II, *Laborem Exercens* (Vatican City: Libreria Editrice Vaticana, 1981), sec. 4, http://www.vatican.va/content/john-paul-ii/en/encyclicals/documents/hf_jp-ii_enc_14091981_laborem-exercens.html. Emphasis mine.
2 *Ibid.* Emphasis mine.

an external object, presupposes a specific dominion by man over "the earth," and in its turn it confirms and develops this dominion. It is clear that the term "the earth" of which the biblical text speaks is to be understood in the first place as that fragment of the visible universe that man inhabits. By extension, however, it can be understood as the whole of the visible world insofar as it comes within the range of man's influence and of his striving to satisfy his needs.

A transitive verb is a verb that requires a direct object; logical transitivity means that if *a* implies *b*, and *b* implies *c*, then *a* implies *c*. In a similar way, John Paul II characterizes the objective dimension of work with the word "transitive," which highlights the linear nature of the *objective dimension* in which the person works on external objects. This section introduces two other important qualities of work. First, there is the time-less nature of work. John Paul II does not mean to imply that specific jobs or precise types of work are always static through time. Rather, his point is that the objective dimension of work has been present through-out all periods of history and will remain relevant in any future phases of human development:

The expression "subdue the earth" has an immense range. It means all the resources that the earth (and indirectly the vis-ible world) contains and which, through the conscious activ-ity of man, can be discovered and used for his ends. And so these words, placed at the beginning of the Bible, never cease to be relevant. *They embrace equally the past ages of civi-lization and economy, as also the whole of modern reality and future phases of development*, which are perhaps already to some extent beginning to take shape, though for the most part they are still almost unknown to and hidden from him. While people sometimes speak of periods of "acceleration" in the economic life and civilization of humanity or of indi-vidual nations, linking these periods to the progress of sci-ence and technology and especially to discoveries which are decisive for social and economic life, at the same time it can be said that none of these phenomena of "acceleration" exceeds the essential content of what was said in that most ancient of biblical texts.[3]

A second important quality of work introduced in Section 4 is that it has both *collective (e.g., universal) and individual* aspects. This distinction, and the reality that work encompasses both, becomes vitally important in John Paul II's later development and presentation of the subjective dimension of work:

> As man, through his work, becomes more and more the master of the earth, and as he confirms his dominion over the visible world, again through his work, he nevertheless remains in every case and at every phase of this process within the Creator's original ordering. And this ordering remains necessarily and indissolubly linked with the fact that man was created, as male and female, "in the image of God." This process is, at the same time, *universal*: it embraces all human beings, every generation, every phase of economic and cultural development, and at the same time it is a process that takes place within *each human being,* in each conscious human subject.[4]

Figure 1 illustrates this distinction between the individual and the collective aspects of work:

FIGURE 1

Individual

Collective

3   *Ibid*. Emphasis mine.
4   *Ibid*. Emphasis mine.

A simple illustration highlighting the reality that work contains both individual and collective components. Figure 1 represents a benchmark that is expanded in Figures 2 and 3.

Section 4 of *Laborem Exercens* also highlights the specific historical epochs through which the objective dimension of work has developed:

> There thus emerges the meaning of work in an objective sense, which finds expression in the various epochs of culture and civilization. Man dominates the earth by the very fact of *domesticating animals*, rearing them and obtaining from them the *food and clothing* he needs, and by the fact of being able to extract various natural resources from the earth and the seas. But man "subdues the earth" much more when he begins to cultivate it and then to transform its products, adapting them to his own use. Thus *agriculture* constitutes through human work a primary field of economic activity and an indispensable factor of production. *Industry* in its turn will always consist in linking the earth's riches—whether nature's living resources, or the products of agriculture, or the mineral or chemical resources—with man's work, whether physical or intellectual.[5]

The historical epochs detailed in the encyclical correspond closely to those historical stages summarized by Wilber as foraging, horticulture, agrarian, industrial, and informational stages.[6] Wilber[7] also includes a prediction about those future stages "which are perhaps already to some extent beginning to take shape, though for the most part they are still almost unknown to and hidden from him."[8]

The development of advanced technologies, which corresponds to the most recent stage of development of work, has been accompanied

5   *Ibid.* Emphasis mine.
6   Ken Wilber, *Integral Spirituality: The role of spirituality in the modern and postmodern world* (N.p.: Integral Spiritual Center, 2007).
7   *Ibid.*
8   John Paul II, *Laborem Exercens*, sec. 4.

by both positive and negative outcomes. Upon closer examination, these outcomes represent aspects of an actual *relationship* between technology and the person. Inquiring into the nature of this relationship raises a number of questions; the ethical nature of these questions leads us directly into the subjective dimension of work.

Section 2: The Subjective Dimension of Work

While Section 5 of *Laborem Exercens* details the *objective* dimension of work, which has progressed through "various epochs of culture and civilization," Section 6 begins the encyclical's unpacking of the *subjective* dimension of work. Work in the objective dimension involves the person operating on an external object; work in the subjective dimension involves the work as a creative process operating on the agent performing the work. That is, the objective dimension of work is *transitive* in nature while the subjective dimension of work has a *reciprocal* nature because the process returns to the person as an inherent end.[9] Just as the creative Word of the Father goes forth and fruitfully returns, so the creative process of work bears the mark of its Creator in its subjective character.

A. Self-Actualization and the Subjective Dimension

Because the human person tends toward self-actualization and because meaningful work is an integral piece of self-actualization, the person is therefore also the subject of work:

> Man has to subdue the earth and dominate it, because as the "image of God" he is a person, that is to say, a subjective being capable of acting in a planned and rational way, capable of deciding about himself, and with a tendency to self-realization. As a person, man is therefore the subject to work. As

9   "So shall my word go forth out of my mouth: it shall not return unto me void, but it shall accomplish that which I please, and it shall prosper in the thing where I sent it" (Isaiah 55:11).

a person he works, he performs various actions belonging to the work process; independently of their objective content, these actions must all serve to realize his humanity, to fulfil the calling to be a person that is his by reason of his very humanity.[10]

Therefore, any work-related ethical question must begin with a proper consideration of the subjective dimension of the person and the subjective dimension of work. John Paul II tells us that the reality of the subjective dimension is rooted in our biblical understanding of the person:

> And so this "dominion" spoken of in the biblical text being meditated upon here refers not only to the objective dimension of work but at the same time introduces us to an understanding of its subjective dimension. Understood as a process whereby man and the human race subdue the earth, work corresponds to this basic biblical concept only when throughout the process man manifests himself and confirms himself as the one who "dominates." This dominion, in a certain sense, refers to the subjective dimension even more than to the objective one: this dimension conditions the very ethical nature of work. In fact there is no doubt that human work has an ethical value of its own, which clearly and directly remain linked to the fact that the one who carries it out is a person, a conscious and free subject, that is to say a subject that decides about himself.[11]

The recognition that there exist both objective and subjective dimensions of work immediately raises the question of how each dimension relates to the other, and which is more important. The decisive answer given by John Paul II may be incomprehensible to some economists:

10 John Paul II, *Laborem Exercens*, sec. 6.
11 *Ibid.*

> ... the basis for determining the value of human work is not primarily the kind of work being done but the fact that the one who is doing it is a person. The sources of the dignity of work are to be sought primarily in the subjective dimension, not in the objective one. Such a concept practically does away with the very basis of the ancient differentiation of people into classes according to the kind of work done. This does not mean that, from the objective point of view, human work cannot and must not be rated and qualified in any way. It only means that the primary basis of the value of work is man himself, who is its subject. *This leads immediately to a very important conclusion of an ethical nature: however true it may be that man is destined for work and called to it, in the first place work is "for man" and not man "for work."* Through this conclusion one rightly comes to recognize the pre-eminence of the subjective meaning of work over the objective one....[12]

This does not imply independence between the work performed and its *economic* value. It also does not preclude the wage paid from reflecting the marginal value of the work. John Paul II is making a deeper point and stating that the primary value of work is *not economic at all*. More specifically, the wage itself represents a secondary value of work. This is a challenging teaching, particularly within finance and economics where monetary compensation is assumed to be the singular motive for engaging in work. The subjective dimension, which John Paul II argues should be pre-eminent, is totally absent in financial and economic models. Section 6 concludes with a foreshadowing of why the subjective dimension of work is pre-eminent:

> On the other hand: independently of the work that every man does, and presupposing that this work constitutes a purpose—at times a very demanding one—of his activity, this purpose does not possess a definitive meaning in itself. In fact, in the final analysis it is always man who is the purpose of the work,

12   *Ibid.*

whatever work it is that is done by man—even if the common scale of values rates it as the merest "service," as the most monotonous, even the most alienating work....[13]

This line of thought continues in Sections 11 and 12, which provide a more detailed philosophical foundation for the primacy of the subjective dimension of work. Section 11 discusses the historical conflict between labor and capital, which began as a very real social conflict during the industrial revolution when workers "put their powers at the disposal of the entrepreneurs, and these, following the principle of maximum profit, tried to establish the lowest possible wages for the work done by the employees...."[14] The way in which the conflict played out as an ideological conflict between liberalism and Marxism, between the ideologies of capitalism and scientific socialism and communism, and the way this was transformed by political means into a systematic class struggle, is thoroughly documented elsewhere. It is not the focus of John Paul II in this encyclical. His focus is a more fundamental and foundational inquiry into the nature of work itself.

The key starting point in this inquiry is a recognition of the great reality of work, which is closely linked with man as the subject of work, since man himself develops through work. The development of the subjective dimension begins with the acknowledgement that all of the resources of economic production originate as a gift, freely given, from the Creator to mankind:

> In every phase of the development of his work man comes up against the leading role of the gift made by "nature," that is to say, in the final analysis, by the Creator. At the beginning of man's work is the mystery of creation. This affirmation, already indicated as my starting point, is the guiding thread of this document, and will be further developed in the last part of these reflections.[15]

13 *Ibid.*
14 *Id.*, sec. 11.
15 *Id.*, sec. 12.

In the historical conflict between labor and capital, the ideology of capitalism set the rights of capital over the rights of labor; the ideology of
communism took the opposite position. In Section 12, John Paul II highlights the instrumental nature of capital, and argues for the primacy of
the person over things. All of the means of economic production have
gradually developed through man's cumulative experience and intellectual powers. Thus, all of the technology and capital that are at the service
of work (e.g., "instruments") are the result of work. Capital is only an
instrument, a collection of things:

> All the means of production, from the most primitive to the ul-
> tramodern ones—it is man that has gradually developed them:
> man's experience and intellect. In this way there have appeared
> not only the simplest instruments for cultivating the earth but
> also, through adequate progress in science and technology, the
> more modern and complex ones: machines, factories, laborato-
> ries, and computers. Thus everything that is at the service of
> work, everything that in the present state of technology consti-
> tutes its ever more highly perfected "instrument," is the result
> of work ... We must emphasize and give prominence to the pri-
> macy of man in the production process, the primacy of man over
> things. Everything contained in the concept of capital in the strict
> sense is only a collection of things. Man, as the subject of work,
> and independently of the work that he does—man alone is a per-
> son. This truth has important and decisive consequences.[16]

B. The Primacy of the Human Person

John Paul II does not equate this primacy of labor over capital to an endorsement of communism. He argues that the dichotomy or separation
of labor and capital is philosophically impossible, and the historical conflict between labor and capital was a false choice that obscured the fundamental nature of work. The implications of the priority of labor over

16 *Ibid.*

capital are properly understood only when work itself is properly understood. Hence the need for a foundational development of the subjective dimension of work. Each dimension (the subjective and objective) contains both individual and collective aspects of work, and this 2 x 2 dichotomy is illustrated in Figure 2.

FIGURE 2

This figure illustrates how the subjective and objective dimensions of work each contain individual and collective components. The "collective + subjective" dimension is labeled "inter-subjective"; the "collective + objective" dimension is labelled "inter-objective." This framework will be used in Figure 3 to illustrate several determinants of human well-being that also have financial value implications for firms.

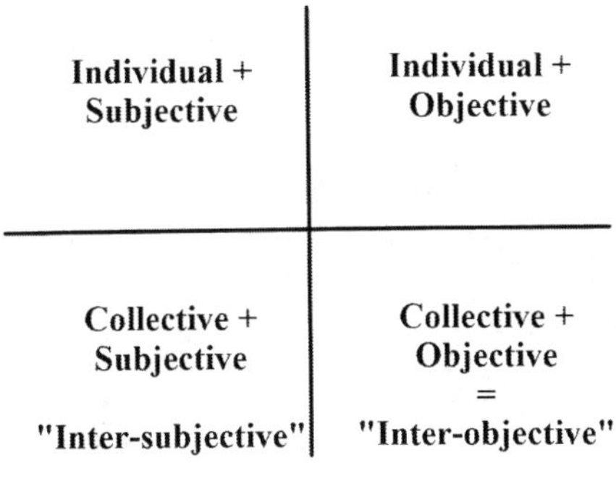

Individual + **Subjective**	**Individual +** **Objective**
Collective + **Subjective** **"Inter-subjective"**	**Collective +** **Objective** = **"Inter-objective"**

Section 3: First and Second Things

Sections 7 and 13 of *Laborem Exercens* focus on the values necessary for a proper framing of the relationship between labor and capital. A key idea is that the original and perennial errors of capitalism occur when the right ordering of values is reversed. This reversal, or inversion of primary and secondary values, leads to what Oliver O'Donovan calls a "totalizing of market theory" in which "… we are sometimes forced to treat as a loss what any sound philosophy regards as gain. Work, for example, a good gift of God and an experience of a person's intellectual and physical powers, is spoken of by the negative term 'labor' in order to represent the relation of worker and employee as an exchange rather than a partnership."

John Paul II begins Section 7 with a focus on the right ordering of values, and the inversion of primary and secondary values. The biblical understanding that originates in the Book of Genesis is obscured, or even reversed, in the modern materialistic civilization which

> ... gives prime importance to the objective dimension of work, while the subjective dimension—everything in direct or indirect relationship with the subject of work—remains on a secondary level. In all cases of this sort, in every social situation of this type, there is a confusion or even a reversal of the order laid down from the beginning by the words of the Book of Genesis: man is treated as an instrument of production, whereas he—he alone, independently of the work he does—ought to be treated as the effective subject of work and its true maker and creator. Precisely this reversal of order, whatever the program or name under which it occurs, should rightly be called "capitalism"—in the sense more fully explained below.[17]

Section 7 also highlights that this error can occur in any economy or market in which the person is subordinated to the instruments of production, which includes capital:

> Everybody knows that capitalism has a definite historical meaning as a system, an economic and social system, opposed to "socialism" or "communism." But in the light of the analysis of the fundamental reality of the whole economic process—first and foremost of the production structure that work is—it should be recognized that the error of early capitalism can be repeated wherever man is in a way treated on the same level as the whole complex of the material means

17 *Id.*, sec. 7.

of production, as an instrument and not in accordance with the true dignity of his work—that is to say, where he is not treated as subject and maker, and for this very reason as the true purpose of the whole process of production.[18]

A. The Historical Origins of the Error

Understanding the origins of the error and its historical emergence is the focus of Section 13. John Paul II asserts that from a philosophical viewpoint, the historical conflict between labor and capital was framed as a false choice. Elevating capital over labor can never be philosophically right, nor can it be reconciled with a Christian understanding of the person. In fact, "capital cannot be separated from labor; in no way can labor be opposed to capital or capital to labor, and still less can the actual people behind these concepts be opposed to each other...."[19] Any economic system that contains both labor and capital can be accurate only by ensuring the priority of labor over capital. Again, John Paul II emphasizes that this requires a foundation that explicitly recognizes both the objective and subjective dimensions of work. The person is always the subject of work that is conditioned by capital. But capital itself is never itself a subject, not even a nebulous or impersonal subject:

> Opposition between labor and capital does not spring from the structure of the production process or from the structure of the economic process ... All that we can say of everything in the production process which constitutes a whole collection of "things," the instruments, the capital, is that it conditions man's work; we cannot assert that it constitutes as it were an impersonal "subject" putting man and man's work into a position of dependence.[20]

Thus, nothing inherent in the production process requires labor and capital

18 *Ibid.*
19 *Id.*, sec. 13.
20 *Ibid.*

to be in opposition. The philosophies of economism and materialism separated labor and capital and set them in opposition by considering human
labor exclusively according to its economic purpose. The historical roots
of this are described in Section 13:

> This consistent image, in which the principle of the primacy
> of person over things is strictly preserved, was broken up in
> human thought, sometimes after a long period of incubation
> in practical living. The break occurred in such a way that
> labor was separated from capital and set in opposition to it,
> and capital was set in opposition to labor, as though they were
> two impersonal forces, two production factors juxtaposed in
> the same "economistic" perspective. This way of stating the
> issue contained a fundamental error, what we can call the
> error of *economism*, that of considering human labor solely
> according to its economic purpose. This fundamental error
> of thought can and must be called an error of *materialism*, in
> that economism directly or indirectly includes a conviction
> of the primacy and superiority of the material, and directly
> or indirectly places the spiritual and the personal (man's ac-
> tivity, moral values and such matters) in a position of subor-
> dination to material reality.[21]

Economism pre-dated materialism, and pre-framed the issue by viewing
labor in a non-humanistic way. But even dialectical materialism is incapable of thinking about human work in a way that supports the primacy
of man over capital:

> ... the fundamental issue of human work, in particular for the
> separation of labor and capital and for setting them up in oppo-
> sition as two production factors viewed in the above mentioned
> economistic perspective; and it seems that economism influ-
> enced this non-humanistic way of stating the issue before the
> materialist philosophical system did. Nevertheless it is obvious

21 *Ibid.*

that materialism, including its dialectical form, is incapable of providing sufficient and definitive bases for thinking about human work, in order that the primacy of man over the capital instrument, the primacy of the person over things, may find in it adequate and irrefutable confirmation and support.[22]

Interestingly, John Paul II states that this error did not originate in the philosophy or economic theories of the eighteenth century, but originated in the whole of economic and social practice of that time. It was a "practical error" or an error that eventually made its way into formal philosophies, and it was during the Industrial Revolution that society focused on the means (increasing wealth) while ignoring the ends (humans) who should be served by wealth:

> Obviously, the antinomy between labor and capital under consideration here—the antinomy in which labor was separated from capital and set up in opposition to it...—did not originate merely in the philosophy and economic theories of the eighteenth century; rather it originated in the whole of the economic and social practice of that time, the time of the birth and rapid development of industrialization, in which what was mainly seen was the possibility of vastly increasing material wealth, means, while the end, that is to say, man, who should be served by the means, was ignored. It was *this practical error* that struck a blow first and foremost against human labor, against the working man, and caused the ethically just social reaction already spoken of above. The same error, which is now part of history, and which was connected with the period of primitive capitalism and liberalism, can nevertheless be repeated in other circumstances of time and place, if people's thinking starts from the same theoretical or practical premises.

The only chance there seems to be for radically overcoming this error is through adequate changes both in theory and in

22 *Ibid.*

practice, changes in line with the definite conviction of the primacy of the person over things, and of human labor over capital as a whole collection of means of production.[23]

B. The Subject/Object and Fact/Value Dichotomies

The dichotomy and separation of the objective and subjective dimensions of work is related to the fact/value dichotomy that accompanied the early twentieth-century movement of logical positivism. In fact, logical positivism contributed to the marginalization and elimination of the subjective dimension of work from models in economics and finance.

Wilfred Pareto and Lionel Robbins were influential advocates of "value-free" economic models designed to explain how things are (e.g., positive economics). The positivists argued that science must be concerned exclusively with facts and therefore cannot contain normative vocabulary. For example, Robbins argued that interpersonal utilities cannot be compared because doing so requires one to make a value-based assessment of the individuals in question.[24] But, as pointed out by Little, any attempt to draw a sharp line between fact and value turns out to be impossible.[25]

The positive economic models thus developed with a focus on explaining how people actually behave, eliminating any framework or vocabulary that might consider how people *should* or *could* behave. Thus, the models focused exclusively on the objective dimension of work. (In defense of the positive economists, this assumption may have reflected accurately the economic reality of profit-maximizing behavior. Such behavior had developed during the long period of incubation of the previously described "practical error" in which capital was elevated to a dominant position over labor.)

---

23 *Ibid.*
24 Lionel Robbins, *An Essay on the Nature and Significance of Economic Science* (London: Macmillan and Co., 1932).
25 Daniel Little, "*Review of the end of value-free economics*, edited by Hilary Putnam and Vivian Walsh. Routledge, 2011," *Erasmus Journal for Philosophy and Economics* 5, no. 1 (2011), 87–92.

But what was not accurate, and did not reflect the reality of the person, was another more subtle assumption Robbins made about work itself.[26] For example, Robbins describes a "man dividing time between production of real income and enjoyment of leisure."[27] Though man wants both, he cannot fully satisfy his wants of each, and he has to choose one over the other. "Everywhere we turn, if we choose one thing we must relinquish others which, in different circumstances, we would wish not to have relinquished" and therefore "Economic Science is that which studies human behavior as a relationship between ends and scarce means which have alternate uses."[28] At one level, these statements simply capture the elementary notion of opportunity cost that is central to economics. Yet this framework also invokes a subtle assumption: labor is fundamentally a means to an end, not an end in itself. Work has no meaning outside of the income it provides.

C. The Scientific Evidence

These assumptions are directly at odds with the findings of modern social science. Diener and Seligman survey the scientific evidence-based determinants of human utility and human flourishing and find that while material and physical resources are one determinant, other key determinants exist.[29] Among these are physical and mental health, a democratic and stable society, reputation, meaningful relationships, transcendent purpose, goal value congruence, and meaningful work.[30] According to

---

26 Robbins, *Nature and Significance of Economic Science.*

27 *Id.*, 12.

28 *Id.*, 15.

29 Ed Diener and Martin Seligman, "Beyond Money: Toward an Economy of Well-Being," *Psychological Science in the Public Interest* 5, no. 1 (July 2004), 1–31.

30 For references to the large body of literature documenting these determinants of human well-being, see Martin Seligman, *Authentic Happiness* (N.p.: Atria Books, 2002); Martin Seligman and Mihaly Csiksentmihalyi, "Positive Psychology," *American Psychologist* 55, no. 1 (2000): 5–14; Ed Diener and Martin Seligman, "Beyond Money: Toward an Economy of Well-Being," *Psychological Science in the Public Interest* 5, no. 1 (July 2004): 1–31; Albert

the Gallup World Poll, the number one determinant of human happiness is not wealth, not health, not even family; it is a "good job": meaningful work done in the company of people we care about. Gallup CEO Jim Clifton notes: "What the world wants is a good job. This is one of the most important discoveries Gallup has ever made."[31] These determinants are illustrated in Figure 3, also presented in Friesen,[32] and arranged according to the individual-collective and subjective-objective categorizations in Figure 2.

Note that the subjective determinants of well-being, as illustrated on the left-hand side of Figure 3, correspond directly to the subjective dimension of work and include meaningful work, goal-value congruence, transcendent purpose, and meaningful relationships. Figure 3 helps illustrate the simple reason these value-relevant determinants of well-being are excluded from models in economics and finance: they all belong to the subjective dimension of work. Models that omit the subjective dimension simply cannot incorporate these aspects of work or human utility.

FIGURE 3

Figure 3 illustrates the determinants of human utility, or "flourishing", described by Diener and Seligman[33] and arranged according to the 2x2 matrix illustrated in Figure 2. The collective+subjective dimension is

Bandura, *Social Foundations of Thought and Action: A Social Cognitive Theory* (Englewood Cliffs, NJ: Prentice Hall, 1986); Fred Luthans, Bruce Avolio, James Avey, and Steven Norman, "Positive Psychological Capital: Measurement and Relationship with Performance and Satisfaction," *Personnel Psychology* 60, no. 3 (2007): 541–72; John Paul II, *Centesimus Annus* (Vatican City: Libreria Editrice Vaticana, 1991), http://www.vatican.va/content/john-paul-ii/en/encyclicals/documents/hf_jp-ii_enc_01051991_centesimus-annus.html; and Tyler VanderWeele, "On the Promotion of Human Flourishing," *Proceedings of the National Academy of Sciences* 114, no. 31 (2017): 8148–56.

31 Jim Clifton, *The Coming Jobs War* (Omaha: Gallup Press, 2011).
32 Geoffrey Friesen, "Human Flourishing and the Subjective Dimension of Work," *Faith & Economics* (Forthcoming).
33 Diener and Seligman, "Beyond Money."

labelled "intersubjective" while the collective + objective dimension is labeled "interobjective." Note that the subjective dimension of work is illustrated on the left-hand side of Figure 3 and includes meaningful work, goal-value congruence, transcendent purpose, and meaningful relationships.

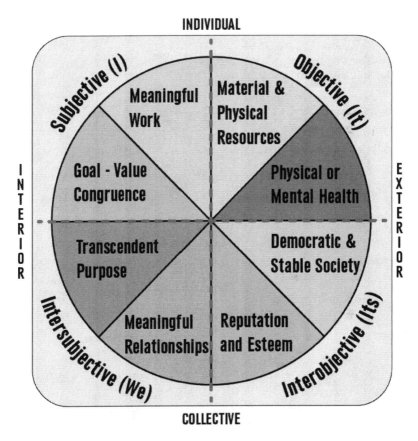

© 2020, Geoffrey C. Friesen

D. A Closer Look at the Historical Error

It is useful to see exactly what Robbins says about the assumption that work cannot be regarded as inherently meaningful, because this helps us know where to begin the error correction process:

This, then, is all that lies behind the occasional appearance of the homo œconomicus—the purely formal assumption that in certain exchange relationships all the means, so to speak, are on one side and all the ends on the other. If, e.g., for purposes of demonstrating the circumstances in which a single price will emerge in a limited market, it is assumed that in my dealings in that market I always buy from the cheapest seller, it is not assumed at all that I am necessarily actuated by egotistical motives. On the contrary, it is well known that the impersonal relationship postulated is to be seen in its purest form when trustees, not being in a position to allow themselves the luxury of more complicated relationships, are trying to make the best terms for the estates they administer. *All that it means is that my relation to the dealers does not enter into my hierarchy of ends. For me* (who may be acting for myself or my friends or some civic or charitable authority) *they are regarded merely as means.* Or, again, if it is assumed—which in fact is usually done for purposes of showing by contrast what the total influences in equilibrium bring about—that I sell my labor always in the dearest market, *it is not assumed that money and self-interest are my ultimate objects*—I may be working entirely to support some philanthropic institution. *It is assumed only that, so far as that transaction is concerned, my labor is only a means to an end; it is not to be regarded as an end in itself.*[34]

The assumption about work never being an end in itself is hard-wired into nearly all models of competitive markets and applied to nearly all models of the firm in finance. But it contradicts both biblical wisdom and modern social science, as well as empirical evidence regarding economic value creation in the modern firm. As Diener and Seligman note:

… economic indicators were extremely important in the early stages of economic development, when the fulfillment of

34 Robbins, *Nature and Significance of Economic Science,* 89. Emphasis mine.

basic needs was the main issue. As societies grow wealthy, however, differences in well-being are less frequently due to income, and are more frequently due to factors such as social relationships and enjoyment at work.[35]

The reason these factors are so difficult to include in finance models is because they require a fundamental re-ordering of our understanding of value and the economic relationship between humans, wealth, and work, and they specifically require a model that integrates *both* the objective *and* subjective dimensions of human work.

One consequence of eliminating the subjective dimension of work from economic models is that it also eliminates the foundation for "win-win" economic situations. Trade-off logic describes situations where benefits to one party necessarily come at the expense of the other. Engagement logic captures win-win situations, where benefits to one party also lead to benefits for the other. The subjective dimension of work is the foundation for engagement logic. When the legitimacy of the subjective dimension was denied, Robbins recognized that this also implied the impossibility of win-win situations. The axiomatic rejection of the possibility of win-win situations can be seen in the famous debate between Lionel Robbins and Sir Josiah Stamp. Robbins paved the way for the *ex ante* rejection of win-win situations by arguing that since such situations cannot *always* exist, economists are justified in assuming that they *never* exist.

The background was an on-going debate in England about the extent to which historical artifacts and monuments should be preserved during industrial expansion. This debate reached its apex in the early 1930s at the time both men's public influence was high. Robbins first characterizes Stamp's position:

> Sir Josiah, who has done so much to maintain sweetness and light in our times, is anxious to preserve the countryside and to safeguard ancient monuments. (The occasion of the paper was a decision on the part of his railway company not to

35   Diener and Seligman, "Beyond Money."

destroy Stratford House, a sixteenth-century half-timbered building in Birmingham, to make room for railway sidings.) At the same time, he believes that Economics is concerned with material welfare. He is, therefore, driven to argue that "indifference to the æsthetic will in the long run lessen the economic product; that attention to the æsthetic will increase economic welfare." That is to say, that if we seek first the Kingdom of the Beautiful, all material welfare will be added unto us. And he brings all the solid weight of his authority to the task of stampeding the business world into believing that this is true.[36]

Next, Robbins points out what he believes to be the flaw in Stamp's viewpoint but not before first mischaracterizing Stamp's position. Stamp merely argued that win-win situations might *sometimes* exist. Robbins argues that because such situations do not *always* exist, economists are justified assuming that such situations *never* exist:

> It is easy to sympathize with the intention of the argument. But it is difficult to believe that its logic is very convincing. It may be perfectly true, as Sir Josiah contends, that the wide interests fostered by the study of ancient monuments and the contemplation of beautiful objects are both stimulating to the intelligence and restful to the nervous system, and that, to that extent, a community which offers opportunities for such interests may gain in other, "more material," ways. But it is surely an optimism, unjustified either by experience or by a priori probability, to assume that this *necessarily* follows. It is surely a fact which we must all recognize that rejection of material comfort in favor of æsthetic or ethical values does not *necessarily* bring material compensation. There are cases when it is *either* bread *or* a lily. Choice of the one involves sacrifice of the other, and, although we may be satisfied with our choice, we cannot delude ourselves that it was not really

36 Robbins, *Nature and Significance of Economic Science,* 28.

a choice at all, that more bread will follow. It is not true that all things work together for material good to them that love God. So far from postulating a harmony of ends in this sense, Economics brings into full view that conflict of choice which is one of the permanent characteristics of human existence. Your economist is a true tragedian.[37]

Perhaps the real tragedy is that win-win situations, rooted in the subjective dimension of work, were eliminated from economic thinking for nearly a century after this debate. What Robbins' argument fails to make room for is the possibility of reciprocal determinism in economics,[38] or more specifically the feedback between the realization of certain ends and the means by which those ends are themselves produced. Robbins sees this clearly and articulates it:

What has happened, of course, is that adherence to the "materialist" definition has prevented Sir Josiah from recognizing clearly that Economics and Æsthetics are not in pari materia. Æsthetics is concerned with certain kinds of ends. The Æsthetic is an end which offers itself for choice in competition, so to speak, with others. Economics is not concerned at all with any ends as such. It is concerned with ends in so far as they affect the disposition of means. It takes the ends as given in scales of relative valuation, and enquires what consequences follow in regard to certain aspects of behavior.[39]

Robbins' view is limited to precisely what John Paul II referred to as the "transitive" dimension of work, with man operating on external objects to earn a wage, which is a means to other ends. Robbins rejects

37 *Id.*, 28–29. Emphasis mine.
38 Albert Bandura, *Social Foundations of Thought and Action: A Social Cognitive Theory* (Englewood Cliffs, NJ: Prentice Hall, 1986); Robert Shiller, *Narrative Economics: How Stories Go Viral and Drive Major Economic Events* (Princeton: Princeton University Press, 2019).
39 Robbins, *Nature and Significance of Economic Science,* 29.

the possibility of meaningful work by assuming that the subjective dimension *does not* and *cannot* exist.

Section 4: Work, Self-Actualization, and Integral Human Development

In another publication I have noted "a key empirical discovery by modern social science is that people progress systematically through stages of growth and development and meaningful work arises or emerges as a key source of human growth—and key determinant of human 'utility'—only after other needs are met."[40] These stages characterize the physical stages of development that occur over the human life span as well as intellectual and cognitive stages, psychosocial development, stages of moral development, faith, and consciousness

A. Stages of Human Development

The relevance of this scientific insight for finance and economics is that the agents in economics and finance models are always at the same stage of development across all of these different dimensions. To see this, think about an individual characterized by a formal-operational level of cognitive development.[41] The corresponding moral stance focuses upon law and order, the importance of the social contract, and individual rights.[42] The corresponding sense of self is ordered toward conscientious conformity and pursuit of individual interests.[43] The corresponding consciousness emphasizes exterior realities and exterior action.[44] Maslow notes that the person at this stage of development possesses "esteem

---

40 Friesen, "Human Flourishing and the Subjective Dimension of Work," 22–23.

41 See, e.g., Jean Piaget, *The Psychology of Intelligence* (Totowa, NJ: Littlefield, 1972).

42 Lawrence Kohlberg, *Essays on Moral Development, Vol. I: The Philosophy of Moral Development* (San Francisco, CA: Harper & Row, 1981).

43 Jane Loevinger, *Ego Development* (San Francisco: Jossey-Bass, 1976).

44 Jean Gebser, *The Ever-Present Origin,* trans. by Noel Barstad with Algis Mickunas (Athens: Ohio University Press, 1985).

needs" such as developing a positive reputation and the respect of others, prestige, accomplishment, and material wealth.[45] There is also a strong drive for exterior achievement.[46]

In another publication I have noted that the human needs associated with *these developmental stages* accurately correspond to the economic agents in current finance models.[47] That is, the agents in finance models reflect a *particular* stage of human development. Diener and Seligman explain that this stage of human development characterized the era when neoclassical models in economics and finance were developed.[48]

But this very limited vision of the person that dominates economics and finance is inconsistent with a true understanding of our human nature, as described in the publication *Oeconomicae et pecuniieariae quaestiones*:

> The human person, however, actually possesses a uniquely relational nature and has a sense for the perennial search for gains and well-being that may be more comprehensive, and not reducible either to a logic of consumption or to the economic spheres of life.[49]

Part of having an appropriate vision of the human person is recognizing the reality of human growth and integral human development. The agents in economic models may learn, but Bayesian learning is not the same as interior or moral growth and development. This meaning of the word "growth" is absent in economic vocabulary.

---

45 Abraham Maslow, *Motivation and Personality* (New York: Harper & Row, 1970).

46 Clare Graves, *Levels of Human Existence*, Seminar Transcript, Washington School of Psychiatry, October 16, 1971 (N.p.: ECLET Publishing, 2002).

47 Geoffrey Friesen, "Human Flourishing and the Self-limiting Assumptions of Modern Finance," *Journal of Business and Professional Ethics* (Forthcoming).

48 Diener and Seligman, "Beyond Money."

49 Congregation for the Doctrine of the Faith Dicastery for Promoting Integral Human Development, *Oeconomicae et pecuniieariae quaestiones (Considerations for an Ethical Discernment Regarding Some Aspects of the Present Economic-Financial System)* (Rome: N.p., 2018), sec. II.9.

Let us return to the economic agent *homo economicus*: the next stage of development for the agent includes a need for learning, growth, aesthetic appreciation, and self-actualization;[50] an emphasis on principles of justice, equity, and human rights;[51] the growth into autonomy (Quinn and Thakor, 2019),[52] a state in which one is not only able to synthesize or integrate apparently distinct ideas, but also recognizes an inherent autonomy or emotional interdependence with others;[53] and an emphasis on human relationships.[54]

Abraham Maslow was one of the first to highlight the notion of "self-actualization," which he defines as the realization of personal growth, being fully engaged in one's work, and living out one's mission. In short, a desire "to become everything one is capable of becoming" is one of the highest human needs.[55] One sees a close connection to the human described by John Paul II as "a subjective being capable of acting in a planned and rational way, capable of deciding about himself, and with a tendency to self-realization."[56]

B. The Fact/Value Dichotomy

The objective/subjective dichotomy arose during the same historical period as the broader fact/value dichotomy in social sciences. Interestingly, the division of work into objective and subjective dimensions corresponds almost one-to-one with a division of human needs into deficiency and growth needs. A feeling of *lack* motivates human action concerning deficiency needs (e.g., "I am thirsty, so I seek water"). As deficiency needs are satisfied, the motivation for further action *decreases* (e.g., "I

50 Maslow, *Motivation and Personality*.
51 Kohlberg, *Essays on Moral Development, Vol. 1.*
52 Richard Ryan and Edward Deci, "Self-determination theory and the facilitation of intrinsic motivation, social development, and well-being," *American Psychologist* 55, no. 1 (2000); 68–78.
53 Loevinger, *Ego Development.*
54 Graves, *Levels of Human Existence.*
55 Maslow, *Motivation and Personality.*
56 John Paul II, *Laborem Exercens*, sec. 6.

am no longer thirsty, so I no longer seek water"). With growth needs, a feeling or sense of fulfillment motivates human action. The satisfaction of growth needs increases motivation for further action. Learning, meaningful and engaging work, self-actualization, and the pursuit of the transcendent are concrete examples of growth needs.

In another publication I have noted that the reason that economic agents are not fully human is because "economic man" does not seek self-actualization.[57] When the subjective dimension of work is eliminated from economic models, the result is that growth needs are implicitly assumed not to exist. This is the practical explanation for why economic and financial models almost never include growth needs. This tradition dates back at least to the work of Robbins described earlier,[58] as well as Weber[59] and Fisher.[60] In this tradition, human growth needs and the subjective dimension of human work are assumed to be *reducible* into the objective dimension.

The practical result is that finance and economics models lack the necessary framework for thinking about the dignity of human work. Worker utility or worker well-being is modeled as a simple function of wealth and leisure. Wealth and leisure are in turn assumed to be inversely related (e.g., the more time I spend working the less leisure time I have left). In the neoclassical model of the firm, a wage is set sufficiently high to entice the agent to work, but no higher: the equilibrium wage is just high enough to compensate for the disutility of labor, and in equilibrium the worker's participation constraint is "binding." This means that overall utility of the worker is no higher (or only marginally higher) by working than not working. This leaves us in a state of "model poverty," without a framework that captures the subjective dimension of work, incapable of even thinking about the creative process of work operating on the person.

57 Friesen, "Human Flourishing and the Subjective Dimension of Work."
58 Robbins, *Nature and Significance of Economic Science.*
59 Max Weber, "'Objectivity' in Social Science," in *Sociological Writings*, ed. Wolf Heydebrand (New York: Continuum, 1994).
60 Irving Fisher, *The Theory of Interest* (New York: The Macmillan Company, 1930).

C. The Logic of Engagement

The "principal-agent framework" is a term used in economics and finance to describe the relationship between the owner (principal) and manager (agent) of a firm. Under trade-off logic, actions that benefit the principal always come at the expense of the agent. Compensation is paid to the risk-averse agent who responds by providing costly effort. The principal-agent relationship is an inherently adversarial *either/or* relationship, where benefits to one party come at the expense of the other. In another publication, I have noted that because human engagement and human dignity are associated with growth needs (not deficiency needs) they are incompatible with the conventional economic logic of costly effort.[61]

In contrast to the logic of costly effort, the logic of engagement captures a framework in which actions benefitting the agent can also benefit the principal. A "new" source of human utility is a sense of meaning, engagement, or higher purpose. What is different about engagement is that increases in the utility of the agent are associated with increases in the output of the firm, as illustrated in the Figure 4 which is also presented by me in another paper.[62] While "objective effort" is costly to the employee but beneficial to the firm's owners, "subjective engagement" can lead to higher utility for the agent *and* improvements in firm performance that benefit the principal.

The new logic supplements existing economic logic and conventional models; it does not replace them. Economic trade-offs, rooted in human deficiency needs, do not go away. At the same time, they cannot fully describe the human person or the firm, because growth needs are a part of human reality. It is possible to promote human flourishing *and* create value, but only if the subjective dimension of human flourishing has legitimacy in financial and economic decisions. The formal implications of this integrated framework are worked out in detail in another paper of mine.[63]

---

61 Friesen, "Human Flourishing and the Subjective Dimension of Work."
62 *Ibid.*
63 Geoffrey Friesen, "Finance, human flourishing and the logic of stakeholder engagement," Working Paper, University of Nebraska-Lincoln (2020).

Figure 4: The Logic of Costly Effort and the Logic of Engagement

The right-hand side illustrates the impact of costly effort on worker utility (top figure) and firm output (bottom figure) and corresponds to the existing financial and economic framework. The left-hand side illustrates the impact of engagement on worker utility (top figure) and firm output (bottom figure).

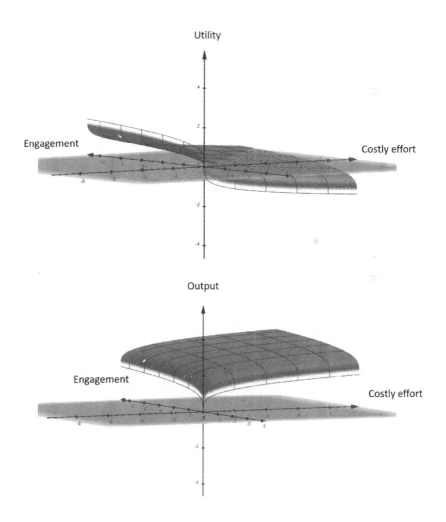

Discussion and Conclusion

It is through an explicit recognition of the subjective dimension of work that the worker fully realizes his "calling to be a person that is his by reason of his very humanity."[64] The integration of the subjective and objective dimensions of work into economics and finance models does not require that existing models be discarded, but that models be expanded so that both dimensions coexist in a properly ordered framework with the subjective dimension being primary. As John Paul II states, "The only chance there seems to be for radically overcoming this error is through adequate changes both in theory and in practice, changes in line with the definite conviction of the primacy of the person over things, and of human labor over capital as a whole collection of means of production."[65]

Integration of the subjective dimension into models in economics and finance is partially important because these models inform our thinking and influence the framing of important decisions. These decisions, in turn, help to shape our social and business environments. Thus, the assumptions embedded in our models can actually affect the world. As discussed above, the historical separation of the objective and subjective dimensions of work has led to the development of economic models that completely ignore the subjective dimension. In turn, the elimination of the subjective dimension from models has helped shape an environment where the role of work in the development of the person lacks legitimacy. The use of "self-limiting" models creates a self-fulfilling reality that reinforces the original error; the discarded subjective dimension of work becomes unimportant, irrelevant, or even imaginary. *Laborem Exercens* is a reminder of a timeless truth our current models have discarded:

> ... the Church has always proclaimed what we find expressed in modern terms in the teaching of the Second Vatican Council: "Just as human activity proceeds from man, so it is or-

64   John Paul II, *Laborem Exercens*, sec. 6.
65   *Id.*, sec. 13.

dered towards man. For when a man works he not only alters things and society, he develops himself as well. He learns much, he cultivates his resources, he goes outside of himself and beyond himself. Rightly understood, this kind of growth is of greater value than any external riches which can be garnered...."[66]

---

66 *Id.*, sec. 26.

- Fr. Giulio Maspero is Professor of Dogmatic Theology and Vice Dean of the Faculty of Theology at the Pontifical University of Santa Croce.
- Patricia Ranft is Professor Emerita of History, Central Michigan University.
- Angela Franks is Professor of Theology, Saint John's Seminary (Boston).
- Deborah Savage is Professor of Theology and Director of Catholic Management Theory and Practice at Franciscan University of Steubenville.
- Msgr. Martin Schlag is Professor of Catholic Studies and Professor of Ethics and Business Law, Alan W. Moss Endowed Chair for Catholic Social Thought, and Director of the John A. Ryan Institute for Catholic Social Thought at the University of St. Thomas (Minnesota).
- Rev. Richard Turnbull is the Director of the Centre for Enterprise, Markets and Ethics, Oxford, and visiting Professor at St Mary's University, Twickenham.
- Michael Naughton is Professor of Catholic Studies, Koch Chair of Catholic Studies, and the Director of the Center for Catholic Studies at the University of St. Thomas (Minnesota).
- Christopher Michaelson is Professor of Business Ethics and Law, the Opus Distinguished Professor of Principled Leadership, and the Academic Director of the Melrose and The Toro Company Center for Principled Leadership, University of St. Thomas (Minnesota).
- Javier Pinto-Garay is Assistant Professor of Business Ethics at ESE Business School, Universidad de los Andes, and President of the Association of Business and Organizational Ethics of Chile.
- Alvaro Pezoa Bissieres is Academic Director of the ESE Business School and Professor of Ethics and Business Humanism at the Universidad de los Andes and is a Research Fellow at the W. Michael Hoffman Center for Business Ethics at Bentley University.
- Gonzalo Flores-Castro Lingán is Professor of Philosophy and Organizational Behavior at the Universidad Católica San Pablo.
- Geoffrey Friesen is Associate Professor of Finance at the University of Nebraska-Lincoln.

Index

Note: Page number with an f indicates a figure. Page number with an 'n' indicated the information is in the notes

Abraham, covenant with, 18
acceleration processes, 193, 193n14
acquired contemplation, 121
The Acting Person (Wojtyla), 165–66n6
action theory, 212, 214–18, 220–23
Adam
    creation of, 85–86
    descendants of, 16
    good and evil, 13–16
    Adam's preternatural gift, 86n23
    relationship with the earth, 11
Adam of Dryburg, 42
Adelaine, Duchess, 43
Aelred of Rievaux, 47
affirmation of ordinary life, 63–68
agriculture, 146, 152, 229
agriculture revolution, 35, 57–58
almsgiving, 62
Ambrose, 27–30
Ancrene Wisse (rule for women recluses), 49
anxiety, 131, 132, 133
Apollinarism, 22–23
Apostolicam Actuositatem (Vatican II), 69
Aquinas, Thomas. *See* Thomas Aquinas, Saint
Arianism, 22
Aristotelian doctrine of form identity, 9

Aristotelianism, 222
Aristotle, 12, 61, 116
Arnold, Matthew, 68
artificial intelligence (AI), 191
Asia, 178, 204
Augustine, Saint, 2, 28–31, 182
Augustinian theology, 66
automation, 191
automatization, 206–8, 207–8n50
autonomy, 98, 180, 185, 196, 207, 207–8n50, 250
avarice, condemnation of, 61–63

Babylon, 7, 17–18
Bacon, Francis, 66, 78–79
Baldwin of Ford, 46–47
Balthasar, Hans Urs von, 70
Bardeen, John, 194
basic system model, 215f
Basil, 26, 27
Beatrice of Tuscany, 42, 43
Beatrijs of Nazareth, 54
Beguines (apostolic group), 52–53
Benedict XVI, Pope Emeritus (previously Ratzinger, Joseph), 90, 140
Benedictine monasticism, 35
Benedictine Rule, 40, 46
Berkhof, Louis, 140
Bernard, Margrave, 43
Bernard of Clairvaux, 47

Bernard of Cluny, 36
Bible
    development and use of, 136–38
    New Testament (*See* New Testament)
    Old Testament (*See* Old Testament)
    rest, understanding of, 9, 28–30
    work, understanding of, 7–12, 18–22
big data, 191
blockchains, 191
The Book of Divine Works, (Hildegard), 50
Book of the Rewards of Life (Hildegard), 49
Bosch, Vicente, 122
Bouchard, Constance, 48
Bowie, Norman E., 185, 187–88
Brattain, Walter, 194
Brenkert, George, 207–8n50
Buddhism, Buddhist, 111
Burkhart, Ernst, 128
Busa, Roberto, 195n20
business, 97–98, 110, 151–52
business ethics, 4–5
Business Ethics Theory, 189–192, 211
Buttiglione, Rocco, 74, 76

Calvin, John
    biographical information, 135–36
    Commentary on Genesis 2:15, 138, 140
    Commentary on Romans, 156
    Commentary on the Harmony of the Evangelists, 139
    common grace, 141
    cosmological principle, 139
    creation and human work, 138–39
    exploitative business practices, 152
    gifts enabling creativity and innovation, 144
    hardship and work, 146
    Institutes of the Christian Religion, 135, 140
    labor for the glory of God, 151
    natural law, 141–42
    oversight of the family, 154
    state, role of, 156
    talents, use of, 141
    value of work, 146–47
Calvinism, Calvinists, 65, 66, 146
Canon Law, Contemporary Catholic, 126n53
Canons Regular movement, 41–42
Capital (Marx), 73
capitalism, capital
    antinomy, labor and capital, 239–240
    as collection of things, 148, 234
    description of, 93
    economic system and, 99–100, 236–37
    error of, 203n40, 243–48
    goods for society and, 97–98
    ideological conflicts, 233
    labor, relationship with, 150, 203n39, 233–34, 237–240
    laissez-faire, 92, 94, 99
    owners of capital, 96–97
Caritas in Veritate encyclical (Benedict XVI), 90, 140
Carmelites, Order of, 56
Catechism of the Catholic Church
    mystical state, 122
    private ownership of goods, 97n55
Cathars (apostolic group), 52
Catherine of Louvain, 54
Catholic Social Teaching (CST), 189–192, 201–2, 213–14
Catholic Social Thought
    complementarity, as mission, 82–84

documentary heritage of, 80–81
feminine and masculine genius, 84–90, 89n31
reordering principles of, 92–102
socio-economic context, 90–92, 99
women and, 80–82
Catholicism, Roman Catholicism
Contemporary Catholic Canon Law, 126n53
contributions in the Church, 79–80, 102–9
spiritual work in medieval era, 146
state, role of, 158
view of 'call,' 70, 147
Centesimus Annus encyclical (John Paul II), 4, 79–80, 92–102, 114, 191
Chalmers, Thomas, 158
change, effects of, 216
character
formation of, 1–2, 168, 170
inductive character, 179–180
moral character, 164, 172
normative character, 213–14
social character, 200–201
subjective character, 170, 230
transcendent character, 173
China, 178, 204
Christian, work ethic, 2–3, 56
Christian eschatology, 35–37, 35n2, 36n3
Christian humanism, humanism, 3–4, 6–7, 22–31
Christian Social Congress, Amsterdam (1891), 135
Christifideles Laici, Apostolic Exhortation, (John Paul II), 69, 83
Christina of St. Troud, 54
Church. *See* Catholicism, Roman Catholicism; Protestant(ism)
Church Fathers
Eastern humanism, 22–27

overview, 6–7
postmodernism hope, 31–33
Western humanism, 27–31
work, exile of, 12–18
work, redeemed, 18–22
work, teachings on, 7–12
Cistercians, 45–48
Ciulla, Joanne, 184–85
civil government, 155–58
civil justice, 156, 201
class struggle, 233
Clement of Alexandria, 116
clerical reforms, 43, 43n37
clerics, activities of, 44, 126n53
Clifton, Jim, 242
Cluny
Damien influenced by, 37–38
French Benedictine monastery, 35–37
cognitive development, 248
collective aspects of work, 228–29, 228*f*, 235*f*, 243*f*
Commentary on Genesis 2:15 (Calvin), 138, 140
Commentary on Romans (Calvin), 156
Commentary on the Harmony of the Evangelists (Calvin), 139
Commercial Revolution, 56, 58
common good, 141, 158, 189–190
common grace doctrine, 140–42
Communism, 73–74, 92–93, 234
community life, dimensions of, 92
Compendium of the Social Doctrine of the Church
feminine genius, 89–90, 89n31
"The Human Person and Human Rights," 82–84
overview, 80–82
Confessions (Augustine), 182
contemplation
acquired versus infused, 121

action and, 123
Catholic tradition on, 116–123
contemplative leadership, eight Cs of, 111, 111n7
John Paul II's magisterium and, 112–15
meaning of, 113, 119–120
in middle of the world (active live), 123–133
social consequences of, 130–32
corporations
    business practices, 190
    international, 192, 200–205
Cosden, Darrell, 147, 149
cosmological principle, 139
creation
    Adam, 85–86
    care of, as mission, 10
    Eve, 87–88, 87n27, 88n29
    God's plan for, 2–3, 6–7
    human work and, 138–39
    through God's word, 19, 137
    of wealth, 91, 94, 97
    of women, 11
Cross, of Christ, 95, 116, 161
culture
    of life, 81, 103
    popular culture, 10, 34
    Western culture, 40, 42, 49, 56
    of work, 200, 202

Damian, Peter, 37–47, 55
Dante, Alighieri, 37
de Sales, Francis, Saint, 3, 64, 123
de Vitry, Jacques, 52, 53
decision-making criteria, 214–17, 221, 223
delegation, of work, 178
democratic capitalism, 92n37
developmental stages of human development, 248–250
Diener, Ed, 241, 242, 244–45, 249

Dies Domini, Apostolic Letter (John Paul II), 133
digital revolution, 194–95
digital technology, 191, 194
dignity, human dignity
    subjective dimension of, 132, 232
    wages and, 207
    work design and, 211
    of the worker, 58–59, 148–155
disciplinary society, 66
Divine Comedy (Dante), 37
divine filiation, 127, 132
D'Oignies, Marie, 53
Dominican Order, 56, 118
dominion
    biblical text, 230–31
    defined, 197–98
    mandate of, 138

earth, resources of, 227–28
ecology
    moral, 168–69, 171–72
    spiritual, 180
economic science, 225, 241
economic system
    capitalism (*See* capitalism, capital)
    Catholic social teaching and, 92
    family, priority of, 153–54
    globalization and, 150–51, 200–205, 211
    human dignity and, 175, 191
    labor over capital, priority of, 237
    Marxism (*See* Marxism)
    overview, 224–25
    unemployment and, 209
    values and, 99
economic value, 224–25, 232
economics
    first and second things, 235–248
    integral human development, 248–253

objective (transitive) dimension of
  work, 225–230
  overview, 224–25
  subjective dimension of work,
  230–35
economies of scale, 204n42
economism, 148, 203n39, 238
economistic view of work, 148, 225
economy and related terms, 240
efficiency
  of action, 216–18
  delegation and, 177
  Taylorism and, 20
Einstein, Albert, 171
Elizabeth of Spalbeck, 54
employees, 175–181, 206–10, 207n50
employers, 150, 152, 155, 175, 184
employment
  automatization and substitution,
  205, 208–9
  dignity of work and, 207
  technology and, 143, 201
  See also unemployment
engagement logic, 245, 252–53, 253*f*
Engels, Frederick, 73–74
England, 56, 245
enterprise, entrepreneur(ship), 142–
  45
equity, 2, 250
eschatology
  Bernard of Clairvaux, 47
  Cluniac, 35–37, 35n2
  Damian's social theology, 37–38
  Rule of St. Benedict, 46
  types of, 36n3
  work theology and, 59
Escrivá, Josemaría
  contemplation and, 111–12, 118–
  19, 121–133
  John Paul II and, 4
  mandate of dominion, 138
  ordinary work and, 3

ethics
  business ethics, 4–5
  Business Ethics Theory, 189–192,
  211
  Christian work ethic, 56
  decision-making criteria, 221
  moral virtues and, 117, 117n25,
  222
  nature of work and, 186
  *Protestant Ethic and the Spirit of
  Capitalism* (Weber), 61
Evangelical Quarterly (Hart), 138
Evangelii Gaudium (Apostolic Exhortation, Francis), 82
Evangelium Vitae encyclical (John
  Paul II), 106, 114
Eve
  creation of, 87–88, 87n27, 88n29
  good and evil, 13–15
Exameron (Ambrose), 29–30
exploitation, exploitative, 151–52,
  204n43, 205

The Fable of the Bees (Mandeville),
  63
fact/value dichotomy, 225, 240–41,
  250–51
faith
  in God, 114, 151
  in Jesus Christ, 64, 134, 162
  stage of human development, 248
  women of, 82, 103
Familiaris Consortio, Apostolic Exhortation, 81
family
  priority of in economic system,
  153–54
  Wages and Other Social Benefits
  (John Paul II), 153
farming, 41, 43, 170
Fathers of the Church. *See* Church Fathers

Feast of Corpus Christi, establishment of, 53, 54
finance
    fact/value dichotomy, 240–48
    first and second things, 235–248
    integral human development, 248–253
    monetary compensation, 232–33
    objective (transitive) dimension of work, 225–230
    overview, 224–25
    subjective dimension of work, 230–35
first causes, 7–12
Fisher, Irving, 251
5G technology, 191
Flores-Castro Lingán, Gonzalo, 5, 212
Fordism, 206
The Forge (Escrivá), 125
Fourth Industrial Revolution, 184
Francis, Pope
    Evangelii Gaudium, 82
    Laudato si,' 78, 140
    technocratic paradigm, 4, 114n14
    women, role of, 103
Francis of Assisi, 55
Franciscan Order, 53, 54–56
Franks, Angela, 4, 60
free bargaining, role of, 97
Free University of Amsterdam, 136, 157
freedom
    benefit of work, 45
    choices by humans, 23–24, 108
    in economic sector, 93
    of indifference, 73
    institutions fostering, 2
    responsibility and, 114
    from work, 12
Friesen, Geoffrey C., 5, 224, 243*f*

Gallup World Poll, 242

Gaudium et Spes (Vatican II), 112–13
Genesis, 8–18, 32n82, 136–140
genetic engineering, 191–92
genius (charism) masculine/feminine, 84–90, 89n31
Geoffrey of Hanlawe, 42
The German Ideology (Marx & Engels), 73
gift, 31–32, 94, 94n44
globalization, 150–51, 200–205, 211
God, Creator
    gift to mankind, 233
    plan for creation, 2–3, 6–7
    relationship with humans, 11–12
    as Truth Itself, 38
Godfrey, Catherine, 5
Godfrey of Tuscany, 43
Gospel
Calvinists and, 65–66
Catholic social teaching and, 136, 190, 191
    as first book of meditation, 128
    of John, 19–21, 28–30
    Puritanism and, 65–66
    women and spirt of, 103
gospel of work, 137, 146, 161
Grandy, Gina, 111
gratuity, law of, 104–5
Greek mythology, material world and, 7
Gregg, Samuel, 201
Gregory, Brad S., 60–63
Gregory of Nyssa, 23–25, 30
Gregory the Great, 117
"The Grumbling Hive, or Knaves Turn'd Honest" (Mandeville), 63
Guardini, Romano, 78
Guerric of Igny, 46
Guibert of Hoyland, 47
Guilla, Empress, 42–43

Hahn, Scott, 13
Hall, Joseph, 64

happiness, 104, 242
Hart, Ian, 138–39, 146
health care, 154
Hegel, Georg Friedrich Wilhelm, 4
Hennely, Alfred T., 113
Herman of Tournai, 48
Heschel, Abraham Joshua, 169
Hildebert of Lavadin, 42
Hildegard of Bingen, 48–52
holiness, 3, 46, 119, 122, 126
Holy Spirit, 19, 140
homo economicus, 244, 249
Hsieh, Nien-hê, 207–8n50
Hugh of St. Victor, 42
human beings
    developmental stages of, 248–250
    dignity and (*See* dignity, human dignity)
    relationship with God, 11–12
    three elements of, 23–24
human development, integral human development, 248–255
human flourishing, 100–102, 241–43, 243*f*
"The Human Person and Human Rights" *(Compendium of the Social Doctrine of the Church)*, 82–84
human rights, 250
human wellbeing, determinants, 235*f*, 243*f*
humanism
    Christian humanism, 3–4, 6–7, 22–31
    eastern church fathers, 22–27
    western church fathers, 27–31
humanity, in work, 198–200
Humbert of Romans, 52
Humiliati (apostolic group), 52–53
Humphrey of Llanthony, 42

Iacocca, Lee, 42, 169, 170, 173
IBM developments, 195n20

Ida of Léau, 54
Ida of Louvain, 54
Ida of Nivelles, 54
idleness, 65, 132
idolatry, 15, 17–18
Ignacio, Javier, 189
Ignatian theology, 66
Ignatius of Loyola, 118
Illanes, José Luis, 117–18
incarnational theology, 49–50
inclusion, 2, 58n99
Index Verborum (Busa), 195n20
individual aspects of work, 228–29
Industrious Revolution, 61–63
industry, 192–93, 229
infused contemplation, 121
inheritances of work, 200n34
injustice, 42, 114, 115, 130–31, 202
    See also justice
Institutes of the Christian Religion, (Calvin), 135, 140
insurance, 154
integral human development, 248–255
interiority, 9, 71, 132, 199
international corporations, 192, 200–205
International Labor Organization, 149
internet of things (IoT), 191
Isaac of Stella, 47
Israel, 18, 144

Jesus, Jesus Christ, Christ
    divine nature, 28
    double filiation, 19–20
    work, life of, 19–20
Jewish Sabbath. *See* Sabbath
job design, 176–77
John Paul II, Pope
    Centesimus Annus encyclical, 4, 79–80, 92–102, 114, 191
    Christifideles Laici, Apostolic Exhortation, 69, 83

Dies Domini, Apostolic Letter, 133

on dignity of the worker, 58–59, 207

early life experiences, 3–4

Evangelium Vitae encyclical, 106, 114

Familiaris Consortio, Apostolic Exhortation, 81

Laborem Exercens encyclical (*See Laborem Exercens*)

Letter to Women, 84

Mulieris Dignitatem Apostolic Letter, 4, 81

Theology of the Body, audience talks, 60n1, 85n20

women, role of, 103

John XXIII, Pope, Saint, 175, 190

Judaism, 2

See also Jewish Sabbath

Juliana of Mont Cornillon, 53–54

justice

civil justice, 156, 201

in economic sphere, 80–81, 112, 153

in monasteries, 44

Pontifical Council on Justice and Peace, 81, 147

principal of, 250

prophetic justice, 130

social justice, 42–43, 57, 80–81

See also injustice

justification, works and, 46

Kant, Emmanuel, 221

Kennedy, Robert, 165

Keynes, John Maynard, 2, 209

Kingdom of God, 3, 66, 131

knowledge, power and, 78–79

Kuyper, Abraham

biographical information, 135–36

calling to work, 147

cosmological principle, 139

on family, 154

Free University of Amsterdam, 136, 157

gifts and common grace, 144

labor for the glory of God, 152

Lectures on Calvinism, 157

The Social Question and the Christian Religion, 152

state, role of, 157–58

talent in the workplace, 141

vocations, 154–55

labor

biblical perspective, 9

capital, relationship with, 150

division of, 43–44, 74

as intransitive, 75

types of, 46–47

Webster's definition, 36

labor substitution, 205, 208–10, 211

labor unions, 54, 151

Laborem Exercens (John Paul II)

as Christian humanism, 6–7

criticisms on, 162

Elements for a Spirituality of Work, 158

objective dimension of (*See* objective dimension of work)

opening paragraphs, 135

operational principle, 212–14

protestant appreciation, 134

publication of, 3–5

scripture, use of, 136–38

subjective dimension of (*See* subjective dimension of work)

Wages and Other Social Benefits, 153

laissez-faire capitalism, 92, 94, 99

laity

Catholic tradition on, 147

duty of, 44–45, 127

John Paul II on, 69
Lao Tzu, 168n11
Laudato si' (Francis, Pope), 78, 140
law of gratuity, 104–5
lay brothers and sisters, 40–41, 43
Leader(ship)
    business leadership, 210
    contemplative leadership, 111, 111n7
    institutional leadership, 177
    subjective dimension of, 176–78
learning, 216–18, 222
Lectures on Calvinism (Kuyper), 157
LeGoff, Jacques, 54
leisure, 132–33, 251
Leo XIII, Pope, 92, 134, 135, 175
Letter to Women (John Paul II), 84
Lévinas, Emmanuel, 111
Lewis, C. S., 173
Little, Daniel, 240
liturgy, liturgical
    dimension of biblical text, 8–9
    Genesis and, 10
    liturgy of the hours, 113
    monastic communities, 40
logos, 25
London Dock Strike (1889), 135
Lonergan, Bernard, 167
López, Javier, 128
López, Pérez, 5
love, 103–6, 119–120, 129–132
Love and Responsibility (Wojtyla), 77
Lumen Gentium (Vatican II), 69, 160
Lutgard of Aywieres, 54
Luther, Martin, 64, 139

machines, 184, 196, 198
MacIntyre, Alasdair, 111, 170–71, 222
man. *See* human beings; men, masculine; person, personhood
Mandeville, Bernard, 63
Manning, James Cardinal, 135

Marengo, Luigi, 209
Margaret of Ypres, 54
Maritain, Jacques, 3, 123, 165n4
Maritain, Raissa, 123
market, 62, 96–97, 99
market globalization, 192
market mechanisms, 97n54
market theory, totalizing of, 235–37
Marx, Karl, 2, 4, 68
Marxism
    Capital, 73
    human person and, 94, 99
    ideological conflict, 233
    labor and, 73–75
    modernity, human labor and, 69, 70, 75
    technological determinism, 201, 211
Maslow, Abraham, 248, 250
Maspero, Giulio, 2, 6
Mater et Magistra (John XXIII), 175
materialism, 148, 202–3, 203n39, 238–39
matter, spiritual origin of, 8
meaningful work, 183–88
means of production, 93, 195–96, 195n21, 203n40, 205
meditation, 111
men, masculine
    genius of, 84–90, 86n23, 86n26, 89n31
    parenthood, tasks of, 104–5
mercantilization, 202, 204n42
Merton, Thomas, 3, 120, 123, 123n45
metaphysics of labor
    Industrious Revolution, 61–63
    ordinary in being, 69–72
    ordinary life, affirmation of, 63–68
    overview, 60–61
    spirituality of labor, 72–77
Michaelson, Christopher, 4, 183

Middle Ages, medieval
    Cistercians, 45–48
    Cluny, 35–37
    connotation in popular culture, 10
    Damian, Peter, 37–45
    reflections, 56–59
    women's contributions, 48–56
migrant, migration, 151
Miller, David, 147
mindfulness, 111
mission
    care of creation and, 10
    complementarity as, 82–84
    human's expulsion from paradise
        as, 14
Monasticism, monk
    Cistercians, 45–48
    Cluny, 35–37
    Fonte Avellana, 37–38
    lay brothers and sisters, 40–41
    legislation on canonical life, 41–
        42, 41n24
    renewal of, 35
moral, ecology, 168–69, 171–72
moral orientation, of work, 167–171
moral virtues, 117, 117n25, 222
Moses, 138
Mulieris Dignitatem, Apostolic Letter
    (John Paul II), 4, 81, 88
Mysticism, mystical, 39, 44, 47, 121–
    22

Nadal, Jeronimo, 118
natural law, 141–42
nature of work and enterprise, 142–
    45, 186, 227–28, 230
Naughton, Michael, 4, 163
negative learning, 218, 220
neuroscience, 191
New Testament
    contemplation, 116
    Gospel (*See* Gospel)

ontological depth of God's work,
    9
Paul's epistle (*See* Paul, apostle)
reaffirmation on work, 6
work redeemed, 18–22
Noah, 16–17
nobility
    barred from commercial profes-
    sions, 54
    engaging in manual labor, 57
    responsibility to social injustice,
    42–43
Nolan, Kim, 111
Novak, Michael, 92n37
Novo Millennio Ineunte, Apostolic
    Letter (John Paul II), 114–15

objective dimension of work
    Catholic and Protestant traditions
    on, 146
    dignity of work and, 132
    external or material sense, 95
    human wellbeing determinants,
    235f, 243f
    meaningful work and, 183–88
    means of building things, 165
    sense of work, 218–19
    as transitive, 225–26
O'Donovan, Oliver, 235
*Oeconomicae et pecuniariae quaes-
    tiones* (document), 249
Okonjo-Iweala, Ngozi, 108
Old Testament
    creation through His word, 19, 137
    Genesis, 8–18, 32n82
    occupations listed in, 160
operational relationship, 217–18
opportunity, in work, 205–10
Opus Dei, 124
ordinary life
    affirmation of, 63–68
    in being, 69–72

organizational problem, of work, 194
Origen, 116

Paglia, Camille, 86n26
parenthood, tasks of, 104–5
Pareto, Wilfred, 225, 240
Parmenides, 7
participation, in work, 205–10
"Passionately Loving the World" (Escrivá), 121–25
Paul, apostle
    charity, in light of truth, 90
    epistles of, 40, 137, 160
    first Corinthians, 30
    Pauline anthropological tripartition, 23–24
    Thessalonians, 24–25
    on work, 21–22
peace
    civil justice and, 156
    God's path to, 133
    mindfulness understood as, 111
    See also Pontifical Council on Justice and Peace
Pelagianism, 65
pensions, 154
Pérez López, Juan Antonio, 5, 212–18, 220, 222, 223
person, personhood
    aesthetic personalism, 71–72
    dignity of (*See* dignity, human dignity)
    law of gratuity and, 105
    primacy of, 132, 192–200, 203n39, 234–37
Person and Act (Wojtyla), 71
personalist principle, 222
Pezoa Bissieres, Alvaro, 4, 189
phenomenological description of work, 164–67
Physica (Hildegard), 50
Pieper, Josef, 132

Pinto Garay, Javier Ignacio, 4, 189
Pius XI, Pope, 175, 191
Pius XII, Pope, 103
Plato, 7, 9, 116
Platonic metaphor, 39
Platonic mythology, 10
politics, 62–63, 62n10, 90, 108, 126, 161–62, 186
Pontifical Council on Justice and Peace, 147
Poor Catholics (apostolic group), 52
Poor Lombards (apostolic group), 52
postmodernism, 31–33
poverty, poor
    definition of, 91
    model poverty, 251
    Pope Leo and, 135
    preferential option for the poor, 90–91, 92n37, 100–102
    voluntary poverty, 55–56
prayer, 128–29
    See also contemplation; meditation
preferential option for the poor, 90–91, 92n37, 100–102
principal-agent framework, 252–53
private ownership of goods, 97n55
private property, 74, 93, 97, 98
profit
    maximizing, 150–51, 204n43, 205, 233, 240
    short-term, 107
    subjective dimension of, 170–71
    Taylorism and, 206
profit economy, 52, 98
property (private), 74, 93, 97, 98
prosperity, 91, 94, 97, 210
Protestant Ethic and the Spirit of Capitalism (Weber), 61
Protestant(ism)
    authoritative framework and, 162
    Calvin (*See* Calvin, John; Calvinism, Calvinists)

common grace, 140–42
common themes of, 134–36
creation mandate, 138–140
Kuyper (*See* Kuyper, Abraham)
natural law, 141–42
nature of work and enterprise, 142–45
soteriology and, 62
spiritual elitism, 64–65
work, as calling to holiness, 3
work and value, 145–46
Puritanism, 65–66, 76

Quadragesimo Anno encyclical (Pius XI), 191

Ranft, Patricia, 3, 34
Ratzinger, Joseph (later Benedict XVI), 60–61, 68
reciprocal determinism in economics, 247
Reell Precision Manufacturing, case study, 178–181
Reformation, Protestant
soteriology and, 62
spiritual elitism, 64–65
work, as calling to holiness, 3
relation
constitutive, 11
gratuitous, 13
operative, 220
relationship
capitalism and labor, 150, 203n39, 233–34, 237–240
Creator/human, 11–12
operational, 217–18
structural, 217–18
Rerum Novarum encyclical (Leo XIII), 92, 134–35, 150, 154
responsibility
business leaders, 210
communal, 34

freedom and, 114
moral, 199
nobility's, 42–43
personal, 55, 143, 156
shared, 177
rest
biblical perspective, 9, 28–30
in eschatological terms, 46, 47–48
Sabbath and, 77, 154
resurrectional theology, 49–50
retirement, 169
Richard of Hexham, 42
"Rights and Duties of Capital and Labor" *Rerum Novarum*, 92, 134–35, 150, 154
Robbins, Lionel, 225, 240–41, 243, 245–48, 251
Robert of Grosseteste, 53
robotics, 191, 198, 199
Roman Catholic. *See* Catholicism, Roman Catholicism
Romuald of Ravenna, 37
Rosenbrock, Howard, 176
Rule of Benedict, 40, 46
The Rule of Clare of Assisi, 55
Ruskin, John, 163n1

Sabbath
contemplation and, 133
Jesus and, 20, 29
Jewish Sabbath, 9–10
work and rest, 77, 154
salary. *See* wage, wages
salvation, through family and work, 16
sanctification, sanctifying, 24–25, 41, 57, 125, 128
Savage, Deborah, 4, 78
Sayers, Dorothy, 138
Scarchilli, Frank, 5
Schlag, Martin, 1, 27, 110
Schotte, Gerald E., 218

Schwanda, Tom, 110–11
Schwartz, Adina, 187–88
Scola, Angelo, 104
Scripture. *See* Bible
Second Vatican Council (Vatican II)
    Apostolicam Actuositatem, 69
    Christian humanism program, 3
    Gaudium et Spes, 112–13
    Lumen Gentium, 69, 160
secular, secularity
    laity's duty, 44–45, 127
    monastic communities and, 38, 43
    work and, 22, 35, 119, 124
self-actualization, 230–34, 248, 250
self-determination, 166n6
self-realization, 250
Seligman, Martin, 241, 242, 244–45, 249
Sen, Amartya, 91, 97n54
Sertillanges, Antonine Dalmace, 212–13
Shaftesbury, Lord, 158
Sheen, Fulton, 108n87
Shockley, William, 194
sin
    Christ Redeemer and, 125, 161
    common grace and, 140
    contemplation and, 115, 120
    Noah, new beginnings and, 17
    original sin, 14, 15, 89
Sisemore, Timothy A., 110–11
slavery, condemnation of, 26, 32, 132
Sliwa, Martyna, 111
social injustice, 42–43, 57, 80–81
The Social Question and the Christian Religion (Kuyper), 152
social theology, development of, 38–40
social virtues, 82, 102
society
    communist, 73
    disciplinary, 66

divisions in, 44–45
goods for, 97–98
medieval society, 35–37, 54–57, 54n91
women's contributions, 83, 105–9
socio-economic context, Catholic Social Thought, 90–92, 99–102
solidarity, 97n55, 114, 190
spiritual ecology, 180
spirituality
    business literature on, 110
    Cluniac eschatological, 35–37
    contemplation and, 115, 119
    of labor, 72–77
    of work, 112–13, 131, 158–162, 171–74
Stamp, Josiah Sir, 245–47
state, role of, 155–58
stewards, 39
steward(ship), 39, 43, 97n55, 114, 140
Stoicism, 66
structural relationship, 217–18
subjective dimension of work
case study, 178–181
    Catholic and Protestant traditions on, 146
    collective and individual aspects, 228–29, 228*f*, 235*f*, 243*f*
    dignity of work and, 132, 232
    as framework for insights into, 163–64
    human person, primacy of, 132, 234–38
    human wellbeing determinants, 235*f*
    institutional form, 174–78
    meaningful work and, 183–88
    moral orientation, 167–171
    overview, 181–82, 219–220, 224–25
    person performing the work, 95–96

phenomenological description, 164–67
reciprocal nature of, 230
scholarly use of, 4, 5
self-actualization and, 230–34
spiritualty of work, 171–74
transitive dimension (*See* transitive dimension of work)
Women's work and, 79
subject/object dichotomy, 240–41
subsidiarity, principles of, 190, 201
substitution, labor, 205, 208, 211

Taylor, Charles, 60–61, 63–68
Taylorism, 206–7
The Teaching of Luther and Calvin about Ordinary Work (Hart), 138
technology, technological
automatization, 206
business ethics theory and, 191–92, 211
dangers of, 143, 193
displacement the human person and, 79, 184
globalization and, 200–205
for the good, 192–200
as man's ally, 143
primacy of man over things, 192–200
substitution, labor, 205, 208, 211
telecommunication, 193, 194, 201
teleopathy (confusion of aims), 132
Thatcher, Margaret, 92–93n39
theology, theological
Apollinarism, 22–23
resurrectional theology, 49
Theology of the Body, audience talks, 60n1, 85n20
Therese of Lisieux, Saint, 64
Thomas Aquinas, Saint
avarice and, 61

clerics, commercial activities of, 126n53
contemplative life, 117–18
eschaton and this life, 128–29
Index Verborum and, 195n20
metaphysical anthropology of, 85n20
non-burdensome work, 64
Tolstoy, Leo, 167
trade, of goods
as human right, 97n54, 99–100
humanitarian and, 126
international, 48, 155
responsibilities, 134, 144
trade-off logic, 245, 252
trades, working, 27, 45, 171
training and development, in work, 178
transistors, invention of, 194–95, 201
transitive dimension of work, 75, 164, 193n15, 225–230, 247–48
Trinity, 19
Turnbull, Richard, 3, 134

unemployment, 151, 208–10
See also employment

value, work and, 145–46
value-free economic models, 225, 240
Vatican II. *See* Second Vatican Council (Vatican II)
Vico, Giambattista, 68
virtue, virtues
almsgiving, 62
in business, 98
Catholic Social Teaching and, 189–190
moral virtues, 117, 117n25, 222
social virtues, 82, 102
Von Hildebrand, Dietrich, 107n86

wage, wages
dignity of the worker, 207

equilibrium wage, 251
exploitative business practices 152
global impact, 150
supporting families, 153
value of work and, 232–33
Wages and Other Social Benefits
(John Paul II), 153
Wahlstedt, Bob, 178–180
Waldensians (apostolic group), 52
Watson, Thomas J., 195n20
wealth
  as existential and material, 100
  good wealth, 165, 171, 210
  Industrial Revolution and, 239–
  240
  leisure and, 251
  maximization of, 170
  source and creation of, 91, 94, 97
Weber, Max, 61, 251
Wilber, Ken, 229
William of Newburgh, 42
Wilson, James Matthew, 72
win-win situations, 245–47
Wojtyla, Karol (later John Paul II)
  The Acting Person, 165–66n6
  Love and Responsibility, 77
  Person and Act, 71–72
  personalist principle, 222
  subjective dimension of personal
  living, 196–97
  work, defined, 2
Wolf, Susan, 188
women
  Catholic Social Thought, 80–82
  contributions in society and public
  life, 105–9
  contributions in the Church, 79–
  80, 102–9
  creation of, 11
  feminine genius, 84–90, 89n31
  High Middle Ages contributions,
  48–56

marketplace participation, 96–97
mothers, role of, 153–54
parenthood, tasks of, 104–5
ways of knowing, 105n80
work
  Biblical understanding of, 7–12,
  18–22
  as calling to holiness, 3
  Catholic tradition on, 3
  collective and individual aspects,
  228–29, 228f, 235f, 243f
  complexities of, 1–2
  delegation, 178
  dimensions of (*See* objective dimension of work; subjective dimension of work)
  economistic view, 148
  in eschatological terms, 57
  exile of, 12–18
  exploitative business practices,
  151–52
  as God's plan for creation, 2–3
  inheritances of, 200n34
  international corporations, 192,
  200–205
  job design, 176–77
  materialistic view, 148
  meaning of, 95
  meaningful work, 183–88
  moral orientation of, 167–171
  nature of, 142–45
  organizational problem, 194
  Oxford English Dictionary definition, 1
  phenomenological description of
  work, 164–67
  Protestantism and, 146–48
  redeemed, 18–22
  spirituality of, 110–13, 158–161
  (*See also* contemplation)
  technology and, 5
  timeless nature of, 227–28

training and development, 178
as transitive (*See* transitive dimension of work)
value and, 145–46
work management, 206
worker
dignity of (*See* dignity, human dignity)
family and vocation, 153–55
methodological reflections, 161
rights and responsibilities, 149–153
role of the state, 155–58

workplace
conditions at, 183, 187–88
objective elements in, 184
participation regardless of merit, 141
subjective dimension of workers, 175
women in, 81, 89–90, 105

Yeoman, Ruth, 185, 187–88
Yvette of Huy, 54

Zambrano, María, 34